# Praise for <u>In Session</u>

A beautifully written, sensitive portrayal of the complexity of the therapeutic relationship. [Deborah Lott] gives voice to countless women who have struggled to find themselves through this intimate process with another. This is a book I will recommend to my patients. It should be required reading for all therapists.

> — *Alice Brand Bartlett, Edward Greenwood Professor, Karl Menninger School of Psychiatry and Mental Health Science*

A very valuable contribution to our knowledge of the therapy experience, through its privileging and focusing on the client's experiences.

> — *Laura S. Brown, Ph.D. ABPP, Immediate Past President, APA Division of Psychology of Women, author of* Subversive Dialogues: Theory in Feminist Therapy

Invaluable reading for both patients and therapists. Deborah Lott provides a wonderful exploration of the treatment process through the eyes of both partners in the therapeutic relationship. Anyone contemplating entering therapy as well as those in therapy who have questions about their treatment should read this book.

> — *Marion F. Solomon, Ph.D., author of* Love and Marriage in an Age of Confusion *and* Narcissism and Intimacy

This book is "must reading" for psychotherapists, women, and for the people who care about them. It is a sobering look at the challenges faced by women in therapy, and yet it offers hope through guiding us past risks and danger to the promise of healing.

> — *Gary Schoener, Clinical Psychologist, author of* Psychotherapists' Sexual Involvement with Clients

Deborah Lott's book reads like a novel, has the sweeping vision of great social criticism and delivers the emotional support of the best of self-help books. Every woman in therapy and every social worker, psychologist or psychiatrist who treats women should take a giant step forward by reading *In Session* cover-to-cover.

> — *Keith Ablow, M.D., Forensic Psychiatrist, author of* Denial

# In Session

# In Session

## The Bond Between Women and Their Therapists

Deborah A. Lott

Marie M. Cohen, Ph.D., Editorial Adviser

W. H. Freeman and Company
New York

*Text Designer:* Cambraia Magalhães

Library of Congress Cataloging-in-Publication Data
Lott, Deborah A.
  The bond between women and their therapists / Deborah A. Lott;
with Marie M. Cohen.
      p.    cm.
  Includes index.
  ISBN 0-7167-3562-8 (cloth)
  1. Psychotherapist and patient. 2. Women–Psychology. I. Cohen,
Marie M. (Marie Marguerite) II. Title.
  [DNLM: 1. Professional–Patient Relations. 2. Women—psychology.
3. Psychotherapy personal narratives. WM 460.5.W6 L884b 1999]
RC480.8.L68   1999
616.89′14—dc21
DNLM/DLC
for Library of Congress                                    98–52301
                                                              CIP

Printed in the United States of America

First printing, 1999

W. H. Freeman and Company
41 Madison Avenue, New York, NY 10010
Houndmills, Basingstoke   RG21 6XS, England

*To my mother,* Evelyn Budnitzky Lott *(1917–1995), for never telling me that I was asking too many questions.*

*To my husband,* Gary Edelstone, *for sustaining me with the faux* New York Times *stories in the morning, the jazz riffs at dusk, the dreamy puns in the middle of the night, and the promise of a future.*

# Contents

# In Session

# Introduction

I began to think about psychotherapy in earnest nearly twenty years ago. Having returned to my hometown of Los Angeles after several years working in book publishing in Boston, I was at a crossroads. I wanted to write professionally but feared I'd never be able to support myself. I'd come home because my father, after years of physical and mental illness, was dying. I was hoping to make some peace in our relationship, some peace with the psychological consequences of having had a crazy father. I joined a writers' group and I embarked on psychotherapy.

It turned out that several other members in my group were also in therapy. Some turned to therapy to help them cope with the insecurity of the writer's life; a few were struggling valiantly to exorcise childhood demons; one was determined to stop having impossible relationships with men. As we shared manuscript drafts and rejection slips, we also began to share therapy war stories.

It struck me that our exchanges resembled nothing so much as accounts of love affairs. We felt the same urgent need to get every detail straight, every word right ("and then she said . . . , and then I said . . ."). We could be unduly vulnerable to our therapists' actions, assigning profound importance to their seemingly trivial remarks. Sometimes we felt like first graders admiring our teachers; at other moments we resembled adolescents in the throes of a crush. On some days, we reported our reactions with an anthropologist's detachment; other days we'd find ourselves totally in their sway.

Our appraisals of the process wavered: Therapy had already changed us remarkably; therapy was the biggest waste of time and money imaginable. Our therapists were brilliant; our therapists were con artists. We questioned exactly what it was we were paying for—insight? empathy? ways of changing our own thinking? the therapist's knowledge, objectivity, skill, or simply his or her presence as a captive listener?

We found the very structure of the therapeutic relationship problematic. It was inherently unequal: We needed our therapists more than they needed us, they were much more important to us than we were to them, and the whole alliance was sustained only by our paying considerable fees. This artifice made us uneasy. To what extent was this even a *real* relationship, and if it wasn't real, *what* exactly was it? It wasn't friendship and yet it was different from any other professional relationship we had ever had. It was intimate and at the same time formally conscribed; it encouraged us to expose ourselves while imposing tight constraints on the encounter.

Worse, some of us felt as if we couldn't even say who our therapists were. All we knew for sure was how they conducted themselves during sessions. We shuddered to think they might be capable of leading "double lives" and that outside of the therapy room they might not be so kind, compassionate, and patient.

"For all I know, he could be an ax murderer!" Carla exclaimed one day, after having seen one too many old Hitchcock movies. She found it even worse to imagine that her therapist might simply be like some of the men she knew who drank too much and cheated on their wives. Jeannie worried that her soft-spoken, unflappable young woman therapist was silently making judgments she knew better than to share. If our therapists were playing roles and were different people outside the consulting room, why did that seem to invalidate our therapy? Why did it matter so much to us that our therapists be who they appeared to be?

The so-called "boundaries" of therapy, the rules of the game, were also bewildering. Why did Amy's therapist offer routine end-of-the-session hugs while Nancy's flinched if Nancy got any closer to her than ten feet? Why did Pat's therapist chat amiably about her own life while Nancy's turned every question into a question? What accounted for these differences, and which made for better therapy? Why were shifts in the boundaries, such as when Amy's therapist asked her to go down to the corner with her to get coffee, so disconcerting?

And so, on some late evenings, after the official writers' group meeting ended, some of us retired to a local coffee shop to commiserate and to analyze and reanalyze each perplexing client–therapist exchange. Despite our misgivings and confusion about the process, we made one clear and unanimous observation: Sharing our stories and appreciating the commonality of our experiences—even those that seemed crazy—provided a certain, albeit comic, relief.

Being one-on-one in the therapy room could lead to a dizzying loss of perspective, an inability to trust oneself. Bringing another person into the room, even after the fact, could clarify matters. In fact, talking about our therapy together proved to be one of the most therapeutic aspects of the whole process.

Over the next few years, I found my niche as a health journalist and began to tackle the professional psychotherapy literature. It offered some explanation for the experiences of the women in my group. The intensity of clients' feelings and the centrality therapists assumed in their clients' internal lives were attributed to *transference*. Early in his career, Freud reported discovering a phenomenon by which clients transfer onto the therapist their most primal feelings. These were emotions first formulated for significant figures in the past, notably parents. The blankness of the therapist, the resemblance between the parent and therapist's authority, could evoke these transference feelings. According to Freud's theory, therapists were stand-ins, the feelings directed at them unresolved remnants of their clients' most profound and unresolved feelings from infancy and childhood.

Freud also offered a second, slightly more commonsense explanation of transference as the application of "stereotype plates." According to Freud, people had a tendency to unconsciously create and then globally apply these templates, which had been forged in early childhood relationships. These internal models shaped people's perceptions and expectations in all the significant relationships that came afterward. They influenced how we picked our lovers, how we responded to criticism from an authority figure, how we interpreted the unspoken cues that pass between strangers. In short, these templates provided the emotional rules for how to function in relationships.

The most important aspect of Freud's transference theory, perhaps, was the role he assigned it in psychotherapy. The therapeutic relationship provided an ideal arena for the client to observe her own templates in action. By looking at her interactions with her therapist, she could come to understand and then modify these sometimes negative repetitive patterns.

Once I'd started to think about transference, I saw evidence of it everywhere in the stories my group members had told. When Jeannie's therapist became pregnant, Jeannie felt pierced by sadness and jealousy. As a woman of thirty-seven who ached to be a mother but had no serious romantic prospects, she would have expected to envy her therapist's maternity. What caught Jeannie off guard was also feeling envious of her therapist's unborn baby!

Carla related an odd perception she had during sessions. Whenever her therapist turned to a side table and tapped out the contents of his pipe, her eyes went to his hands. For a flash they became her father's. There was something about the gesture and her therapist's turning away from her as he spoke that filled her with an ancient melancholy.

Angela, who had grown up with five siblings, hand-me-down clothes, and an always exhausted mother, hated coming into her sessions and sitting down on a chair warmed by its former occupant. "I feel like screaming, '*Who's* been sitting in *my* chair?'" she roared, sounding like one of Goldilocks's three bears. The sibling rivalry of Angela's past made her resent the very idea that her therapist had any clients other than her.

The theory of transference seemed to explain the depth of clients' feelings in psychotherapy. It also made sense of our tendency to keep repeating certain behaviors in our lives, even when those actions were counterproductive. Until people became aware of their patterns, they were likely to apply the same templates over and over again, to keep attempting to master the past by repeating it.

But as I read the literature and looked back on the experiences of my writers' group, it also began to seem to me that a complicated, and often dogmatically interpreted, theory had quickly subsumed direct, naturalistic observation of the full gamut of clients' experiences. Notably absent from the professional literature were clients' descriptions of what it felt like to be in the difficult and asymmetrical relationship called psychotherapy. Why hadn't anyone, particularly someone who was not a therapist and might have less of a theoretical ax to grind, asked women, who formed the majority of psychotherapy clients, about this experience? Although a number of clients had written memoirs of their psychotherapy, no journalist had ever looked at a large, representative group of clients' experiences in order to reveal the common threads.

In my writers' group, many of our perceptions of our therapists were idiosyncratic and tied to personal history. Others seemed to reflect more universal wishes, a deeper yearning for meaning and even transcendence. Many of us harbored a secret wish to be understood perfectly and loved completely in a way that no human had ever loved us before; this was a love with a redemptive potential. I wondered just how universal this wish was in women's psyches and what part it played in our therapy and in our lives. Surely such wishes would have influence outside of therapy: on the lovers we chose, the marriages we walked away from, on our whole relationship to power and autonomy.

When I considered the experiences of women in therapy, I also saw that the therapeutic relationship was not only a locus for reenacting the past; it also had a tendency to become emblematic, paradigmatic. It was easy to believe that if we could not get it right in the therapy relationship, we might never get it right anywhere. Conversely, getting it right in therapy seemed to promise that all the relationships that followed would be better. The therapy relationship could take on a symbolic weight exceeding that of other intimate alliances. If our therapists failed us or betrayed our trust, that would also have emblematic meanings: Whom would we ever be able to trust again?

If transference contributes to the intensity of clients' feelings, what the individual therapist says and does also matters tremendously. If Carla's therapist had not been so impossible to read, she would not have had the same ax murderer fantasies about him. If Jeannie's therapist had not arrived at a session bearing Bloomingdale's bags loaded with baby items, Jeannie might not have felt so jealous of her therapist's unborn child.

The more recent professional literature takes a *relational* view. It acknowledges that what goes on between client and therapist derives as much from the vicissitudes of their unique connection as it does from the influences of the client's past. Therapists also bring their own history, biases, and emotional proclivities to the consulting room. Thus, *countertransference* is as significant a factor in the equation as is the client's transference. But simply acknowledging that the therapist is also human does not solve the problem that clients often face of having to discern what belongs to the therapist and what belongs to them. A single question—"How do I know if it's me or my therapist?"—was the source of much of the agonizing within my writers' group. If a therapist, in whom a client has imbued so much authority, attributes the client's reaction to her history, who is she to argue? Transference is a concept that can be turned against the client, used to discredit her perceptions and validate the therapist's. This, as well as the authority that clients must imbue in them in order to engage freely in the process, gives therapists a lot of power.

As I began to research this book, I saw that a lot of the dilemmas that clients experience in the therapy relationship revolve around issues of the therapist's power and its mystification. Transference may make the therapist seem powerful and mysterious, as our parents must have seemed when we were children. But therapists also have very real power over clients' lives. By accepting the role of client, an individual gives the therapist permission to explain her own behavior to her, to see in her what she cannot see in herself. The more the therapist knows about the client, the more exposed the client feels in the therapist's presence, the more invested the client feels in the relationship, and the more power the therapist gains in relation to her.

Therapists have concrete power as well. They can recommend or prescribe medication, deem people sane or insane, even restrict their freedom or mobility. Inequity in power is a very important factor in the relationship between clients and therapists, and many therapists do not seem to understand all the ramifications of this asymmetry.

Others simply do not use their power responsibly. Why don't more therapists explain to their clients how therapy works and how long the process is likely to take? Why don't the principles of informed consent that apply to all other medical procedures seem to apply to psychotherapy? If informed consent applied, therapists would be obligated to lay out the risks and alternatives to psychotherapy at the outset, just as does a physician recommending a course of treatment. Therapists' seeming reticence to disclose what they know, and to own up to what they don't know, has unnecessarily mystified their power and the whole psychotherapeutic process.

Several years after my writers' group first began to talk about therapy, one of the women confided that a prior therapist had committed an extreme abuse of power, a severe violation of the therapeutic boundaries, by having sexual relations with her. There seemed no limit to the sorrow and shame that attended Michelle's disclosure. When she told us how her beloved and ailing therapist had, after several years of kind and helpful treatment, taken pornography out of his desk drawer and asked her to perform a sexual act on him, her voice took on the quality of a small child who had been betrayed by a parent.

I had been harboring a kindred secret. During my first few months back in Los Angeles, I had consulted a practitioner still in training to receive his therapist's license. A bear of a man with a shaved head, D. was a former Zen monk and a perennial guru who took his power very personally. He spouted platitudes authoritatively, looked at me with big, soulful eyes, and burned sandalwood incense during sessions in his home office.

Soon my therapy had collapsed into a brief sexual encounter. Perhaps I had wished that by having sex with a father figure I might magically resolve my troubled relationship with my own father or find a better father to replace him. When the encounter proved disturbing and disorienting instead, I shrugged off the psychological damages, deeming it a failed experiment. Only months and years afterward did I appreciate the psychological consequences of the event and the complex ways it confounded my later efforts to seek counsel. Surely what happened with D. is part of what compelled me to write this book.

My experiences in therapy, and the experiences of my writer-colleagues, make it clear that the relationship between women and their therapists can be an arena for abuses of power as well as for growth and understanding. The relationship is a genuine bond, and yet it has the potential to take on symbolic meanings. Boundaries seem crucial for limiting the therapist's power and preventing client exploitation, and yet there has always been considerable controversy over their proper delineation.

Several years after my writers' group disbanded, my own therapy ended. Overall, I found therapy a beneficial and often moving experience. I made the most progress when I gave up the fantasy of my therapist's being perfect and accepted that he could misunderstand my feelings, make mistakes, and still help me. Much of my therapy occurred outside of sessions in my own processing of our exchanges and my own reconsideration of the lessons of my childhood. In some respect I incorporated my therapist as a new voice inside; there was the therapist who sat across from me in his office and the therapist I carried around with me in my head, someone to whom I could address what was too frightening, too disorganizing to think about by myself.

This process of using the therapist as an internal icon is scarcely addressed in the professional literature, particularly from the client's point of view. How do clients internalize their therapists—as voices, images, icons of support? How are these internalized icons brought to bear in the client's life? And what can this process teach us about the way people use other people inside their heads? Surely the people who are important to us exist as much as internal icons as they exist as in-the-flesh others.

After therapy, I saw more clearly the ways in which my responses reflected my childhood experiences. I also recognized that other people's assumptions and perceptions were far more idiosyncratic than they initially appeared. Sometimes now I think it a miracle that human beings are able to establish a consensual reality at all—when the individualistic meaning of those exchanges threatens to turn all encounters into a Tower of Babel. We may think that we share a common, objective reality with others, but in fact, we all perceive through the filters of our childhoods. As a result of therapy, I am better able to discern the presence of those filters, to distinguish what belongs to the past, what belongs to the present, what belongs to the other person, and what belongs to me.

My fascination with the psychotherapeutic process has persisted, as have my questions. I decided to write this book to explore further how women actually experience the relationship with their therapists. I set out to expand the dialogue that began in my writers' group to encompass a much larger and more diverse group of women. I felt certain that I could write a book that no therapist could write because as a journalist I would be freer to ask the hard questions, freer to question the basic assumptions that underlay the field, freer to explore the disagreements among various schools of thought.

In addition to surveying and interviewing women in therapy, I also wanted to consider the professional literature more systematically and to take the questions I had been thinking about for so many years to some of the field's leading psychotherapists and thinkers. I had so many questions: How much of transference theory has ever been validated by any sort of empirical research? What are the alternate explanations for why women tend to fall in love with their therapists? Do the women who fall in love resolve their feelings in the neat fashion described in the professional literature? How important are boundaries, and what is the relationship between boundaries and power? Why do boundaries carry such an incredible charge for clients? Are there ways of thinking about the therapeutic relationship that will empower women as therapy consumers?

I have made a few assumptions that readers may want to keep in mind while reading this book: The relationship between therapist and client takes place in a realm poised between everyday reality and the symbolic. It is a genuine bond, and it exists also in the more symbolically charged realm in which transference operates. When therapists lose sight of this symbolic realm, they may miss therapeutic opportunities and cause their clients pain. On the other hand, some of the dilemmas that clients experience derive from the actual constraints and frustrating conundrums posed by the very structure of the relationship. These should not be denied either.

What the therapist offers is always in some ways an *approximation*. It can never be *true* love; it is always to some extent an *approximation* of love. It has resonances of other significant relationships—parent–child, brother–sister, lover–beloved, but it is not exactly like any of them. It does not have in-the-world viability; it is always delicately balanced between the symbolic and the real. It is important for clients and therapists to appreciate and protect the fragile approximations that characterize their relationship.

There is something inherently tragic about the client–therapist relationship. The therapist can never bring all of herself into the room, the client will long for what she can never get, the relationship is doomed to end. But treating the bond as either ordinary friendship or as a strictly professional exchange of goods and services only diminishes its therapeutic potential and hurts the client.

Like a shipboard romance or a summer camp friendship, the client–therapist relationship derives some of its energy from its built-in limitations. To remain therapeutic, the boundaries must be clear. When the boundaries start to slip, the relationship threatens to turn into something else. When boundaries fail, the full brunt of the therapist's needs emerge and endanger the primacy of the client's interests. Clients need to be able to rely on consistent, predictable boundaries to set the frame for a relationship that does not abide by the rules of any other sort of bond.

Good therapists are able to bring the essence of their real selves into the therapy room without having their needs compete with the client's. They are able to be authentic while maintaining clear boundaries. Some of the most moving poetry ever written was composed within rigid forms. In some respects therapy is an art, and it depends, as poetry does, on a structure for its meaning.

Many books in recent years have "trashed" psychotherapy, decrying the lack of science supporting it, the failures in the profession's self-regulation, the tendency for faddism, the enormous potential for client abuse. One could argue that there is ample evidence to support these critiques. The state of psychotherapy practice in America today virtually cries out for these sort of "Emperor Has No Clothes" exposés.

Too many people with too little training promise quick cures to people in distress. Those who need the most help are often those with the least money, and so they wind up seeing the least trained counselors. Simplistic gimmicks abound and attract a following before they are appraised with any degree of care, let alone scientific scrutiny. Treatments that are effective for one diagnosis are generalized and popularized and diluted and then misapplied to every other population of patients. The same ideas that Freud discarded one hundred years ago, such as the curative power of simple abreaction of traumatic memories through hypnosis, surface and resurface under slightly different guises.

In the course of writing this book, I heard about every variety of bizarre and arcane practice being performed under the aegis of psychotherapy, often by licensed practitioners. The turf battles among the various professionals practicing psychotherapy—psychiatrists, psychologists, social workers—ensure that no one body is responsible for policing or regulating the industry. It is too easy for practitioners to blame laxness in practice on the "other" disciplines.

But if my own therapy experience taught me anything, it is that the world is a complicated and imperfect place, and being an adult means not trying to reduce it to black and white. When I think about therapy, I am reminded of Woody Allen's joke about his uncle who thought he was a chicken. No one in the family could bear to tell him this was a delusion—they needed the eggs. I'm afraid that in the case of psychotherapy, we women still need the eggs.

The stories in this book amply illustrate that a therapist who does the job well gives the client a profound gift. For all its flaws, I do not believe we have yet found the alternatives to replace psychotherapy—not in psychotropic medication, not in self-help programs, not even in the currently popular spiritual movements.

As the principal users of psychotherapy, women clients must demand reform, more systematic inquiry, and more rigorous training and oversight of therapists. They must lobby licensing boards to take disciplinary action against therapists who don't play by the rules and must bring civil suits when those boards fail to serve the public interest.

But women in therapy must also recognize how their own wishes to be cured, their own fantasies of magical transformation, contribute to the mystification of the profession and leave them ripe for exploitation. To be better informed consumers, women need information. Only through a deeper understanding of the client-therapist relationship can women gain more power in their own therapy. In the years since I first began to write about medicine, a great deal of information formerly reserved to physicians has come into the patient's arena. Knowledge and shifts in attitude have brought patients into the medical decision-making process to an unprecedented degree. Psychotherapy seems to be the last holdout—its secrets still mystified, its practitioners reluctant to invite clients into a genuine dialogue about the process itself.

For too long, the therapy relationship has been hermetically sealed. While women in small circles like my writers' group talk about therapy with one another, the stigma surrounding mental illness and its treatment continues to inhibit broader discussion of the issues. Like women in dysfunctional families, women in therapy tend to blame themselves for whatever craziness transpires in their relationships with their therapists.

In this book, a large and diverse group of women share their stories. These stories provide some much-needed models of what good—and bad—therapy looks like. Perhaps this book will lead to more systematic and scientific inquiry into the issues raised; perhaps it will empower women to take a more active role in their own therapy.

At the very least, a woman reading this book will quickly find out that she is not the only one who has been perplexed by the therapeutic process, not the only one who has fallen in love with a therapist, been enraged by a therapist, or longed to be mothered or fathered or magically transformed by a therapist. I doubt if there is a single woman in therapy who has not sometimes wished for a third person in the room, another perspective on that charged one-on-one interaction. I hope this book will begin to provide that witness.

# About the Research for This Book

To expand the dialogues about therapy that had begun in my women writers' group, I set out to survey more systematically a large and representative group of women who had been in psychotherapy. Case histories have always been written by therapists, and so tell only half of the story. I wanted to give women in therapy the opportunity to tell the other half, and then I wanted to consider how boundary and transference issues figured into their narratives. Although I felt strongly that the book I could write as a health journalist would be very different from the book any practicing therapist would write, I thought it was important to have a seasoned therapist at my side.

While producing an educational film about the emotional issues involved when a doctor discloses a cancer diagnosis, I met Dr. Marie Cohen, a UCLA-affiliated psychologist. Her doctoral research on the doctor–patient relationship provided the basis for the film, and Marie was an expert on the subject. She was also a very gifted psychotherapist. She had a strong psychoanalytic background but was also a feminist and an original thinker. I asked Marie to be my editorial adviser because I knew that she would be willing to consider theoretical "truths" from all vantage points.

Marie and I designed a five-page questionnaire that we tweaked several times during the course of the research on the basis of the responses we were getting and some of our respondents' direct suggestions. We asked some general questions: "Why did you go into treatment?" "How long did your treatment last?" "Please rate the degree to which you found it helpful (very helpful, somewhat helpful, etc.)." "What was the most helpful aspect of the process?"

A few of our questions allowed for yes/no or multiple choice answers, but for the most part the survey asked for longer narrative responses. Our main focus was on how women felt about the process and about being in the client–therapist relationship, how they felt deep down about their therapists. Our questionnaire may have lacked some scientific precision, but it did afford respondents the chance to talk about those very issues that could easily slip through the cracks in the usual psychotherapy outcomes studies. We were looking for the subjective response, for those feelings about therapy that respondents might never have had the opportunity to articulate before, for those feelings that a woman might consider unusual or shameful. Had the respondents ever felt attachment, dependency, or love for their therapists? What about anger or hatred? How would they describe those feelings? Did they ever dream or fantasize about their therapists? Did they ever have sexual or romantic dreams or fantasies? What part did their therapists play in their interior lives? When did they think about them? Did they every carry a particular visual image of them around in their heads?

How did they conceptualize the boundaries of their therapy, and how did they feel about those boundaries? Did the therapist ever breach them, and if so, what was the impact? Did they themselves ever breach the boundaries or feel tempted to breach them? If a woman had strong feelings for her therapist, could she discuss them freely within the context of the therapy? Was this process helpful? Were such feelings ever labeled "transference" by the therapist? Did the women feel that their therapists' feelings or reactions ever got in the way of the therapy? When that happened, did their therapists take responsibility? Were they keeping secrets from their therapists? What *couldn't* they talk to their therapists about? Had their therapists ever done or said anything they considered inappropriate? What did they know of their therapists' lives outside of therapy? How did they find out? What else did they want to know? Did they ever feel they already knew too much?

With the help of a research assistant, I distributed the questionnaires widely. I mailed them with introductory letters to many of the psychotherapy training programs in the country asking for help in finding respondents. Some of these programs require that trainees embark on a course of psychotherapy before becoming therapists themselves, and I thought that trainees might be more willing to talk openly about the process. By including them, we also thought that we might offset the anticipated criticism that self-selected respondents would tend to be people with an anti-therapy ax to grind. As a result of this outreach, 64 respondents out of the total 274 are therapists or therapists in training themselves.

As other means of locating respondents, I placed advertisements in the classified section of publications likely to be read by women. The newsletter of the American Association of University Women proved particularly fruitful. I advertised in campus newspapers and alumni association magazines. For this reason, quite a few of the respondents are well-educated professionals; among them are professors, teachers, and graduate students. The survey also includes a group of incarcerated women undergoing a form of psychotherapy as part of their rehabilitation.

We put up flyers in bookstores and in health clubs and clinics where women congregate. A notice on several psychology bulletin boards on the Internet garnered a few respondents.

I received well over 400 inquiries from all over the country, and 277 women actually returned the completed questionnaire. We eliminated three questionnaires from our tabulation because many questions were left blank or the answers suggested more serious mental illness than seemed to fall in the scope of our sample. We also received one questionnaire from a man who wished to be heard on the subject.

In the end, we tabulated the questionnaires of 274 women. Fifty-two respondents came from California; 19 from New York; 13 from Massachusetts; 10 from Washington state, at least one from every other state, and one from the United Kingdom. Respondents ranged in age from nineteen to seventy-six with an average age of forty-one. Many respondents volunteered more than the completed questionnaire itself: Some sent appendices of ten pages or more;

others included the daily journal entries they had recorded while in therapy.

From the questionnaires, I culled many of the shorter quotes that appear in the book. With the help of a computer data analyst, we performed some rudimentary quantitative analysis, some of which appears in text.

Drawing from those respondents who checked a box on the questionnaire indicating a willingness to be interviewed, I contacted and formally interviewed 120 women either in person or over the telephone. Once word got out that I was writing the book, I was also besieged by women I knew and friends of friends, and even total strangers, who wanted to tell me their therapy stories. I could not go to a dinner party or a bridal shower or any other social event without someone telling me a therapy story.

I also contacted several support organizations for women who have had sexualized relationships with their therapists. Some of the stories of sexual transgressions came from these contacts. Since I solicited this information intentionally, the data from these women are not included in the data analysis.

The women who provided the longer stories in the book were all interviewed at some length, some for as long as eight or ten hours over the course of weeks or months. These were women who'd had particularly strong experiences in therapy—good and bad—women who were still in a quandary over something that had happened in therapy, women who were particularly articulate or particularly motivated to tell their stories.

I will never forget Elsa. Now in her seventies, Elsa provided a personal psychotherapy history that nearly corresponded to the history of psychotherapy in America since the 1940s. She was in the office of a close colleague of Wilhelm Reich (dressed in her underwear, a requirement of the therapy, which included a bodywork component) when the federal government came to remove the orgone machine. She witnessed America's love affair and disenchantment with classic psychoanalysis; she observed and sometimes participated in the humanistic revolution of the 1960s and 1970s. And she has since watched the cognitive-behaviorist movement grow, along with the twelve-step programs of the 1990s. Elsa was there as each movement brought its own vocabulary and concept of the therapist–client encounter, its orthodox and maverick practitioners. An optimist by nature, Elsa concluded in her interview that she had learned something useful from each of these therapeutic encounters.

Elsa's story provided much-needed perspective as I probed and prodded and pushed my subsequent interviewees. How did they perceive the therapist's power and their own power vis-à-vis the therapist? How did they feel about the built-in limitations of the relationship? Finally, how would they tell the story of their own therapy? Did it have a beginning, a middle, and an end? How were their stories different from the stories their therapists would tell? What did they wish they'd known when they first went into therapy? What would they like to tell therapists?

The women I interviewed seemed sincerely dedicated to improving the practice of psychotherapy and to helping educate other women. Some participated because they hoped that the very process of the interview might finally bring them clarity. A few took their interview transcripts back with them to their therapists and used the material in their therapy. Several confessed that they were participating in the hopes that their therapists would read the book and finally get the message they had been unable to convey in their therapy. Some decided after the fact that they had disclosed too much and withdrew their participation from the project. For a few women, telling me what had happened in their therapy probably served as a form of revenge against their therapists.

In general, the women were remarkably open, generous with their time, and courageous in their quest for self-knowledge. When their therapy had gone badly they wanted desperately to understand why. Even those women who had the most successful therapy experiences found the relationship between therapist and patient perplexing. My respondents (with the exception of some of those who were therapists themselves) nearly unanimously reported that they knew too little about therapy going in and that they often turned to the professional literature for answers. Clients complained that they had been inadequately prepared for the intensity of the feelings they would undergo during the process. Even those therapists who identified themselves as psychoanalytic sometimes seemed uncomfortable discussing the feelings their clients developed for them. The women I spoke to also shared considerable concerns about how the therapeutic boundaries served, or failed to serve, their needs.

Case histories written by therapists bear the same relationship to my respondents' accounts that a fairy tale like Cinderella might bear to a real life love affair. Case histories, from Freud's first accounts of young women with hysteria to the therapy "tales" that were all the rage a few years back, are a literary form, with a beginning, a middle, and an end. Most have a key memory that is uncovered, a central mystery that is solved. Once this pivotal climax occurs, everything else is denouement. The patient breaks free of her psychological shackles and lives a healthier life. Not surprisingly, the therapist-protagonist (who is also the author) is usually kind, wise, perceptive—if not omniscient—in short, the hero of the story. When women tell their own therapy stories, they do not always have a neat beginning, middle, and end. Change does not progress in a cumulative, linear fashion. The therapists are not always wise, heroic, or perceptive. Some stories remain stuck in the middle, die for want of a hero, or end with mysteries yet to be uncovered, work yet to be done. Many women must find a way, *despite* their therapists, to become the heroes of their own therapy stories.

Marie Cohen and I read over the interview transcripts that provide the text for these stories and discussed them from multiple vantage points. Then I took the questions these narratives raised to some of the country's most renowned therapists. Among them were Keith Ablow, Judith Armstrong, Margaret Baker, Alice Brand-Bartlett, Glen Gabbard, Janet Hadda, Constance Hammen, Michael Kahn, Richard Loewenstein, Gary Schoener, Irene Stiver, Michael Sussman, Charles Wahl, and Drew Westen. (See the Acknowledgments for a complete list of interviewees.) They provided some good answers and, in true therapeutic fashion, more hard questions.

I edited the interviewees' stories for length and clarity but attempted to retain the actual chronology of events. These stories are in the interviewees' own words, with some minimal changes made for the sake of clarity or condensation. I have changed identifying characteristics—names, places of residence, physical descriptions, sometimes professions—to protect the interviewees' anonymity. In the case of the therapists in the stories I have changed names and some identifying characteristics for the same purpose.

# 1

# The Story of Anna O.

*I, a native German girl, am now totally deprived of the faculty to speak, to understand, or to read German. . . . The physicians point it out as something very strange. . . . In the first 2 months of my sojourn here, I had shorter or longer absences, which I could observe by myself by a strange feeling of "timemissing." . . . When I do not read I am laying, not always very quiet, occupied with my thoughts. . . .*

A fragment from *Report by Bertha Pappenheim ("Anna O.") on Her Illness* (1882)

Anna O. was a slight, dark, intense woman of twenty-two when psychiatrist Dr. Josef Breuer first paid a call to her family's well-groomed townhouse in Vienna. Known as the doctor with the "golden touch" in the local Jewish community, Breuer, at forty-three, had a long, soulful face, a full beard, and soft probing brown eyes. Suffering from "hysteria," Anna O. was about to embark on an experiment that would become psychotherapy, and would describe it for the first time as the "talking cure."

Unfortunately, Anna O., whose real name was Bertha Pappenheim, never told her own therapy story, leaving only the fragment excerpted here as an account. Although she delineated her symptoms in florid detail, she hardly commented on her treatment and said nothing about her relationship with Dr. Breuer. But it is this relationship, with its intimations of love and abandonment, for which she is most remembered. The events that transpired between Breuer and Anna O. drove Sigmund Freud to conceptualize transference and linked the story of Anna O. forever after with its discovery.

The "Case of Fraulein Anna O." comprises one chapter in *Studies on Hysteria*, the book that Breuer coauthored with his young colleague Sigmund Freud in 1895, more than a decade after Anna's treatment. Practitioners rarely write case histories to flaunt their failures, and true to the form, Breuer attests that Anna O. was "cured" by the psychotherapy that they had together devised and that their relationship came to a happy conclusion. The Anna O. of the case history, like her sisters who people the other chapters, now seems a nearly mythic figure, the young female hysteric of the late-nineteenth-century case study. Like the vampire women in the fiction of the period, she was afflicted by mysterious symptoms: screaming fits, trances, paralyses, blindness, pain that traveled capriciously from one part of the body to another, periods of lost time, and lapses in identity.

Because Anna O. left so little in the way of an account herself, I tell her story here to set a context for exploring women's relationships with their psychotherapists. Anna O.'s story highlights both the potential and the dangers of psychotherapy and raises many of the same dilemmas with which women in therapy continue to grapple.

When Breuer arrived at the Pappenheim residence, he learned that Anna O. had spent the past few months as her father's night nurse, a role daughters of the period were obliged to perform. Night after night, while the rest of the household slept, Anna remained poised at her father's bedside. Sigmund Pappenheim, at fifty-seven, was dying from an abscess of the lung, probably a complication of long-standing tuberculosis. In an effort to ease his breathing, a surgeon came periodically and inserted a long needle to drain fluid from his lung. Once the autocratic head of his rule- and ritual-bound Orthodox Jewish household, Sigmund Pappenheim was reduced to helplessness, a thin specter against the starched white bed linens.

Anna made a devoted nurse. Vigilant for any change in her father's breathing and perhaps dreading the approach of the Angel of Death (said in Jewish folklore to hover around the bed of the dying), Anna tried not to slip into her usual reveries. Forbidden as a girl to pursue any education beyond high school, Anna found life in her father's house intolerably monotonous. As rebellion seemed futile, she escaped internally to what she called her "private theatre." Lately this theatre had spun out of control. Cheerful fairy tales had turned into epics of horror habited by skeletons and serpents. One day in the entryway of a relative's home she was horrified to look into a mirror and see reflected back not her own face but her father's transfigured by a death's head.

Her first physical sign of illness was a persistent barking cough, perhaps a sympathetic echo of her father's hacking. A multitude of sensations soon took over her body, adhering to no law of physical causality. The muscles of her neck and arm went rigid. Her right leg—as numb as if it had been injected with anesthetic—extended and rotated inward in spasm. Intermittently deaf and unable to focus her eyes, she perceived the walls of her room to be falling over. She relinquished her nursing post and assumed the role of the patient.

Breuer was quickly taken with Anna, particularly, in his words, with her "penetrating intuition," her "great poetic and imaginative gifts," and her "sympathetic kindness." He began to pay daily, sometimes twice daily, visits. He sat at her bedside for hours, transfixed by her most secret thoughts; took her for evening rides in his carriage; held her hand; and spoonfed her peaches. His devotion was unusual; most physicians were wary, if not contemptuous, of their hysterical female patients. As Anna had patiently nursed her father, Breuer now nursed her.

Anna had begun to experience what psychotherapists today call dissociative states, during which she lost continuity in time and awareness of her present surroundings. During these *absences*, she seemed dispossessed, the chaste and obedient Jewish daughter transformed into an unkempt, raging, wild woman. The sacred institutions of family, religion, and medicine received equal shares of her scorn. She hallucinated and screamed words in a hodgepodge of languages, railed at her mother and servants, threw her bed cushions at them, and tore the buttons off her bedclothes. "I have a real self and an evil self," she said.

Sigmund Pappenheim had been the dominant force not only in the Pappenheim household but also in Anna's psyche. She was passionately "fond of him," according to Breuer, and he, in turn, "pampered" her. Although certainly of marriageable age, Anna O. revealed no romantic interests. "The patient, whose life became known to me to an extent to which one person's life is seldom known to another, had never been in love," wrote Breuer. "The element of sexuality was astonishingly undeveloped in her." Perhaps no other man could rival Sigmund Pappenheim in Anna's affections, and yet Anna must have resented the limits on her life exacted by loyalty to him.

An accepted treatment for hysteria at the time was to induce a hypnotic trance and then provide a post-hypnotic suggestion that the hysteric give up her symptoms. Patients sometimes complied, but the effects were temporary. Breuer attempted a variant of this technique by entering into Anna's seemingly self-induced trances. He repeated her ramblings back to her and she picked up the thread and narrated the terrors that passed before her. They centered on a girl sitting watch over a deathbed. After purging herself of these disturbing images, Anna became, according to Breuer, "calm and cheerful." She called this rudimentary form of psychotherapy the "talking cure" and also referred to it as "chimney sweeping."

Anna was improving until her father died, which was to Breuer "the most severe psychical trauma that she could possibly have experienced." For several weeks Anna's mother had deceived her about his deteriorating condition. When she realized that she had been in her own words "cheated out of a glance and a final word" from her father, she reacted with "a violent outburst of excitement," then moved into a "greatly changed state." Members of her family looked like "wax figures." Her mother became a "stove" that gave off unpleasant heat.

Only Breuer remained real and human. "Only for me was she invariably present," he wrote. She always recognized Breuer's voice, Breuer's face; he was the link to reality, to the world of others, to survival itself. She ate only when Breuer handfed her. Breuer's treatment may have consisted of talking, but the cure appeared to reside in *who* was doing the *listening*—Anna talked only to Breuer, and only when Breuer responded did she feel better. Freud was to claim years later that in the case of Anna, "the personal emotional relationship between doctor and patient was after all stronger than the whole cathartic process."

But Breuer seemed to have remained impervious to the impact of his presence on Anna's symptoms. He attributed the positive results to the method of the "talking cure," never recognizing how much of the "cure's" efficacy resided in Anna's feelings for him and in the bond between them. Nor did he ever acknowledge the seeming depth of his own feelings for Anna.

Breuer postulated his own theory about the nature of Anna's illness and her presumed "cure," concluding that she had suffered numerous traumas during the course of nursing her father and had been forced to suppress the associated "affects." Breuer's notion of affects was close to the contemporary definition of "emotions," except affects carried a sort of electrical or physical charge. When affects could not be expressed, their bound-up energy expressed itself in hysterical symptoms. Anna had never been free to express the horror and grief she felt watching her beloved father deteriorate and die. Breuer theorized that fully recalling the traumatic events and fully expressing the associated affects would completely alleviate her symptoms.

Over the years, therapists have been more inclined to look at the specifics of Anna's relationship with her father. Many have wondered about her internal conflict about that relationship and about her inability to admit her conflictual feelings to herself. Some therapists today suggest that Anna must have suffered specific childhood traumas and deprivations beyond the ordinary horrors of watching a father die to experience the symptoms that she did. Whatever the truth, therapists today are in agreement on one point: Anna's distress had more than a little to do with her relationship with her father, and her "cure" had a great deal to do with her relationship with Breuer.

Breuer's account reveals that Anna's symptoms all began in exchanges with her father: She fell deaf after failing to hear and comply with his request for a glass of wine; she became unable to focus her eyes after being unable to tell him the time because she could not see her watch face through her blur of tears. Whenever she failed her father, she developed a self-punitive symptom. Each of these symptoms seemed a capsular representation of her internal conflict about compliance and rebellion.

Whether Breuer or Anna dictated the termination of her therapy is unclear, but their last session was planned in advance, and Breuer set the scene. Rearranging the furniture in the room to resemble Sigmund Pappenheim's sickroom, he placed Anna in a chair beside the bed, poised to once again serve as night nurse. In his written account, Breuer doesn't reveal where he stood, what lines he spoke, what part he played in Anna's drama. Regarding himself as sympathetic observer, director, perhaps, Breuer missed the extent to which he had become a character in Anna's play. Perhaps he was her father's symbolic stand-in, the man who would survive the sickroom scene, the beloved she would not lose.

Ever Breuer's cooperative patient, Anna produced the final traumatic memory: Late one night she had been sitting alone at her father's bedside. The sound of his irregular breathing filled the room; he was delirious; no cold compress could control his raging fever. Anna was panic stricken, praying the surgeon would arrive on the train in time to drain her father's lung and forestall his death once more.

As the hours passed, Anna "fell into a waking dream." She saw a monstrous black snake coming from the wall to bite her father, and when she went to beat the snake off, she could not move her arm against it. Apparently her arm had fallen asleep over the back of the chair. When she looked down at her recalcitrant hand, her fingers had turned into little snakes, her fingernails into death's heads. Her own hand, which should have been the agent of her father's rescue, had turned into the symbol of his destruction, a graphic, living representation, perhaps, of her internal conflict.

This sickbed incident, according to Breuer, accounted for Anna's lingering paralysis—the arm that she had not been able to move to help her father remained unmovable. Once she remembered the trauma and expressed the associated affect, the full horror she had suppressed at her father's bedside, she could move her arm again and her remaining symptoms vanished. Here was the emotional catharsis that signaled the climax of their work together. With Anna seemingly on her way to a complete recovery, Breuer exited her life.

## The Epilogue

Breuer's summation is tidy—too tidy. Psychotherapy has never been this simple. Years later, Freud claimed that his by-then estranged mentor had left out a critical epilogue. He reported that Anna's mother sent for Breuer on the very evening after the final session. Breuer arrived to find his patient twisting and writhing on the floor, groaning and clutching her abdomen. When Breuer leaned over her and asked what was wrong and she recognized the calm, soothing voice that had become so familiar, she replied, "Now Dr. B's baby is coming." In a letter to writer Stefan Zweig in 1932, Freud wrote that Breuer became "seized by conventional horror . . . took flight and abandoned the patient to a colleague."

Recently discovered hospital papers suggest that Anna's illness lingered long after her so-called final catharsis and that Breuer himself admitted her to a distant and secluded sanitarium. She continued to receive treatment for her hysteria as well as for the dependency on chloral hydrate and other narcotics that Dr. Breuer had, perhaps unwittingly, fostered.

Freud added his epilogue from the vantage point of several additional years of clinical experience and a growing theoretical agenda. For Freud, the events in the epilogue gave vivid proof of *transference*, a phenomenon by which Anna O. transferred early and unresolved feelings for her father onto Breuer. Her hysterical pregnancy suggested to Freud that she had not been as "sexually undeveloped" as Breuer had contended—that, in fact, the feelings transferred were fundamentally sexual and that she had been harboring them for Breuer throughout the course of her treatment. When he abandoned her, her unconscious longings for reunion, and perhaps revenge, emerged in the form of a hysterical pregnancy.

Moreover, Anna's love was just one instance of a larger phenomenon that Freud had observed among his patients in psychoanalysis. In the years since Breuer had treated Anna, a number of Freud's otherwise decorous Viennese lady patients had suddenly thrown open their arms and proclaimed their love for the good doctor. More invested in his analytical ability than in his own attractiveness, Freud interpreted these proclamations of love rather than taking them personally. According to Freud, patients *transferred* feelings—unconscious, primitive feelings that they had developed for significant figures in infancy and childhood—onto the analyst. It was the therapeutic relationship itself that evoked this transference; transference-love "derived from the analytic situation, not the person of the therapist." In assuming the role of authority and confidant, the analyst became a symbol for the projection of the client's deepest drives and desires. Transference feelings were potent and had a volatile potential—hence the high drama of the final scene between Anna O. and Josef Breuer.

Nor were therapists immune. Freud also claimed that the psychotherapeutic relationship as well as the client's transference were apt to stir intense and unresolved feelings in the *therapist*. This *countertransference* was equally dangerous. When therapists did not help clients understand their own feelings and instead reacted to these feelings, fireworks were likely; when patient and therapist acted out their transference and countertransference feelings, disaster could ensue. Anna O. had fallen in love with Breuer, and he had reciprocated, lost his scientific objectivity, and fled out of fear and shame.

In Freud's view, there was only one appropriate and therapeutic approach to transference: dispassionate interpretation. The analyst must never fall under the spell of transference by taking too personally the role in which the patient had cast him. And the analyst must be careful not to gratify the transference feelings, but to help the patient understand their unconscious origins. Only by recognizing their roots in primitive drives could the patient resolve and then renounce these feelings in favor of more adult fulfillments.

Whether in love or simply out of his depth, the moralistic and high-minded Breuer never used the "talking cure" again. Treating

Anna O. had wreaked havoc in his personal life, he complained in a letter to his friend Auguste Forel in 1907: "It was impossible for a general practitioner to treat a case of that kind without bringing his activities and mode of life completely to an end. I vowed at the time that I would *not* go through such an ordeal again."

If Freud first observed transference as a phenomenon—the intense feelings of need, vulnerability, rage, and desire that developed among women in psychotherapy—he quickly conceptualized it as a set of theoretical and untestable ideas about a phenomenon. The psychoanalysts who followed developed an ever-more arcane body of writings on the subject, making it difficult to differentiate the phenomenon of transference as it is experienced from all the psychoanalytic ideas about it. In this book, I try to get back to these feelings as women in therapy actually experience them, as Anna O. might have written about them if she'd had the chance.

So what sense can modern readers make of Anna O.'s relationship with Dr. Breuer? Did she really fall in love with him, and if so, does Freud's transference theory adequately explain her love? The concept certainly explains the relationship's intensity as well as Anna's apparent shift of affection from her father to Breuer. The relationship's charge, its significance for her, derived partly from its resonance with her earlier relationship with her father. It would seem that in her relationship with Breuer, Anna may have been both reenacting her relationship with her father and attempting to resolve it.

Clearly, transference theory can illuminate some aspects of Anna O.'s relationship with Josef Breuer. But to talk about their relationship strictly in terms of transference is reductive. Breuer fulfilled needs in Anna that had long gone unmet. He allowed her to speak the unspeakable, to express her deepest feelings without fear of censure, to behave in the most socially unacceptable fashion. He responded always by attempting to understand her in her own language, by validating that her language had merit and meaning in the world. He knew her to the extent that one person seldom comes to know another, and this intimacy, while skewed one way, was genuine.

When Anna O. revealed herself completely, and Breuer seemed to accept and understand her completely, how could that *not* feel like love? Losing Breuer, particularly without his acknowledging the significance of her loss, was not just a repetition of the loss of her father, but was an occasion for grief and, perhaps, rage in its own right.

To even engage in the talking cure with Breuer, Anna had to make a leap of faith, investing Breuer with the power to help her. The very strength of her wish to be helped, the very act of giving herself up to the wish, evoked her deepest longings and desires. She allowed Breuer entrée into her most interior life, and he embraced the intimacy. Their relationship became emblematic of what any relationship with another person could provide, important beyond its literal limits. If Breuer loved her, she was lovable; if he did not, then she would be alone always. As the one she turned to for help, the one who understood her completely, Breuer's actions and words were bound to take on undue significance.

Anna may have wondered how Breuer could have performed such loving ministrations and then have had the power to just walk away. In fact, Breuer had considerable power that Anna did not. He had freedom of movement, authority in the world, the status that came with being a male member of the Viennese bourgeosie. And he had power over Anna: the power to get her out of her father's house, at least temporarily; to prescribe treatments; to administer drugs; to touch and examine her body; to disclose or deny information; to negotiate with the world on her behalf. He had the power to commit her to an asylum against her will, to tell her story and have the world accept it on his terms.

To be intimate with Breuer was to share in his power, to feel that her life, her personal meanings, had an impact on someone else. To lose Breuer was to be returned to her father's house and to silence. Even as their work together gave Anna a way to reveal feelings that had been submerged, her feelings for Breuer became submerged, and the emotional importance of their relationship became an unspeakable secret between them. When Anna could not express her feelings directly, she resorted to her usual medium of expression—her body—and enacted them in the form of a fantasied pregnancy.

It is hardly surprising that Anna might respond to Breuer's abandonment with a cry of pregnancy—a baby was one way that a woman could prove to the world what had gone on between her and a man. To be carrying Breuer's baby would be incontestable evidence of the intimacy that they had shared.

If Breuer had been brave enough, had found the language, to discuss the significance of their relationship, he and Anna might have come to a better understanding of its symbolic and realistic significance. They might have seen in their bond a distillation of Anna's wishes, needs, and feelings about love and might have been able to use that understanding to help her resolve some of her earlier relationships and the conflicts she had about the direction of her life. Perhaps if Breuer could have acknowledged his own feelings, and the fear that finally drove him to bolt, he could have worked with Anna to prevent the final dramatic enactment and Anna's subsequent relapse.

## Flying Without a Net

As psychotherapy pioneers, Josef Breuer and Anna O. were making up her treatment as they went along. They began with no mutually understood boundaries, no structure to circumscribe their exquisite, profound, and potentially dangerous connection. Therapeutic boundaries might have delineated Breuer's power and limited some of his behaviors. Moonlight rides, repeated physical contact, and spoon-feedings might have been too provocative, resembling too closely the care that children receive from their parents and lovers receive from their loves. These acts, in conjunction with such intense psychological intimacy, might have suggested to Anna that Breuer's love was absolute, not limited, his commitment eternal, not finite. She might well have imagined she was about to get her perfect mate, the culmination of her every wish.

Breuer's unboundaried interactions with Anna may have looked too much like true love, or rather a perfect love, beyond the limitations of mortals. Without a structure to define their relationship, this promise of perfect love and redemption hung over their relationship, leaving Anna vulnerable to victimization. As kindhearted as Breuer may have been, he did not take full responsibility for the power that comes with the psychotherapist's role, and he never acknowledged his own symbolic weight in Anna's psychic life.

## A Rorschach Test for Therapists

The "Case of Fraulein Anna O." has served as a veritable Rorschach test for therapists of every generation since, with theorists interpreting and reinterpreting it through the shifting filters of history. They have reexamined Anna's illness, her treatment, and her relationship with Dr. Breuer. She has been rediagnosed according to every possible paradigm, her symptoms chalked up to pathological grief reaction, borderline personality disorder, and, most recently, dissociative identity disorder. As psychoanalysis has shifted its focus of attention from the father of toddlerhood to the mother of infancy, therapists have seen in her transference more mother and less father.

These shifting interpretations reveal that psychotherapy is prone to fad and fashion, that it occurs in history, that regardless of its scientific claims, it does not take place in a laboratory protected from social forces. In looking at the women's therapy stories in this book, we must remember Anna O. so as not to forget the social context that shapes them.

Years after her treatment with Josef Breuer, Bertha Pappenheim found her own voice. As a leader of the European feminist and social work movements, she devoted her life to disenfranchised women and children. She traveled widely, crusading against the hypocrisy of a bourgeois establishment that held marriage and family sacrosanct while secretly supporting such institutions as black market prostitution of teenage girls. She never married herself and left no indication of ever having had a serious romance. In a poem written in 1911, she expressed her sadness over what was missing from her life:

*Love did not come to me—*
*So I live like the plants,*
*In the cellar, without light.*

Some sources suggest that Pappenheim continued to suffer from psychic distress, perhaps even lapsing into trances at nightfall.

When pressed by journalists to comment on her treatment with Dr. Breuer, Bertha Pappenheim would say only that psychoanalysis was a "double-edged sword."

As we will see, women in therapy today still relate to Pappenheim's mental unrest, to the disjunction between her needs and what society offered by way of cure, and to the complex nature of her relationship with her therapist. They would probably agree with her assessment of therapy as a double-edged sword. About their relationships with their therapists, however, they have a great deal more to say.

# 2

# The Approximate Relationship

In my first week of research for this book, I arranged to interview a well-known psychoanalyst. He had a reputation for being brilliant, for being an iconoclast who could cut through dogma and speak the truth. I arrived for our interview at six o'clock on a Friday night to find his building, which housed mainly psychotherapists, already deserted. His waiting room was dark and paneled in mahogany, accented by a few carefully chosen abstract paintings. I pulled the switch to signify my arrival and waited.

Dr. V. soon appeared at the doorway, a distinguished man in his sixties, tall and dressed in a dark, well-tailored suit, with a nondescript but tasteful tie. He had thick gray hair that he frequently brushed out of his eyes by shaking his head back and a disarming manner of forcing me to be the first one to break eye contact. In his inner office, which was also dark and warm, he sat across the room from me in a big, black leather armchair. I sat on a smaller chair, leaning in intently so as not to miss a nuance. I began by asking Dr. V. to explain transference.

"If you play according to the analytic rules," he said, "the patient begins to relate to you as though she had some prior contact with you, as though you were a person of significance from her earlier life. . . . Of course, transference does not occur only in psychotherapy. We have transference to our neighbors, transference to our friends, but we also have information about them that serves as a reality corrective. Transference is maximized in analysis because the analyst withholds information about himself, refrains from intruding his needs into the therapeutic interaction."

Dr. V. conveyed such a sense of easy authority that I began to imagine that he would answer my questions so completely that I would not have to go through the usual laborious process of gathering information and sorting it out—Dr. V. would tell me everything I needed to know about the relationship between women and their therapists.

"Transference is not just a love feast," he was saying, as I emerged from my daydream. "I tell my patients sometimes that it's like waiting on the corner of 42nd Street and Times Square. If you stand there long enough, eventually everybody in the world goes by. Every human feeling, every need that you could have in any human relationship, is apt to make an appearance somewhere in the relationship with the analyst."

"And what about the analyst?" I asked. "What part do the analyst's feelings play?"

"Hopefully, a good clinician has gone through all the files in his cabinet. He knows where his wellness leaves off and his sickness begins. He tries to see the ways in which the latter affects his judgment about patients and he tries to limit the effects."

As the remaining daylight faded and Dr. V.'s office grew even darker, he seemed to be fading somewhat, too. Greedy for enlightenment, I pounded him with questions. His answers grew less direct, and after a while he began to ramble. I noticed that his hands had begun to tremble, just a bit. But before I could be sure I had seen what I thought I had seen, he folded them into his lap. I wanted so much for him to give me what I needed that I could not allow myself to imagine that he was in any way impaired.

I brought the interview to a close and stood up to leave. Dr. V. smiled graciously, seemingly undiminished. But then as he was walking me out, he grew pale, clutched the door handle in an effort to stabilize himself, and collapsed to the floor. There he was—the analyst of great renown, the man who would answer all my questions, weak and pale, eyes closed, sprawled across the threshold of his office.

My first impulse was less than noble: I wanted to flee. Then a wave of guilty dread washed over me. Had I finally done it—killed an interviewee with my insistent, incessant curiosity? Could I have prevented this from happening? I kneeled down to attend to Dr. V., and in a flash I remembered another day that had not been so clear in memory for several years—the day my father, at age sixty-five, had his final, fatal stroke. I was in my parents' bedroom helping my mother care for him. He had a high fever and was babbling incoherently. While my mother was in the next room, trying to reach his doctor on the phone, I was watching over him. As I wiped his face with a cool washcloth and he grew more and more delirious, I felt nearly paralyzed by fear. As I watched, my father suddenly grabbed his head and his eyes opened wide in terror. Then he began to choke and retch, spewing mucus and saliva. The next minute the terror was gone, his eyes devoid of everything.

I panicked, wanting more than anything else to run out of the room. And then I was overcome by waves of dread and guilt and loss—how could I have watched and been unable to protect him, to stave off this catastrophic torrent of events?

Now, as I kneeled over Dr. V., the entire scene and all my associated feelings flooded over me. And I realized, in an instant, the truth of what Dr. V. had been telling me about transference. I had been ready, primed to plug him into a premade father category. My reactions at his collapse—shock, fear, guilt, the urge to flee—might have seemed nearly universal, but their distinctive coloration derived from my past. If Dr. V.'s collapse reminded me of my father's stroke, and if I reacted in the same way, the deeper motives and emotions that drove my reaction seemed to go back much further to the interactions of early childhood. I suspected that without being consciously aware of it, I had cast Dr. V. as being both like the father I'd had and the father for whom I'd always wished.

"Doctor," I said, lightly touching his arm, "Do you know what is the matter with you?"

After a few excruciating moments, Dr. V. opened his eyes. "I'm diabetic," he whispered. "Can you please get my glucose tablets from my side table?"

His tablets were not on the side table. His pristine, protected analytic office—whose dark surfaces offered no impediments, yielded no information to interfere with the patient's internal process—became the enemy. In a hot panic I cast out any respect for Dr. V.'s privacy, rifling through his papers and foraging through his drawers recklessly. It occurred to me that I was no doubt living the fantasy of many a therapy client who imagines going through her therapist's things in search of some piece of critical personal information.

I finally found the glucose tablets and ran to place one in Dr. V.'s mouth. As it dissolved and the glucose entered his bloodstream, color came back into his cheeks. I sat on the hallway floor beside him, an unspoken injunction against touching him mysteriously having come back into force.

"This never happens to me," he said, "but I had a patient with an emergency and didn't have a chance to eat lunch. Then I got so involved in our conversation I didn't realize I was going too long without eating . . ."

"It's okay," I said. I am a medical writer after all so this shouldn't faze me. "I'm just sorry—"

"There's absolutely no reason to blame yourself," Dr. V. said, his therapeutic instincts kicking in. "In a way I'm glad this happened when you were here, as opposed to a patient. A patient would have been so much more upset. If there's one thing a patient can't tolerate in an analyst, it's his mortality."

I understood what Dr. V. was saying. Our therapists are the objects not only of our projection of feelings and experiences from the past, but also of our wishes for the impossible. We long for our therapists to be perfect, immortal, so that their existence can somehow validate and redeem our own. And we long for these immortal beings to love us perfectly, unconditionally, in a way that we have never been loved before. I had projected onto Dr. V. my experiences with my own father, but I had also projected onto him my wishes for the father I had never had but perhaps imagined I had for a few blessed moments of early childhood—the wise, all-knowing authority, the good father who could impart absolute truth to me pleasurably. I had wished for that from the moment I called Dr. V. and arranged for the interview, but I had not realized how much I had been wishing for it until he collapsed at my feet.

My "session" with Dr. V. gave me an unintentional but nevertheless vivid and personal demonstration of transference. Dr. V. had quickly become a symbolic figure for me, a representative of father-past and father-potential. In our brief encounter, I had revealed little about myself, certainly had not allowed him to see the extent of my vulnerability. Nevertheless, I had felt a great deal about Dr. V. that I never would have recognized had our interview not culminated in such a dramatic fashion. I can only wonder how much more profound my feelings might have been if Dr. V. had been my psychotherapist.

The women I interviewed for this book have experienced profound, intense, seemingly disproportionate, sometimes sublime, and often unmanageable feelings toward their therapists. When women in therapy talk about transference, they are talking about these feelings. Sometimes, their comments make transference sound like an awful disease. A woman who has experienced what she considers transference for one therapist and is beginning treatment with another may dread its onset, be on the lookout for its tell-tale signs, and fight it off like a relapse of the flu. ("Oh, no, I've got transference again!") Other women describe it as a slightly disreputable practice: "I don't *do* transference," one wrote. Before turning to the feelings that women in therapy describe, let's look at the nature of the relationship in which such feelings flourish.

## The Real and the Symbolic

The relationship between therapist and client takes place in a realm poised between everyday reality and the symbolic. Clients know that their therapists are ordinary people, that therapy is what they do for a living. The relationship's limitations are all too apparent. A client sees her therapist once or twice or maybe three times a week in his or her office for forty-five or fifty minutes. For the therapist's services, which are often difficult to quantify or even describe, the patient pays fees. For many women, these fees represent a significant expenditure and make the therapist's services seem a particularly precious commodity.

Contact with the therapist is largely limited to these formal sessions; women in therapy know that good clients do not call their therapists between sessions too often, do not make too many extra demands, do not ask too many probing questions about their therapists' personal lives, or expect therapists to disclose how they really feel about their clients.

The client–therapist relationship is inevitably asymmetrical and involves a certain artifice. It is not natural, after all, for one person to reveal everything about herself and the other to reveal little or nothing, nor is it natural to be intimate in such measured doses. There is something ritualistic about the repetitive structure of sessions, about the way the therapist always opens the door to her office with the same half-smile or clears her throat to indicate that time is up.

This is a bond marked by unresolvable tension and paradox. It is intimate and yet skewed one way; professional and yet highly personal; fueled by the client's hopes and wishes, yet sustained by the payment of fees. More than one woman in my survey compared therapy to prostitution in its dissonant mix of the professional and the private. "Therapy is like seeing a prostitute," Jenna wrote. "Even though it feels awkward and embarrassing you have to hurry up and take your clothes off so you can get what you came for. After you've relaxed some and are feeling extremely vulnerable, you have to be quick about putting your clothes back on, so someone else can use the room."

The room, of course, is not the only issue. Someone else is also going to use *your* therapist. The person you feel so close to, the one who shares the secrets you've never before spoken out loud, will say good-bye and then turn around and share equally special intimacies with others.

In ordinary society, close relationships tend to be symmetrical and to progress along a predictable trajectory of intimacy: The parties spend increasingly more time together, share increasingly intimate and reciprocal disclosures, observe one another in a variety of different settings to assess each other's reliability and trustworthiness.

A seemingly intimate relationship that does not progress along this course, that is not reciprocal, that cannot be tested by the usual social means, that only operates within a very circumscribed sphere is apt to be confusing and frustrating. The simultaneous intimacy and constraints of the psychotherapeutic relationship simply do not jibe; clients tend to feel a certain tension to turn the relationship into the more usual social cast: friendship, romance, family.

To be in therapy is to trust someone about whom you cannot collect the information to protect yourself, whom you cannot observe in the usual social settings. A client's only gauge is how her therapist behaves within the constraints of the role, what she reveals of herself in sessions. It is not surprising then that women in therapy worry a great deal about the authenticity of their therapists. Is this person real or putting on an act? Is compassion something she *does* or the way she *is*? What does she *really* think of me? Can someone be paid to *care*?

There is something paradoxical in the fact that clients are attempting to change, "to move rock," as a woman named Donna put it, in a relationship that is, in many respects, static. No matter how much a client invests in time, revelations, and emotional expressiveness, the relationship cannot progress beyond certain limits. It is doomed to end by design. It is inherently tragic to become so close to someone that you can never completely know and are destined to lose.

Clients also cannot escape the fact that they need their therapists more than their therapists appear to need them. The therapist has many clients, while the client has only one therapist. Therapists matter to their clients more than their clients can matter to them, and they take on symbolic meanings that far transcend the apparent limitations of the relationship. They become symbolic of what their clients need and what they fear, internalized icons, representatives of past figures and future possibilities, the loci of the hope for change. They people their clients' dreams, assume voices in what were once interior monologues, become the mystery men and women in their sexual fantasies.

Sally, a woman who was afraid of flying, told me that when airborne she comforted herself by imagining that her therapist was sitting in the back of the plane, acting as a sort of guardian angel. Randi, who at age twenty-six, had already spent ten years suffering from bulimia, had internalized her father's anger into a voice in her head that often berated her for being "bad." For years her therapist, who was a gentle, grandfatherly man, told her, "You weren't a bad kid, you just had bad luck." Eventually his voice overpowered the cries of "badness." Now, several years after her therapy has ended, she has internalized her therapist as self-acceptance: "It's not so much his voice anymore that I hear, as it is a softening of my own voice in support, a merging of our voices."

Susan, who had a long history of suicide attempts, had a recurring dream in which a personified figure of death taunted and cajoled her to join him by taking her own life. After wrestling with her depression during several years of therapy with a bright and compassionate man, she had the dream again, only this time the figure of death assumed her therapist's face. Together she and Death visited, grieved, and ultimately pitied a gallery of recent suicides. Death urged her to go on living; they would be together soon enough. After the dream, Susan lost the urge to commit suicide.

Therapists clearly take on powerful roles in internal dramas. They are the object of profound love and violent anger, recipients of emotions usually reserved for family members and lovers. But they are not family members, are not—or, at least should not be—lovers. They hold a role unlike any other.

To enter into therapy, the client must make a leap of faith, investing the therapist with her hope for change. By this very leap of faith, the relationship with the therapist becomes emblematic. It constitutes the test case, the mold-breaker, the relationship after which every other relationship will be different. The client may come to believe that if she fails in the therapy relationship, she will fail in every relationship that follows. Conversely, if she can succeed in therapy, she will take that success with her everywhere.

To make the leap of faith necessary to enter into therapy, a client may need to believe that the therapist is more than just another mortal human being, that cure will come through some process more magical than mere conversation. The prospect of change may inspire hopes of some more profound, even spiritual, transformation. As one woman nearing the completion of her therapy said: "I'm grateful because in many respects I feel like a different person now, but sometimes I'm disappointed because he's human and I'll still be human even when I'm done with therapy."

The psychotherapeutic relationship—asymmetrical, concentrated, ritualistic, emotionally intense—is ripe for taking on emblematic, symbolic meanings for the client. It is no wonder then, given the context of the relationship, that the therapist's small acts may assume enormous importance. We can imagine why the therapist might well become the object for the client's expression of everything she has gotten, failed to get, or wanted to get from another human being.

Is the very structure of the therapy relationship a set-up to induce profound feelings? Yes. Clients are susceptible to developing disproportionate feelings because the therapist means so much more to them than they mean to the therapist. The very rules and limits of the therapeutic relationship (confide all to someone who is paid to listen and to behave in a manner that looks like caring although you can never know for sure how much the therapist really cares) are likely to induce profound feelings. Of course, a client is predisposed to be hypersensitive to a therapist's behavior when she relies on the therapist for so much; confides deep, emotional material; must pay dearly for brief snatches of the therapist's time; and is never sure who she really is or how she really feels. As Hannah put it, "The whole situation of deprivation in therapy is a trap—what else can you do but desperately want what you're not allowed to have any of?" To need someone who doesn't need back is emotionally hazardous and apt to inspire intense feelings.

Be that as it may, not every woman in therapy finds the relationship a trigger for deep emotions, and the balance between the therapist as realistic helper and the therapist as symbol is different for every woman. A sizable minority of the women who participated in my research reported having what they considered reality-bound, adult-to-adult relationships with their therapists. They regarded them as sounding boards, coaches, sympathetic listeners, skilled problem solvers, role models, supportive allies. They might have been fond of them and thought highly of them, but they did not think about them a great deal while out of their offices. They did not become inordinately attached to them, nor did they attempt to alter the boundaries of the therapy to satisfy some deeper longings. They didn't want anything beyond what was being offered. They seldom became enraged with them. In short, they never fell in love.

However, for the majority of the women, the relationship with their therapists was much more significant. Of the 274 respondents in my survey, 209 reported having felt "love, attachment, or dependency" for at least one therapist at some point in their lives. Fifty-nine women answered that they had never felt those feelings for any therapist, and six declined to respond. Of the 209 who said they had felt love, attachment, or dependency, 110 used the word "love" or a synonym for it.

These feelings may have been most pronounced in those women who had the most disappointing childhoods, those who entered therapy not to solve finite problems but to change themselves in more fundamental ways, those whose therapies probed deeply into their emotional lives and their childhoods, and those whose treatment went on for several years. In shorter treatments where the emphasis was on particular techniques or methods—for example, in the more practical, cognitive-behaviorally oriented therapy—clients seemed less likely to develop profound feelings.

# The Disproportionate Importance
# of Small Things

In the therapy relationship, small things may take on undue importance. Joanna, a woman in her thirties, experienced a sense of "total abandonment" when her therapist was late to a session. She could reason that the therapist's tardiness certainly didn't mean that she was abandoning her, but that's not how it felt. When Clara's therapist yawned repeatedly during a session, that seemed proof that Clara's life was irredeemably boring. For Nan, the therapist's mildly disheveled office was evidence of his impending nervous breakdown.

In the course of therapy, it is not unusual for a woman to become intensely vulnerable to the therapist's actions, capable of being deeply wounded by an offhand remark, prone to argue at the slightest hint of disagreement. She may need too much for her therapist to always say or do precisely the right thing and may imbue the therapist's saying the wrong thing with untoward consequences.

Joanna made the emotional equation between lateness and abandonment early in her therapy. She says now, "If I couldn't even count on her to show up on time, how could I trust her with my innermost feelings?" Behavior that in the context of a friendship might seem merely impolite or irresponsible becomes, in the context of the therapeutic relationship, proof of the therapist's innate untrustworthiness. The emotional charge is much greater than it would be in the context of friendship, partly because the hope a woman places in her therapist is also so much greater. A woman can observe her friend in numerous situations; all she really has to go on with her therapist, whom she needs to trust so much, is how she performs in the confined limits of the approximate relationship.

The clients who have these feelings are often also aware that their responses seem disproportionate, out of scale with their usual reactions to similar events, and out of keeping with the facts at hand. The client finds herself thinking: Where did *that* come from? What was that about? Why am I feeling this way?

Clara, the woman who found her therapist's yawning so disturbing, explains: "I understand intellectually that I'm overreacting. But I overreact all the same." It has become so important to her that her therapist *not* find her boring that a mere yawn poses a major threat to their connection.

When a woman feels rejected because the therapist has switched her appointment time or enraged because he cannot remember the name of the puppy she had when she was eight or ready to quit because she responded to a telephone page during a session, her reaction has a symbolic dimension. The therapist's actions have come to represent more. What happens in the therapy room has taken on a life-or-death quality.

A woman may find herself in the territory of the disproportionate response when she wants something from the therapist, perhaps his snapshot, an extended session, or to see the house where she lives. Whether the therapist will bend the boundary and grant her desire becomes the overriding focus of their relationship. If the therapist says yes, then the therapist "really" cares about her; if no, then she concludes that the relationship is only about money. Her desire may become insistent, unwilling to accept anything less. "This very particular gratification must come from my therapist right now," the wish seems to say. While a woman's desire may not be overtly sexual, it has the driven quality of sexual need. Like a lover seeking sexual union with her beloved, the client refuses to be satisfied by any other act than the longed-for one.

A client may experience this sort of profound feeling when new information about the therapist threatens her prior assumptions (or illusions). Inez became distraught when she learned that her therapist admired a New Age guru that Inez considered a fraud. Finding out that your therapist votes for the "wrong" candidate, has questionable taste in movies, or appears after a vacation wearing a wedding ring can initiate crises that require the client to reestablish in her own mind who her therapist "really" is. Seeing the therapist out of context can bring a client face-to-face with the disjunction between the therapist's ordinary mortal life and her symbolic needs, between the therapist's outside life and the very private importance the therapist has assumed for her.

A woman in therapy knows, of course, that her therapist has some other life, yet to see him in the supermarket dressed in a Grateful Dead T-shirt and Bermuda shorts, spouse and unruly children in tow, can rouse mixed feelings. One woman who ran into her female therapist in the drugstore picking up a prescription found herself flooded with concern for her health and frightened by the prospect of seeing her in a diminished state. Before that moment she had not realized the depth of her feelings.

The imposed separation wrought by a therapist's vacation may also create a crisis as a woman recognizes just how important her therapist has become to her. While the vacation poses no literal threat to her existence, it may feel as if it does, and she may grieve the separation as she would never grieve the temporary absence of a good friend. A number of women described calling their vacationing therapists' phone machines or driving by their offices to regain some closeness.

## Idealization, Overvaluation

If small acts can take on undue importance in therapy, the therapist himself also may seem grander, larger, more powerful than other mortals. Idealization and overvaluation of the therapist are probably the most common unrealistic assumptions clients make about their therapists. A client may attribute her therapist with those traits most lacking in herself or those that were missing in her parents when she was growing up.

Many women describe the process of idealization or overvaluation as putting the therapist on a pedestal, assuming that he or she is capable of feats beyond the ability of others. A woman may believe that her therapist is perfect, has an ideal life, or can do no wrong. As

Laurie said, "I used to think she was flawless. Only pearls of wisdom fell from her mouth. She had a perfect husband and perfect sex and perfect children." For some clients, this idealization dissipates over time and the therapist achieves more human proportions: "There was a period in my therapy when I was furious that he wasn't perfect and felt deeply wounded if he made mistakes or didn't live up to my fantasies."

A client may resist the process of de-idealization and struggle to hold on to a fantasy of perfection. As Nina, a woman of thirty told me, "When he's not good, I feel like I have to scurry around and put paint on his cracked spots, and I feel really upset when he's not perfect. It's my fault. If only I had been good enough." Some women rail against the therapist's foibles, and her *very right* to have them. Jamie joked about her therapist's attempts to dissuade her of her idealized illusions: "She's just in denial about her own perfection." With some clients, idealization is the peak of the mountain down which the therapist is doomed to slide into a pit of debasement. The therapist who disappoints by not being perfect becomes totally worthless.

Many women see their therapists as larger-than-life, literally, as physically bigger than they are. Some reported observing their therapists shrink as the months progressed. Flo recognized that her therapist could not be as tall as she had assumed when she observed his head clear the top of his door frame. More than one woman reported being oblivious to her therapist's pregnancy, simply not seeing the physical transformation. Elle became aware of having willfully denied her therapist's pregnancy until the ninth month, when the physical changes became impossible to ignore.

Although idealization is common, fantasies of perfection are distinctive and the ultimate meaning of idealization is idiosyncratic. One woman's ideal therapist is someone who's perfectly attuned to her; another's is the exact opposite of her mother; still another's is capable of delivering flawless sex or, alternately, of being perfectly asexual and above desire.

Clients also idealize the nature of the therapist's power, assuming, for example, that perceptiveness is clairvoyance. As Nan said, "There was something magical about the way he understood me." It would seem that the most common illusion is that the therapist must be perfectly well adjusted, and in a completely happy personal relationship, to be effective. Being a good therapist is not seen as a product of knowledge or skill, but as an inherent trait. To find out that the therapist is divorced, estranged from his children, or suffers with his own depression jeopardizes the therapy.

## Attachment and Dependency

Of course, it's only natural to become attached to someone who listens in rapt attention to your life story, who seems dedicated to alleviating your pain and to helping you find the significance of your existence. And yet, the feelings of attachment and dependency that women develop for their therapists often exceed the realistic limits of the relationship.

Meg, a woman in her twenties who'd had a very harsh childhood and an unsatisfying relationship with her own mother, said of her therapist, "I felt that if I could no longer work with her I'd dissolve or implode or explode or something." Felicity, recognizing the infantile quality of feelings like these, wrote, "When we're separated, I feel like there's an umbilical cord between us."

Attachment may extend to the therapist's possessions, which has prompted the comparison to a toddler's security blanket. Psychiatrist D. W. Winnicott called toddlers' "boo-boos" *transitional objects* and interpreted them as reminders of the infant's connection to her mother. The object gains its power through association with the mother, but the child has complete control over its comings and goings. A client may carry the therapist's crinkled business card in her wallet not just so she'll have the therapist's number in case she needs to call him, but as a sort of talisman to ward off harm, an always-present reminder of their connection.

Other clients long to possess something more personal—a photo of the therapist or a memento from the office. When Moira's therapist moved away, Moira kept a pillow from the arm of the sofa in her office. The pillow was a source of comfort, even when looking at the therapist's photograph seemed too visceral a reminder of her loss. Arlene invited her therapist to attend her graduate school graduation and wanted him to let her have a photo taken of the two of them together at the reception. In her fantasy, the photo had to be very small, a private memento that belonged only to her. As a child, Arlene believed that whenever she enjoyed something too much, too visibly, her mother would take it away. Her pleasure in the photo could be kept a secret.

Once attached, some women dread the therapist's abandonment, worrying about the therapist's becoming ill, dropping dead, or leaving town. As one young woman reported, "I fear coming to her office and finding a note that she will no longer be seeing clients."

This sort of sudden termination actually happened to Gail. Her therapist assured Gail early on in her therapy that she had no intentions of leaving her practice. But when her husband was to be relocated, she decided to move in a few weeks and informed her clients in a form letter delivered over a three-day weekend. Gail had never spoken to her therapist in any detail about their own relationship and was unaware of the depth of her attachment until she received the "Dear John" letter.

"It was like a hand grenade being thrown down my chimney," she told me, "and it felt familiar. I started to cry; I couldn't move." Only upon contemplation did Gail realize that the therapist's abrupt departure resonated with her mother's unexpected death on the table during open heart surgery several years before. The threat of impending loss made her feel like an abandoned daughter all over again. More surprising was that she also felt an identification with her mother. "I had feared being taken apart and not put back together again in therapy. When I received this letter informing me that she was leaving I saw myself being left open on the operating room table."

In their session prior to the move the therapist admitted too late that her departure might have had symbolic significance for clients: "I forgot that communications sometimes occur on two levels."

# Therapist's Presence Brings Comfort

For some clients, the mere presence of the therapist brings comfort. The therapist's consistency and tolerance, the reliability and ritualistic quality of sessions, become associated with sanctuary and safety. The therapist's very presence may then induce a state of calm and comfort, in the same way that the mere appearance of mother may calm a lost and screaming child.

The fact that clients do not usually see the full range of their therapists' moods and demeanors may result in their perceiving the therapist as one-dimensional. Whatever mood she projects in a session seems the essential quality of her being. When a therapist is serene in sessions, the client may not assume that she is a multifaceted person who behaves in a serene manner but that she is the very personification of serenity. If, one day, the client should arrive to find the therapist agitated, she may feel as if she has been betrayed.

When Jamie and her therapist both went through a natural disaster, her therapist developed posttraumatic stress disorder (PTSD) and confided her diagnosis in Jamie, who was not sympathetic. "She thought it was funny for a therapist to have PTSD but I didn't. It shook my image of her as unflappable and did not comfort me much at a time when I was pretty freaked out myself. She's my rock, and I look to her to always be steady and calm."

Some patients feel distress at *any* change in the therapist and, by extension, at any change in her office or in the routine of sessions. The therapist must be an icon of consistency and stasis; the therapist must be a Buddha, according to several clients in my study, and the Buddha may not change. Perceiving the therapist as steadfast may even lead to perceptual distortions. For instance, a client may have trouble estimating a therapist's age or may perceive the therapist to be enduring and ageless. A woman who had been in therapy for ten years perceived her therapist as not having aged a day since she started with her, although she knew that perception was unreasonable.

When a therapist redecorates her office, cuts her hair, or adopts a different style of clothing, a client may feel uncomfortable, even outraged. Pat said, "As the seasons changed, the sun would come in the window of her office and I could no longer sit on the couch and would have to move to a chair, and that always bothered me. I didn't like any kind of change with her; I wanted stability."

## Wanting to Be Special

Wanting to be special, not just another client, was a nearly universal desire among the therapy clients in my survey. This wish is often explained in terms of sibling rivalry; the client does not want to share her therapist, just as she may have resented having to share her parent; the client wants to be her therapist's favorite, just as she wanted to be her parent's favorite. But even without thinking in terms of these transference interpretations, wanting to be special is understandable. To see yourself as merely another client is to be reminded of just how skewed the relationship is and of how emotionally dangerous it is to feel so much about someone who is not equally emotionally invested. To be special means to have reached the therapist on some more personal level, to be appreciated for more than one's fees. To be special is to be needed back.

Some clients spend months or even years in therapy attempting to ensure a privileged status as the therapist's favorite patient, best patient, smartest patient, most successful patient, and so on. The strategies for this pursuit vary. When one woman's therapist always laughed when she told him an amusing story, she concluded that she would need lots of good material. For another, being the perfect patient meant making the most progress, so she refrained from telling her therapist about any setbacks. Then there was the woman who tackled therapy as she would a class—she read every book she could find on the subject and employed the professional lingo liberally. I would guess that many a client decides to go back to school and become a therapist herself out of the wish to be special in her therapist's eyes.

# Alike and Different: The Therapist as Standard for Measure

Some women come to focus on their resemblance to and difference from the therapist. The therapist becomes the standard by which to define and delineate the self. A woman may long to be her therapist's exact twin and may thus probe any minor resemblance for proof of deeper kinship. As Pat said, "We decided that I should go to decaf about the same time she started drinking decaf, which made it seem all the more like we were sisters."

Megan, a historian and teacher, became obsessed with the degree to which her therapist was like and unlike her mother and herself. She explained, "I want the person I'm talking to so intimately to have the same values that I have." After putting the therapist through a series of tests to determine if her values were acceptable, Megan felt reassured enough to proceed in the therapy, only to become distraught again when several weeks later the therapist began to wear nail polish. "Every week, a different color! When I realized that painting her nails was important to her, I felt a certain disdain. I was thinking that I knew who she was, and what her taste was, and then I discovered that I didn't know the first thing about it."

Based on inadequate evidence, clients feel compelled to draw conclusions as to how similar their therapists are to themselves. Stephanie, a woman in her fifties, told me, "After ending therapy and moving away, I had lunch with my therapist. As she shared some details of her personal life, I was jarred by the awareness that some of her values were so different from mine. She'd empathized so well with me that I'd fantasized that she was more like me than she really was."

For some women, the fantasy of twinship is closely related to envious impulses. As one young woman explained about her older, seemingly more accomplished, therapist, "She has what I want—she is who I want to be." Counter to the perfect twin fantasy is the fantasy of opposition. Like adolescents, some women only seem able to define themselves by taking an adversarial stand against their therapists. They may argue fine points, criticize her attire, delineate themselves over and over again as distinct from her. In opposition, they gain self-definition.

Fantasies and dreams about putting on a female therapist's clothes or trading clothes were reported by a number of women. These fantasies seemed to be one way in which women worked out their feelings about union and separation. Women fantasized about putting on everything from their therapists' lingerie to their wedding gowns. One woman dreamed: "My therapist was leading me through her closet; it was huge, cozy, and womblike. She was going to lend me clothes."

Identifying with the therapist as a role model can free a woman to accept formerly unacceptable parts of herself. Identification can be particularly important to a client who was never able to identify with her own mother. As one woman in her sixties said, "Dr. P. and I are very much alike and that finally made it okay for me to be an intellectual woman and let go of the shame my mother made me feel about that."

Disproportionate reactions, idealization, wanting to be special—these sorts of thoughts and feelings are indigenous to the approximate relationship. It is normal, natural, and understandable for clients to be hypersensitive to the therapist's behavior because clients need their therapists so much, because they never can be sure who their therapists really are, because the therapist is always prone to taking on symbolic importance. But as universal as these feelings might be, they are also different for each woman, and it is in their idiosyncrasies that their meaning lies.

## Child–Parent

It doesn't take much of a stretch to interpret the feelings I've described as being analogous to those that children feel toward their parents. Children attribute disproportionate importance to their parents' remarks and behaviors because they are so dependent on their love and approval. When a child is five years old, her mother, who is so much bigger and more powerful than she is, who feeds her, clothes her, tends (or fails to tend) to her needs, may well seem larger than life. Children tend to idealize their parents, only to go through a harsh awakening during adolescence when they suddenly recognize their flaws and frailties. Children are attached to and dependent on their parents, define themselves in relation to their parents, and long for their parents to love them and appreciate their particular talents and charms. Some women in therapy have similar feelings. This does not prove, of course, that the feelings that occur in therapy are a direct transference of childhood feelings. We have to acknowledge that these feelings of vulnerability and need are also triggered by the unique set-up of the psychotherapeutic relationship.

Sometimes the client is aware of the historical origins of her feelings. For instance, she may long, as I longed with Dr. V., to compensate for her father's failings by turning him into the good father she never had. In my encounter with Dr. V., his collapse evoked a vivid memory of my father's stroke. As if transported from one traumatic moment back to another, I felt once again what I had felt before, along with a host of other feelings for and about my father. The epiphany of this moment allowed me to recognize that I had unconsciously placed Dr. V. in a parental mold long before he collapsed at my feet.

Some women described this same sort of epiphany, a moment when something about the therapist, or something the therapist says, viscerally evokes an earlier moment from childhood. Suddenly the client feels as if she is five years old again with her fondest wish simply being to hide in the corner under her therapist's desk.

But clients also have childhood feelings without being able to directly connect them to their own histories. Pam wrote, "I wanted him to be available to me all of the time, just like a good mother would be." Moira's feelings were not subtle: "I began wishing my therapist had been, or could now be, my mother." As Cindy described very clearly, "My fantasies about my therapist were about him being my parent. When I was in therapy I felt like his child."

Judy said, "I often have dreams in which she is a mother figure. She is holding an infant, and at the same time, she is my mother." Winnie, a therapist in training, imagined that she was "inside my therapist's gut to be close to him." Two other women in my survey also reported this fantasy of being inside the therapist's body. Another woman expressed conflict about her own childlike feelings: "I didn't like that she was in control but I really wanted her to be the adult and take control."

In contrast to wanting the therapist to be the parent she never had, a woman may assume, despite any strong evidence, that the therapist is like her own mother or father. Elaine described trying to prevent the inevitable: "I was so afraid that my therapist would say something critical like my mother always did that I didn't dare to let her say anything. I just talked and talked."

Defining the extent to which a woman's feelings derive from her own childhood and the extent to which they are generated by the peculiar set-up of the approximate relationship may pose an impossible and unnecessary mission. Ultimately, the feelings cannot be parsed out: They derive from the past, from the unique nature of the approximate relationship, from the very particular dynamics of the relationship between that woman and her therapist. To simply call them transference may be reductive. As Eva said, "My essential trust in him as well as a small sense of his humanness has engendered a good deal of affection which, I think, goes beyond or around transference." Or as a woman who'd been in therapy for a number of years explained, "Of course, I feel a deep attachment to my therapist. I've been through hell and back with his help and support."

## Love

The irrational feeling that women may find the most compelling, the most transcendent, and the most difficult to bear in the therapeutic setting is love. Love in therapy may be an adolescent crush-style obsession, the admiring love of a young child for a parent, the love of a twin for her mirror match, or the gratitude for another's selfless gift of understanding.

Therapy-love is usually attributed to transference, to the projection of feelings from the past. But then again, to be understood, to be heard, to be the focus of another's concern feels like love. How is a woman to reconcile how she feels with the fact that her therapist is a professional providing a service, a professional whose "love" must be paid for? How can she love someone whom she knows in such a limited capacity?

Therapy-love is love, but not quite love. As one woman said, "It is a love with limits." What is most important to understand is that the love that occurs in therapy belongs to the situation—it is a hothouse flower that cannot be taken out of the room and survive intact. The therapist's love is always limited—no therapist can sustain a therapy relationship in which she loves freely because to love freely is to want something back, and to want back is to jeopardize the therapy. Love between two adults requires a two-way relationship, a negotiation of needs, a meshing of realities.

What the therapist offers is always an approximation of love—it cannot reflect her needs as a whole person and still do service to the client. It is a love that is always poised between the symbolic and the real, the present and the past. Accepting a love with limitations, learning to love in the face of conflict and inevitable loss, can be one of the major lessons of therapy. And many women whose therapy was successful have no doubt that they were loved, even if that love could never speak its name.

## The Golden Fantasy

Where there is love in therapy, the golden fantasy may not be far behind. Psychoanalyst Sydney Smith described the fantasy of ideal caretaking and flawless understanding in a classic article. As Smith describes, the golden fantasy is the "wish to have all of one's needs met in a relationship hallowed by perfection." If the golden fantasy is nearly universal, it varies in its intensity and hold on a person's life.

Some people bring tinges of the golden fantasy to every relationship; some only express nuances of it in relationship to their lovers or their children.

It may lie largely dormant, stirred only occasionally by the full-screen image of a movie star that seems to promise total gratification or by a woman's fantasy of her own public adulation or by the first date with someone who seems, initially, perfect. According to Smith, the fantasy always carries within it the same implicit narrative: Once this perfect love was mine but now I have lost it, and I must get it back. This love occurred in an Edenic past that cannot be remembered but that is sensed to have existed. The longing for something that is impossible feels instead like the memory of something that can be recovered.

A client in thrall to the golden fantasy may long for an impossible level of empathy from her therapist. Small misreadings may become imbued with a sense of disproportionate betrayal and loss. Any break in the mental connection—any sign that the therapist is distracted or thinking about something else—may be devastating. As Rhonda, a therapist in her forties said, "She used to pick lint off her skirt during my sessions. That drove me insane. If somebody were rustling papers in a class or conference I wouldn't even notice, but I needed to know that she had the capacity to be *totally* with me."

A characteristic of the golden fantasy is that the provider of this perfectly attuned caretaking must ask nothing in return. "No demand is made on the patient except her capacity for passively taking in," Smith writes. This is a love that is given without having to ask. In therapy, the prospect of being understood, the moments of exquisite attunement, and the attention focused solely on the client may reawaken the fantasy.

The golden fantasy assumes many forms in women's therapy stories. Angela describes it this way: "I didn't want to have to work to pay him." The recipient is passive, and the therapist's love would be spoiled by having to give something in return. Angela goes on, "I wanted to live with him and do nothing but therapy. I wanted to remain in my adult body but not have to deal with any adult concerns, to be *totally taken care of by him in every possible way.*" What Angela wants is something way beyond the sort of modulated give-and-take of adult–adult relationships in the real world.

The golden fantasy is, of course, a *fantasy*, and most women recognize it as such. According to Smith, its origins are in the period of separation-individuation when the toddler feels conflict about giving up some degree of closeness to the mother in exchange for more autonomy in the world. How mother and toddler navigate this period may determine the prominence of the golden fantasy in the adult's psychic life.

For most adults, the rational, mature part of themselves recognizes that the golden fantasy is impossible and that even if it were possible, it would come at a tremendous price in autonomy and freedom. Angela goes on to describe what happened when she discussed the wish with her therapist: "My therapist would ask, 'Do you *really* want that? Let's talk about what that would really be like,' and he helped me to distinguish the part of me that wanted it versus the adult part that really didn't."

Renee is a competent, self-assured cognitive-behavioral therapist in her professional life. In her own therapy she learned the extent to which the golden fantasy was a part of her psychic life. To allow herself the fantasy of receiving this perfect love, she had to imagine herself as the victim of a preceding catastrophic loss. Only then could she feel justified:

> My whole family of origin has been killed. I go down to the family house and I find their bodies and it's a terrible thing and I'm devastated but it's also a huge relief. Now I'm really going to get myself taken care of because I've got this incredible excuse to be needy. My therapist comes in and says, "Oh, my goodness, come with me." He takes me to his house and holds me, just holds me. The big satisfaction is the moment when he says, "I'm going to take care of you," and I have a sense of cathartic release in being able to weep in someone's arms and he doesn't want anything from me.

## Communicating Feelings

Given that the sort of strong feelings described here will arise in therapy, what is the client to do with them? Unexpressed, they can explode in scenes like Anna O.'s final encounter with Dr. Breuer or can stall the therapy. Yet women reported over and over again to me their reluctance to tell the therapist the extent of their feelings. Some clients regarded them as peripheral rather than central, as signs of their own emotional weakness or as side effects of the treatment that they'd rather not expose. Many women believed that disclosing their feelings to their therapists would be even more humiliating and painful than suffering them in silence.

Even one hundred years after Anna O., the psychotherapeutic relationship and the feelings engendered by it are not something that clients and therapists feel comfortable discussing. The second most common answer to the questionnaire item, "I can't talk to my therapist about _____," second only to "sex" in its forbidden quality, was "our relationship" or "my feelings about him/her." As Millie said, "I can't think of anything we can't talk about. Except that we've never talked about how I feel about her."

If sex is taboo and feelings about the therapist are censored, then sexual feelings about the therapist are the most taboo topic in women's therapy relationships. "I mentioned my sexual feelings for him only once, briefly. I wanted them to go away and they did." Sexual feelings for the therapist were by no means universal among my respondents, but when they took hold, they could be relentless and destructive. Fleeting sexual images and fantasies ("I wonder what he looks like naked," "I wonder what she does with her husband in bed") were far more common than was obsessive erotic love. Out of 274 respondents, 107 reported that they had had a romantic or sexual fantasy about some therapist at some time in their lives, 148 answered that they had not, and 19 didn't want to talk about it, even on an anonymous questionnaire.

The expert therapists I interviewed for this book, particularly those of a psychoanalytic bent, insisted that they wanted to hear all about their clients' feelings for them, that those feelings constituted important material for the therapy. But many of the stories women told suggested otherwise, that their therapists became uncomfortable when they directed their intense (and often demanding) feelings at them. Some therapists quickly labeled the feelings as transference, as if that would dispel them. Some used the term transference reductively (it's *only* transference) as a way of disavowing the extent to which those feelings might be triggered by the peculiar set-up of the therapist–client relationship or by the individual dynamics of the relationship itself. Others seemed to think that if they just behaved like regular people rather than superior beings, they could reason their clients out of any unreasonable feelings and fantasies. Perhaps they made too little room in the therapy for the symbolic side of the relationship.

Psychologist and professor Michael Kahn wants his clients to talk about their feelings but has observed that this is not the case with every therapist: "Therapists are geniuses at giving the message, 'If you've got feelings about me, I don't want to hear about them.' A client's negative feelings can be very threatening to a therapist." When these feelings cannot be discussed, they become a dangerous subtext that undermines the therapy. When there is no place for a woman's most powerful feelings, she may feel she has no choice but to leave the therapy.

Women are ashamed and may sense quite accurately that their therapists don't want to hear them say, "I need you to love me," "I wish that you could take care of me," "I'm envious of your other life," "I think about you before I fall asleep every night," "Your face comes into my mind when I masturbate," "I wish you could have been my parent." And yet, expressing these feelings freely to a therapist who is able to hear them and work with them can transform the therapy.

## Renee's Story: You've Got to Ante Up

Remember Renee, whose golden fantasy included a prologue of catastrophic loss? She eventually recounted that narrative to her therapist Nathan, but only after spending several years without telling him anything she was feeling about him.

"I sat there like a teenager with my arms crossed," she said. "Just being really oppositional like I had learned to be with my dad."

Getting nowhere, Renee gave up on individual therapy and joined a therapy group led by her therapist. When she saw how well Nathan responded when others shared sensitive material, she realized that she had been missing something by not telling him more. She returned to individual therapy with him.

Part of what Renee had been suppressing was the fact that she had been seduced by her high school drama teacher. She could not help but regard every other authority figure in the light of this betrayal. When she finally told Nathan about it, "A lot of confusing and intense feelings and sensations kept coming up." Renee didn't trust her own motives—was she dramatizing the events to get Nathan's attention? Why was she trying to seduce him when the affair with her teacher had been so damaging? What was going on?

But Nathan said that it didn't matter. Whatever came up, whatever her motives, he could get through it with her. "Whatever it is, we can work on it," he told Renee. Renee recalls what happened next:

> That was the most healing thing Nathan ever said. It let me let it all go. It enabled me to make a leap in my mind. You're never going to get anywhere with it if you don't ante up in therapy, so I thought, What the hell, and I anted up. "Look," I said, "I've been wanting to seduce you and I've been afraid of you. And I want to be more important to you. . . . And I love you."

Nathan never promised more than the approximate relationship could deliver, but he could accept hearing about all of Renee's feelings, all of her fantasies, and he could help her understand them and work through them. There was something profoundly liberating about that. Nathan told Renee, "I genuinely care about you and I want to help you. Your vulnerable side is your truth and it's important not to hide it."

This was something Renee needed to hear. Without being fully aware of it, she had come to believe that if she gave somebody power over her they would either take advantage of it or abandon her. Nathan didn't do either. In the delicate balance that is the approximate relationship, he was able to be with Renee without wanting anything from her. She came to see that it was "safe to feel anything, to express anything, because he was there solely to take care of me, to do what was best for me, within the structure of the therapy."

When Renee was able to disclose her deepest feelings and fantasies about her therapist, her relationship with him suddenly sprang to life. As Nathan proved that he was able to tolerate hearing them without judging her, exploiting her, or taking her feelings about him too personally, Renee learned to trust him. When he repeatedly did not behave as her parents and others in positions of power had, she grasped the ramifications of the assumptions she had made about power and vulnerability while growing up. Renee's therapist gave her the freedom to express her deepest feelings in an atmosphere of safety, without wanting anything from her for himself, and that was an amazing gift.

Renee realized that she would never seduce Nathan or be "something more" to him outside the room. Inside the confines of his office, within the boundaries of the approximate relationship, she could safely allow herself the vulnerability of loving him and feeling loved.

In ordinary life, our deepest longings and fantasies and fears are played out in the same noisy arena as everyone else's. We jockey for as much fulfillment as possible while continually negotiating and tempering our needs against the needs of other people and the constrictions of reality. We struggle to accept compromises, try to forget our disappointments, keep our fantasy lives hidden from other people. That does not mean that in our heart of hearts we are not always longing for Prince Charming or for the perfect mother or expecting all men to be selfish exploiters if given half a chance.

Therapy removes us from the arena. We can only talk and feel; we cannot act. We can only want; we cannot get. In some natural science museums, there are chambers so quiet that we can hear our own hearts beating, our own blood pulse. Of course, our hearts are beating even when we cannot hear them. The psychotherapy relationship is just such a still chamber. There we can hear the voices of the memories, wishes, and fantasies that have been propelling our actions. When our deepest feelings are stirred by the hope of transformation and come smack up against the built-in limitations of the approximate relationship, they are likely to speak ever more loudly until we start to listen.

# 3

# The Therapist's Power

Maria is an accomplished educator now in her late forties. In the 1970s, when her sense of self was shakier, she went into psychoanalysis with a middle-aged male analyst. About two years into her analysis, she was lying on the couch, recalling some seemingly minor event, when her analyst silently walked around from his chair behind the couch and placed his hand quite deliberately on her breast. He kept it there for a few moments and then withdrew it and returned to his place. Amazingly, neither Maria nor her analyst said a word while this act was taking place nor ever discussed it afterward. He never repeated it. She continued to see him for several more years. If any other man she knew in a professional capacity had put his hand on her breast, Maria would have confronted him immediately about the outrageousness of his behavior. But because it was her therapist who put his hand on her breast and because he did so in the context of a session, she convinced herself that his seemingly bizarre action had some therapeutic intent. Therapy, after all, was a mysterious process, Maria told herself.

"And did you continue to trust him," I asked her, "after he did this strange thing?"

"I'm not sure," she said. "All I know for certain is that at the time I didn't trust myself enough."

Women enter psychotherapy with great hopes and high anxiety. They long for comfort and support, insight and understanding, to feel better and to make fundamental changes in their lives. They suspend disbelief and put their trust in the therapist's presumably superior knowledge. They assume that the therapist will be able to see things in themselves that they cannot see, will help them to change what seems intractable. This very assumption on the part of clients grants therapists a certain power. The therapy professions and society as a whole have failed to delineate clearly the limits of this power, and the history of psychotherapy is rife with stories of its abuse.

Therapists derive their power in part from social ascription. In deeming them experts, society gives them provenance over the psychological domain. Besides treating clients, they are permitted to exercise their authority in a number of other ways. They testify in court as experts about others' psychological states, motives, and capacities. They create and apply measures of mental abilities and mental health for educational institutions and the workplace that have far-reaching consequences for people's lives.

To protect the common good, state licensing boards are supposed to evaluate practitioners' knowledge and skills, set some standards for performance, and pronounce them worthy of treating clients. Licensure is the official stamp of society's approval. We would all like to believe that this licensure means something, that in order to be licensed, therapists must possess a common body of privileged knowledge based on some sort of scrupulously acquired scientific evidence. We would all like to assume that licensed therapists must demonstrate their adeptness at applying this body of knowledge in order to continue to practice.

In fact, there are no common standards to which all licensed therapists adhere. Instead, the field is marked by fragmentation, turf battles, and controversy over even the most fundamental questions. In the *Consumer's Guide to Psychotherapy*, psychologists Jack Engler and Daniel Goleman refer to psychotherapy as an "unregulated industry." This "industry" does not represent a single profession but several in competition with each other. The licensed professionals who practice psychotherapy—psychiatrists, psychologists, social workers, M.A.-level marriage and family counselors—receive very different training and take different licensing examinations.

The licensing examination for a clinical psychologist, for example, tends to be broad and to cover some material completely unrelated to the practice of psychotherapy. According to UCLA psychologist Marie Cohen, the California examination for Ph.D. clinical psychologists, for example, might include only a smattering of questions about managing the psychotherapeutic relationship and relevant ethics. Topics like drug rehabilitation, industrial psychology, psychological testing, and the diagnosis of learning disabilities all receive some attention. This means, for example, that a licensed clinical psychologist conducting psychotherapy could have only a cursory understanding of how to work with a client's transference feelings.

Psychiatry programs also vary widely in their emphases, with neurobiology and psychopharmacology currently dominating the curricula at most medical schools. A psychiatric resident today is likely to have far more experience in prescribing psychotropic drugs than in actually conducting anything but the most practical, problem-oriented sort of short-term psychotherapy.

Clients would like to believe that licensing boards closely oversee the work of practicing psychotherapists. In fact, boards have very limited capacity to oversee practitioners and intervene only when a client files a complaint. Even then, the burden of proof is on the client. Filing a complaint is a time-consuming and often demoralizing process. Although sanctions today are probably stricter than at any other time in the history of psychotherapy, licensing boards still seem inclined to give every benefit of the doubt to the practitioner. They drop many complaints for lack of substantiating evidence. Even when practitioners are found culpable of significant abuses of power, their licenses are rarely revoked. Probation or practice under greater supervision are usual penalties. And these generalizations apply only to licensed practitioners. In many states, no license at all is required to practice psychotherapy. Virtually anyone can hang a shingle and call himself a "counselor" or "therapist."

Despite this absence of common standards for the practice of psychotherapy, therapists often have significant and direct power over their clients' lives. Psychiatrists can prescribe medications that directly affect their clients' physical and mental states. In some situations, a therapist can recommend that a client's children be taken out of her care, sign her into temporary confinement, or persuade the court that she is incompetent to take care of herself.

Therapists have the power to describe and diagnose and name, and their words have power. Whether they are naming a disease like bipolar disorder or a personality type like narcissistic personality, the labels they apply, along with their negative connotations, are liable to stay with a client for life. Clara, a shy and self-effacing woman in her thirties, admired and idealized her therapist Sally, who seemed self-possessed and very sure of herself. Clara told Sally about a period of promiscuity she went through in college. Sally, who regarded herself as a feminist, quickly labeled Clara's short-lived and unsatisfying encounters with men as "sexual abuse." Sally seems to have been operating as much out of a political agenda as out of a concern for the client. The label may have liberated Clara from some of the guilt she still felt over her promiscuity, but it also made her feel like even more of a helpless victim.

Given her therapist's judgment, what was Clara to make of any residual positive feelings she had about her casual sexual encounters? She certainly could not sort out such feelings with her therapist without feeling diminished in her eyes. The label deprived Clara of fully exploring, on her own terms and in her own time, the mixed feelings she still had about her own sexuality.

Therapists' words have power. A therapist can, authoritatively, label a woman's behavior as "self-destructive," or "addictive," or "anti-social" and can so change the way the client thinks about herself. This is because the client accepts the premise that the therapist knows something that she does not know, that the therapist speaks with some kind of special authority. Therapists need to speak carefully because their words have power.

Over the history of psychotherapy, therapists have often misused their power, assuming a privileged relationship to "objective" reality and sanity. Some have used suggestive, even coercive, techniques to gain compliance, modify behavior, or convert a client to their way of thinking. They have directed therapy toward goals that were not disclosed, let alone negotiated, with the client, seemingly under the assumption that the therapist knows best.

Psychotherapy has been too easily co-opted to serve political and social ends. Mental health experts have confused societal convention with psychological norms. In the 1950s, for example, psychiatrists routinely told women that their ambition for accomplishment outside of the domestic sphere was symptomatic of a deep-seated failure to accept their innately passive femininity. Until 1973, the *Diagnostic and Statistical Manual of Mental Disorders (DSM)*, the bible of psychiatric diagnosis, classified homosexuality as pathological, and respectable therapists claimed that they could "convert" gay people to "normal" heterosexual lives. When the mission failed, they blamed the patient rather than the erroneous assumptions underlying the "treatment."

## Mystification of Power

If psychotherapists could definitively link specific effects with each of their techniques and methods, that would go a long way toward clarifying the nature and extent of their power. But uncertainty and controversy remain over which elements work—and how they work—to effect change. Only over the course of perhaps the last thirty years have therapists even become very interested in rigorously measuring the results of what they do. Questions abound as to where the effects lie: Do they derive from insight or simply from being in a supportive relationship? If, as many outcomes studies suggest, the answer is the latter, *what exactly* is it about the relationship that helps? As it stands today, psychotherapy is as much an intangible art as a quantifiable science. With so much that remains unknown and nebulous about psychotherapy and its effects and with therapists often unwilling to admit the extent of what they do not know to their clients, the therapist's power has been subject to mystification.

The symbolic weight borne by the psychotherapy relationship contributes to this power. In the face of the therapist's actual power and authority, the client projects feelings and fantasies onto the therapist, and these projections further enhance the therapist's power. Ultimately it becomes impossible to distinguish the therapist's actual power from symbolic power.

The therapy professions contribute to this mystification with their reluctance to set standards for what constitutes effective therapy. The ongoing internecine battles waged among the different disciplines stand in the way of consensus. And none of the psychotherapy professions has done a particularly good job of educating the public to be better informed consumers. One on one, therapists have also failed to adequately educate their own clients. As Deanna wrote on her questionnaire, "I felt as if we were playing a game but only my therapist knew the rules."

Historically, psychoanalysts have been particularly vague and have offered up strong theoretical rationales for this reluctance to share information with their clients. They have used the theory of transference, in particular, the therapist's importance as a transference symbol, as an excuse for mystification of their power, arguing that a client who knows too much about the process or the analyst loses the freedom to fantasize. "Every question answered is a fantasy lost," analysts are fond of saying. They have even advised new analysands not to read anything about analysis, implying that information might interfere with total engagement in the process.

This patriarchal, anticonsumerist attitude is nicely illustrated by a chapter entitled "The First Contact with the Patient" in *The Technique of Psychoanalytic Psychotherapy*, a two-volume classic text by famed psychoanalyst Robert Langs. The book was first published in 1973 and was reprinted as recently as 1989. Under the heading "The Therapist's Basic Stance," Langs addresses the situation in which a prospective patient telephones and asks what the fees will be before making his first appointment.

Dr. Langs writes, "[I]t is best to be brief and not discuss fees on the telephone, since many patients will use such information to foster their already intense resistances and anxieties." If the patient "persists" in getting this information, Langs writes, he would delineate a possible range of fees, "while making a mental note that this *pressure* suggests possible financial problems, a sense of mistrust, considerable hesitancy, and/or some special degree of *demandingness* [emphases mine]."

When the prospective patient treats psychotherapy as any other professional service and asks how much this service will cost, the analyst attributes the patient's desire to be informed as indicative of some sort of pathology! Based on the reports of women in therapy today, it would seem that many nonpsychoanalytic therapists have embraced the analytic stance in regard to providing information even while discarding much of the transference theory that underlies it.

## Lack of Accountability

Psychotherapy is the most private of professional relationships. In addition to possessing considerable power that has been mystified, therapists also practice without the checks and balances that safeguard other fields. For instance, an incompetent physician's work is more likely to come to the attention of other physicians, laboratories, and pharmacies because physicians leave a paper trail of charts, prescriptions, and laboratory orders. But therapists tend to leave no physical evidence of their interventions. They practice in the sanctity of their own offices, one-on-one with the client, with no witnesses present.

When I talked to therapists about this problem, they lamented over how difficult it is for even another therapist to assess a colleague's clinical work. With the exception of teaching environments that use one-way mirrors so that therapists in training can observe master therapists at work and have their own work assessed, therapists find it impossible to determine what actually goes on in other therapists' offices. In the past, partly in the legitimate interest of protecting the client's confidentiality, many therapists made no tape recordings and kept minimal notes of sessions. With the advent of managed care, therapists are being asked to keep more detailed records. Unfortunately, in the managed care setting, this documentation sometimes comes at the expense of client confidentiality.

Charles McGaw, a psychiatrist in Boston who has worked extensively with women who were sexually abused by their therapists, believes that the whole two-person structure of the psychotherapy relationship may need to change to protect clients. "We may need to introduce third parties into the deal," McGaw said. "Maybe every six months, the two parties meet with a third person. . . . We need to somehow break into the hermetically sealed environment that gets created."

## Giving Up Power

When a women enters the hermetically sealed environment of psychotherapy, her hope and her anxiety are often at a very high pitch. In this state of high anxiety, with her understanding of the therapist's power so unclear, clients tend to give away their own power. Like tranquilized patients being wheeled into the operating room for surgery, clients entering the therapist's domain feel they have no choice but to submit totally.

Educated and otherwise savvy and even skeptical women give up their power and refrain from applying their critical faculties, or their common sense, when they embark on psychotherapy. As Judy said, "I asked fewer questions than I did when someone came to my house to give me an estimate for drapes. I gave the drape man a much harder time."

Even when therapists' actions or demeanor were questionable, as in Maria's case, clients were apt to give them the benefit of the doubt. It was just too frightening to think of one's therapist as incompetent or as harboring ulterior motives. The situation may worsen as therapy progresses. The more time, energy, and feeling a woman invests in her therapy, the more difficult it is for her to acknowledge that there is something wrong with her therapist and that she needs to walk away.

Lacking professionally defined standards for what constitutes legitimate psychotherapeutic practice, women find themselves under the sway of therapists who make up their own standards. Diane, a sophisticated New Yorker, recalled that several years ago, she went to a therapist who operated by an unusual set of rules. Unfortunately, she didn't know how unusual they were because she had no standards by which to compare them.

During sessions, Diane had to sit in a chair diagonally across from the therapist who sat at a desk. "I was supposed to look straight ahead, not cross my legs, keep my arms on the armrest of the chair, and not fidget." The therapist provided a reasonable-sounding rationale for these strictures. "This would allow me to get to my deepest feelings, he said. If I crossed my legs or folded my arms, that was going within myself in a hostile way, instead of opening up to him." Diane remembers, "My fondest wish was just to be able to cross my legs." Still she remembers thinking, "Okay, this must be what it's like to be in therapy." Having no models for a patient–therapist relationship, she was "pretty much willing to believe whatever he told [her]."

Another woman, an accomplished administrator in her fifties, recognized in retrospect that her need for therapy was so urgent when she began treatment that she simply didn't have the time or heart to evaluate a prospective therapist's competence. "I was so desperate I would have talked to a dog," she reports. Fortunately, she happened onto a competent practitioner.

Two contradictory beliefs seem to contribute to clients' relinquishment of power. Women assume that their therapists *have* to be competent because society has given them the authority to perform this particularly sensitive, significant work. We want to believe that society's ascription of power stands for something, so we assume that psychotherapists *have* to be competent, *have* to be ethical, *have* to have a body of well-established knowledge. Otherwise, how could society allow them to practice? Otherwise, how could they have the nerve to charge such exorbitant fees?

The second contradictory belief is that there is nothing rational, measurable, or quantifiable about the therapeutic process anyway, so there is no real way to measure a therapist's competence even if one wanted to. Overwhelmed by the unknown aspects of the process, women simply decide that there is nothing useful that can be discerned rationally. In the most extreme form of this belief, some women I interviewed saw no difference between consulting a therapist and consulting a psychic or an astrologer. One woman even used a psychic to find a therapist! These women credited therapy with no greater veracity than any other form of soothsaying. It's all one big cosmic crap shoot, so they might as well just take their chances, they seem to believe. Since the psyche is irrational and mysterious, someone from the same realm of the irrational—a shaman of sorts—might well be the one best suited to treat psychic distress.

Anthropologist Bronislaw Malinowski's classic study of fishermen on the Trobriand islands in the early part of this century sheds some light on this phenomenon. Malinowski found that the less the fishermen could predict what would happen during a particular voyage, the more likely they were to rely on ritual to ensure their safety. When the fishing trip was dangerous but nothing rational could be done to reduce its risks, the fishermen turned to the irrational.

Perceiving therapy as risky and unknowable, some women also resort to ritual. Because they do not know how to assess a therapist's competence, they look for magical signs that the therapist is the "right one," for an inkling that the therapist is somehow familiar. A woman might take as a sign the art in the therapist's office or may attribute too much importance to her tone of voice over the phone. For Tina, the therapist's choice of a light, feminine gold bracelet was a sign that he would be kind and gentle unlike the domineering men in her family. She put her trust in a piece of jewelry.

Along these lines, twenty-four of the respondents in my survey did not know what degrees or licenses their therapists held. In some cases, they did not even know *if* their therapists were licensed. Most of the women did know, although they did not choose their therapists on the basis of training. Those women who had seen more than one therapist (the vast majority in my survey) were likely to have seen a smattering from the various professions—psychiatrists, psychologists, and master's level counselors—at some point in their therapy histories. Of the therapists reported on, 55 were M.D. psychiatrists; 98 were Ph.D. or Psy.D. psychologists; 57 were master's-level clinical social workers, and 31 were therapists with other master's-level degrees. Ninety-two were male and 172 were female; ten respondents did not identify their therapists by gender.

Sixty-four out of the 274 women in my survey were therapists or therapists in training themselves, suggesting that they would have a greater sophistication about psychotherapy than the general public. In choosing a therapist, the majority did take reasonable precautions by relying on referral from another therapist (55) who was either an acquaintance or the therapist of a friend, the referral of a friend (54), or another professional referral (14). Fifteen women saw therapists at public agencies or clinics, eleven received referrals at work, and eleven saw practitioners at their university clinic and so had limited choices. However, thirteen women turned to the phone book, a rather unreliable source, and another eight picked a therapist on the basis of an advertisement or article in the newspaper.

Once in the office, clients neglected to ask adequate questions about their therapists' training, approach, and experience, even in the first session, and remarkably few therapists volunteered this information if not asked. As a group, clients asked their therapists significantly fewer questions about their qualifications, and the nature of the treatment being suggested, than they probably would have asked another medical practitioner in a comparable situation. Perhaps people simply take physical interventions more seriously than psychological ones. Part of the reason for this reticence may be the stigma that still surrounds mental illness and clients' embarrassment at seeking help. Eager to alleviate their own anxiety, they wanted to get on with the process, and so failed to use the first session as a screening interview.

Most clients also knew going in that there were some questions that therapists would be reluctant to answer, and being unsure just which questions were verboten, they felt inhibited about asking any. Wanting to be "good patients" and not be rebuffed and not seem "resistant" or "demanding" like poor Dr. Langs's patient, many declined to ask for specific information. The irony is that clients are probably in the best position to evaluate a therapist's competence early on, before becoming too emotionally invested in the relationship. As a group, therapists are also most inclined to answer straightforward questions honestly at the first meeting, rather than later when such questions may be presumed to have symbolic meanings.

For example, psychologist Michael Kahn told me that he would "sometimes answer" a question regarding his "sexual orientation . . . at the beginning of therapy, when the client is trying to decide whether I'm the right therapist." So, if a client feels that she needs to know a therapist's marital status, sexual orientation, or personal therapy history, the first session is the best time to ask. If a client feels that she must know a particular piece of information in order to engage in the process, she should never assume that a therapist who declines to answer her question in the initial interview will be any more forthcoming later on.

## The Right to Know

To lessen the negative consequences of the therapist's power advantage, clients need to do all they can to ensure that their therapists are competent and trustworthy. So much of therapy is unknown and unquantifiable that clients have a right to know everything that *can be known* of the parameters of the relationship they are entering. In psychiatrist and author Tom Gutheil's words, clients have a right to know what they are "signing up for." Too many women in therapy find themselves, like Alice, in a Wonderland in which the rules keep changing and they are never certain what might happen next.

This process of qualifying the therapist begins in the initial interview. Most therapists will explain the basic rules of therapy, the fees, hours, setting, what happens in the case of missed or canceled appointments, and the patient's right to confidentiality. It is far less likely for a therapist to delve into her philosophy of treatment or to describe how she defines her role. These are questions the client should ask. She has a right to know how the therapist conceptualizes the process: What will happen during sessions? How directive will the therapist be? What sort of material will the therapist want to discuss? A woman entering therapy should ask the therapist how he or she came to this approach and the major influences on her thinking.

Perhaps most important, she should ask how the therapist conceptualizes the relationship between herself and her clients. What are the appropriate limits of that relationship? To what extent will she be supportive and nurturing, and to what extent does she believe in keeping an emotional distance? The women in my survey often found a therapist's emotional distance upsetting and tended to take it personally, particularly if they were unprepared. A woman entering therapy has a right to know if this is how her therapist is likely to behave and to choose whether or not she wants to enter into a relationship of such intimacy with someone who is relatively unresponsive.

While a client may not understand the finer points of her therapist's discussion of theory, she will be able to discern if her therapist has thought carefully about the matter rather than jumped on the most recent bandwagon, is humble or arrogant, is making claims that sound too good to be true, and is able to acknowledge uncertainty. The best therapists are humble and forthright about their own uncertainties.

Psychologist Marie Cohen says that she would begin to respond to a potential client's question about her therapeutic approach with the following:

> I am a psychodynamic therapist, which means that I am influenced by psychoanalytic theory and am interested in both conscious and unconscious processes. I will want to hear about your dreams and daydreams, fantasies and mental images, as well as about your day-to-day struggles. This branch of therapy places an emphasis on the relationship that develops between the client and therapist. We will use it as a laboratory to explore how you interact with people outside therapy. In this therapy, I might offer interpretations, ways of understanding the underlying meaning of your feelings and behaviors.

In contrast, Connie Hammen, a cognitive-behavioral psychologist at UCLA, might explain:

In cognitive-behavioral therapy, we believe that thoughts are a powerful determinant of emotional states and behaviors. We will focus on identifying your dysfunctional thoughts and directly trying to alter the way you think and behave. This is very much an action-oriented, change-oriented type of therapy. It doesn't rely on the concept of insight to lead to change. . . . I think of the relationship between client and therapist as being egalitarian, supportive, genuine, and collaborative.

But rather than providing these specific sorts of answers, many therapists that my respondents consulted were quick to answer by saying "I'm eclectic" or "I borrow from everything," or "I use whichever approach works best with a given patient," answers that are fairly meaningless to a client but are likely to curtail further discussion. A client can respond to these imprecise answers by asking for examples of what the therapist borrows from or what it means to her to be eclectic. Most important to observe is how the therapist takes the question. Clients should beware of any therapist who becomes defensive when asked what exactly it is that he or she does in the room. Humility is an important characteristic of good therapists and the greatest counter to abuses of power.

Some therapists were noteworthy for providing elegant explanations of how they believed therapy worked and what they brought to the process. They invited questions and encouraged prospective clients to formulate their own goals. A few therapists gave handouts entitled "A Client's Bill of Rights" or "What You Need to Know about Therapy," which clearly laid out the ground rules. Most importantly, from the very first meeting they empowered their clients and respected their right to a measure of control over the therapeutic process.

In the first session, a client should also ask how long the prospective therapist has been practicing, what education the therapist has received, the credentials and licenses held, and if the therapist is receiving ongoing supervision. A supervision relationship means that the therapist consults a colleague on a regular basis about challenging cases. Therapists in the early years of their career should receive supervision, but even more experienced therapists recognize the advantages of having access to a second perspective.

Asking the therapist what she would do in the case of an impasse in the therapy is one way of finding out how the therapist conceptualizes her power in relation to the client's. Does she assume that every problem comes from the client? Does she acknowledge that therapists also bring their own issues to their work? Is she open to the idea of seeking consultation from another therapist or of the client and therapist together seeking such a consultation?

Clients should also ask if their therapists have completed their own therapy. Although this is no guarantee of competence, those therapists who have been in therapy themselves are more likely to be in tune with their own issues and less likely to confuse their issues with the client's. At the very least, they will know what it feels like to sit on the other side of the couch.

A prospective client should ask if the therapist has any plans to leave the area and if she is able to commit to a particular span of time; a year does not seem unreasonable.

More controversial is the question of what personal information about the therapist the client has a right or need to know. Some therapists readily disclose their sexual orientation, marital and parenting status, and ethnic or religious background; others do not.

None of this information is necessarily critical to ensuring a satisfactory relationship; it is quite possible in some cases, as some therapists contend, that clients will be better off not knowing it. A question answered *is* a fantasy lost. However, women entering therapy are adults. They have a right to sacrifice certain fantasies in the interest of greater confidence. Only they can assess the personal risks and benefits of having or not having certain information about the therapist, and they may know better than the therapist what the personal consequences of not knowing might be.

Some gay activists make a very convincing case that homophobia is so rampant that lesbian clients may not be completely safe from the consequences of this bias with a heterosexual therapist. It would be ridiculous to try to imagine a therapist's withholding information as to her gender. Because this is nearly impossible, no one advocates not telling the client if the therapist is male or female, even though some fantasies and feelings are lost by virtue of being in therapy with a man rather than a woman, and vice versa.

One could argue that sexual orientation is as fundamental a definer of identity as is gender itself, and so should not be withheld.

Some psychoanalytically oriented therapists have a tendency to answer every question with a question: Why is it important for you to know? What are your fantasies about the possible answers? How will it affect our relationship? In the spirit of good faith, the client may choose to answer the therapist's counterquestions. However, it may be important at the initial session for the client, who has not truly agreed to engage in the therapeutic process with the therapist yet, to simply say, "I'm trying to gather enough screening information to ensure my chances of therapeutic success and to reduce my risk of being victimized. If you're uncomfortable answering any of these questions, please tell me why."

At the other extreme, a woman should be wary of a therapist who is too eager to volunteer information, particularly about personal issues, childhood history, beliefs, and opinions that don't pertain directly to the work. A therapist too eager to confide in the client in the first session may also have difficulty keeping his needs and interests out of the client's way later on.

Early in the therapeutic relationship is the time to set basic goals; conflicts may arise later if client and therapist have not agreed (perhaps never even discussed) the goals of the therapy. If the client thinks she is paying for a coach to offer enthusiastic validation and support and the therapist thinks the client needs more insight and greater autonomy, conflicts are likely to arise. Client and therapist should agree as to what goals are possible and how long achieving them is likely to take.

## What Women Have a Right to Expect

I have come to the conclusion that women entering therapy need to take this assertive, protective, consumerist stance because they simply cannot assume that a licensed therapist is competent. The majority of women I surveyed ultimately received satisfactory therapy. The problem was that a number had to suffer through less competent, less helpful treatment along the way. One hundred and fifty-six respondents reported that a therapist did something they considered "inappropriate" at some point in their therapy history. Although "inappropriate" is a subjective judgment, much of the behavior consisted of flagrant boundary violations, questionable techniques, and clearly unprofessional practices.

In fact, psychotherapy has become a wastebasket term for any number of reputable and less reputable practices performed by practitioners with varying degrees of training and psychological suitability for their profession. A Ph.D. clinical psychologist with a major university appointment in an urban center channels a deity named "Darocles" during therapy sessions and bills insurance companies for this "service" as if it were psychotherapy. His colleagues know and look the other way. A social worker with a master's-level degree hugs, strokes, and rubs clients and does not even call what she's doing bodywork. A Ph.D. psychologist has an office filled with pewter and porcelain statues of wizards, suggests that he is a wizard himself, and walks out of sessions if clients challenge his absolute authority. An M.A. therapist calls herself a therapist/storyteller and tells clients customized fairy tales supposed to contain the metaphoric nugget of their life stories. Some therapists use hypnosis cavalierly to help their clients "recall" repressed material from childhood or even to regress to past lives in search of the origins of their psychological problems.

A therapist's education or license is no guarantee of competence. It would be reassuring to believe that irresponsible therapists are all unlicensed "cranks," but they are not. Whether some of these "alternative" methodologies have validity is not the point. By calling so many different, unsubstantiated practices psychotherapy, the term becomes absolutely meaningless.

I don't think it is unreasonable to expect that licensed psychotherapists, whether M.D. psychiatrists, M.A. or Ph.D. psychologists, or M.S.W. or Ph.D. social workers, be restricted to a practice based on what has been reasonably established over years of research and clinical work, what would be accepted by a consensus of experienced and well-educated therapists. Therapists who choose to use less-established techniques should be obliged to tell the client that these approaches are experimental or fall outside the domain of what is generally considered psychotherapy. While the field is rife with controversy—over the nature of memory, responses to trauma, the therapist's role, what is psychological and what is biological, the impact of nature versus nurture, and on and on, I do not think that a majority of well-trained and well-educated therapists would sanction the extreme approaches just described under the aegis of psychotherapy. But the problem is that when therapists find out that their colleagues are using such unsubstantiated techniques, they tend not to intervene. Everyone—colleagues, licensing boards, professional associations—waits for clients to file complaints before taking any action, and clients are often the people least prepared emotionally to take action.

Women engaged in psychotherapy must hold the professions responsible for closer study of their own methods and the licensing bodies and legislators responsible for more careful monitoring of practice. Clients have a right to know what to expect when they pay a licensed professional to provide psychotherapy, and they should have a responsive body to address when those expectations are betrayed. Perhaps women need to be less reluctant to file complaints with licensing boards, less reluctant to file civil lawsuits, and more willing to let professional associations know what their members are doing in the sanctity of their offices.

## Obligations of Power

In her book *At Personal Risk*, professor of social work Marilyn Peterson contends that when society grants power to a therapist, it comes with two unspoken obligations. The first is that the therapist put the client's therapeutic needs before his own and make all decisions about the course of therapy in service to the client's needs. The second is that the therapist take responsibility for her power and use it with considerable care. The therapist's greater power means that there is always a potential for abuse in the psychotherapy relationship and a multitude of ways for that abuse to occur.

Some therapists abuse their power by identifying too personally with it, acting as though their power is inherent, a sort of divine right of kings, rather than a function of the role. They might execute their power in arbitrary ways, becoming authoritarian tyrants. Authoritarian therapists abuse their power by behaving as if their perceptions are more valid than their clients', as if being the therapist gives them a monopoly on reality.

Other therapists err in the direction of believing that they can equalize the power imbalance completely. They behave like "regular guys," or "pals" to their clients. Therapists who try to be "pals" might dissuade clients of their transference fantasies immediately, downplay their supposedly superior knowledge, and share their personal pain in sessions. By behaving casually and spontaneously, they think they are giving the client an experience of an equal relationship. In fact, total parity in the relationship is impossible. In a relationship of true parity between adults, both people's needs are equally weighed; the therapist would lose any semblance of objectivity and the client could not afford to be completely vulnerable. A client's willingness to be vulnerable and her trust that the therapist will protect her vulnerability are necessary requirements of effective therapy.

The client pays the therapist to know more and to take care of her interests so that she does not have to guard her own needs as she would in any other human interaction. She can relax and engage fully in the process, knowing that she can rely on the therapist, in Michael Kahn's words, "to watch the store." A therapist cannot be a "pal" and also "watch the store."

A sweet woman named Nancy told me a story about a therapist who became more and more chummy at every session. Nancy was flattered and charmed. Then, in the middle of a session, the therapist complained of a muscle spasm and asked Nancy if she would rub her back. Nancy had many issues about physical contact, was half in love with the therapist, and was confused about her own sexual orientation. She froze on the spot.

In a relationship of true parity, the therapist's request might not seem unreasonable. In a psychotherapeutic relationship, little things take on disproportionate importance. The client should never feel that it is her job to satisfy the therapist's needs. Parity is simply not possible in a psychotherapy relationship because the therapist has to have a certain power, authority, and selflessness to be effective. A woman who starts to feel that her therapist wants something from her—anything other than her engagement in the process—should proceed cautiously and confront the therapist with her perception.

The client is not in therapy to please the therapist, flatter the therapist, amuse or entertain the therapist, or make the therapist feel smart, important, valuable, sensitive, lovable, or needed. It is sometimes difficult for women in therapy to recognize this fact because they are so used to feeling responsible for satisfying everyone else's needs in their personal lives.

Good therapists humbly acknowledge and take responsibility for their own power. By doing so, they are apt to act more carefully and more therapeutically, to empower their clients in more meaningful ways than those who disavow their power, deny it, or think they can completely equalize the power imbalance in the relationship. Good therapists empower their clients by negotiating the terms of the therapy. They explain how they work, why they work the way they do, and the evidence for the effectiveness of their approach. They are open to feedback from the client and adjust their approach accordingly. They acknowledge what they do not know and the uncertainties that remain in the field.

Good therapists do not present their conjectures or intuitions or perceptions as reality. They respect their clients' perceptions as having equal value. They take responsibility for their own feelings rather than blaming them on their clients. They enable their clients to set realistic goals and a time frame for achieving those goals. They do not make grandiose promises or outlandish claims. They do not present themselves as savior figures, gurus, wizards, or magicians. They do not promise to love their clients forever or imply that they are the only people who can help them. They do not pretend that they can go back to childhood with them and be the perfect parents they never had. They agree to consultations when the relationship comes to an impasse. Even in the face of a client's unreasonable accusation, they do not become defensive.

An empowered client feels able to discuss the therapeutic process and her feelings about it freely at the beginning of treatment and at any point along its course. She and her therapist are able to periodically revisit her goals. She feels equally free to discuss her feelings about her therapist and about the vicissitudes of their relationship.

As in dysfunctional families, clients tend to blame themselves for the "craziness" that goes on in their relationships with their therapists and to keep their therapists' secrets. What may empower women clients most may be sharing their therapy stories with each other.

# 4

# Drawing Boundaries

On a steamy August afternoon in an elegantly appointed hotel conference room in Toronto, psychologist Arnold Lazarus took to the podium with the dapper bearings of Cary Grant strolling into the country club dining room for lunch. The occasion was a recent national convention of the American Psychological Association (APA), and the room was packed.

Lazarus had first achieved fame in the 1960s as a leader of the behaviorist movement, which sought to liberate psychotherapy from the unscientific dogma of psychoanalysis. He went on to create multi-modal therapy, a pragmatic approach that claims to incorporate the most effective techniques for behavioral change regardless of their theoretical underpinnings.

Now a trim man in his early sixties, with snow white hair, pink in his cheeks, and an impish smile, Larazarus appears to have retained a boyish delight in making mischief. Recipient of the organization's Distinguished Psychologist Award the prior year, Lazarus was now taking a very public maverick stance on the APA's newly revised Code of Ethics by presenting a paper entitled "How Certain Boundaries and Ethics Diminish Therapeutic Effectiveness." The Code spells out in more specific language than ever before appropriate boundaries for the psychotherapy relationship. It cautions therapists against dual relationships (any other social or business contacts with clients), any sexual contact with current or former clients, and misuse of their greater power in the relationship.

Lazarus attributed his profession's newfound stringency to aggressive risk management rather than to any concern for the client. The APA wanted its members to stay out of trouble, that is, out of the malpractice courtroom and out of the headlines. He portrayed his own interests as loftier: a commitment to the "humane" practice of psychotherapy, to "parity" in the client–therapist relationship, and to a "profound respect" for the client's individuality:

> With some clients, anything other than a formal and clearly delineated doctor–patient relationship is inadvisable. With others . . . a willingness to step outside the bounds of a sanctioned healer will enhance treatment outcomes. Thus I have socialized and partied with some clients, played tennis with others, taken long walks with some. . . . At times I have learned more at different sides of a tennis court or across a dining room table than might ever have come to light in my consulting room.

While describing some of his own steps outside the boundaries, Lazarus explained that his actions were "not based on capricious whims . . . but arose from reasoned judgments that the treatment objectives would be enhanced." Nonetheless, one of the boundary crossings Lazarus described seemed motivated as much by his last-minute need for a tennis partner as by "reasoned judgment." Lazarus "got into trouble," he explained, when he invited a female client who was a therapist herself to join him, his wife, and another colleague for a game of tennis. The client declined the offer and opened her next session with an accusation: "This tennis bullshit," Lazarus quoted her as saying, "What are you trying to pull?"

Further discussion revealed that the woman had used a tennis game as a ruse for seducing her own female client and assumed that Lazarus's motives must be "equally impure." Still, Lazarus saw his own invitation as therapeutically useful because it opened up a discussion of the client's "own massive boundary violation."

Lazarus concluded by chastening his colleagues to not behave like "frightened conformists" but to act with the courage of their most famous predecessors whose boundaries were often fluid. The audience responded with laughter, abundant applause, and a few shaking heads. Afterward, several therapists hurried to the podium to confess *sotto voce* their own boundary crossings.

When *Ethics and Behavior*, a professional journal for psychotherapists, published a slightly toned-down version of Lazarus's talk some months later, six leading practitioners wrote strong dissenting opinions to accompany it. Clearly, the current tide has turned in support of strict boundaries, but Lazarus's challenge is hardly unprecedented. The history of boundaries in psychotherapy has been marked by dissension, controversy, and scandal.

Elsa, one of the women interviewed, told me a personal therapy chronicle, which spanned almost fifty years and reflected the field's troubled history. Now in her 70s, Elsa has undergone everything from a scrupulously formal 1940s psychoanalysis in which the analyst never loosened his tie or spoke her first name to 1970s escapades in the hot tub with a human potential movement guru. It is a testament to her own psychological resilience that she recounted her story to me with equanimity and humor, having found value in each era's therapeutic experiments.

What are women in therapy today to make of these shifts in how psychotherapists have delineated the relationship? Is Lazarus right that rigid boundaries can diminish therapeutic effectiveness? That a cup of tea between therapist and client can sometimes be just a cup of tea like any other, a simple and mundane gesture of civility? What about a dinner party or a game of tennis? Looking back at the history of psychotherapy can give us a better perspective on these questions.

## The History of Boundaries

If Josef Breuer presumably fled when Anna O. fell in love with him, Freud's followers had no hesitation about rushing in where Breuer had feared to tread. They had a propensity for becoming personally, often romantically, entangled with their analysands, often with catastrophic results. If the psychotherapeutic alliance resembled other bonds such as those between doctor and patient, priest and confessor, it was also fraught with dangers all its own. Freud observed rather quickly that this bond could take on all the intense emotions usually reserved for family members and lovers. He responded by developing a therapeutic frame to delineate the role of the analyst and the nature of the relationship. The analyst was a surgeon, a mirror, a blank slate, a scientist who must not obscure the phenomenon being observed with biases, beliefs, or too personal an engagement. Freud's conception of the transference was a major determinant of how he came to delineate therapeutic boundaries.

Freud believed that what was transferred in transference were remnants of aggressive and sexual drives from infancy and early childhood. Frozen in time, bound up in conflict, these primal urges, as well as the internal defenses against them, all came back to life in the transference. The analyst had to be careful not to get drawn into attempts to gratify these feelings, for example, by loving the client back or by trying to provide belated but perfect parenting. To do so could be disastrous; the analyst's job was to help the analysand understand the infantile origin of her strivings and the impossibility of satisfying them fully as an adult.

Neutrality and abstinence became the bywords of analytic demeanor. Neutrality meant that the analyst was to take no sides in the patient's internal struggles. Abstinence meant that the analyst would not get caught up in trying to gratify the client's longings and would refrain from using the patient to gratify his own as well. To do so, he had to guard vigilantly against gratification, to the point of depriving the patient of even the usual human warmth. The analyst was to serve as an impartial object for the patient's transference projections and as an interpreter of those projections as they came up. By obeying these strictures, the analyst would avoid Breuer's error of feeding Anna's transference fantasies and allowing his own countertransference to run amok.

Out of this theoretical rationale Freud drew specific therapeutic boundaries. Sessions were to take place at regularly scheduled times each week and to last for a given period of time, usually fifty minutes. The analysand was financially responsible for a given block of time even if she missed a session or if the analyst was on vacation. Sessions were to take place only in the analyst's office, which also had to be neutral ground, providing no clues about the analyst's personal life that might detract from his usefulness as a transference object. Analysts were to avoid any extra-therapeutic or social contact with their patients. If a patient brought the analyst a gift, his duty was to decline it and to interpret its potentially hidden meanings. For example, a gift might be an unconscious attempt to placate the analyst or a way for a patient to deny her anger toward him.

The medium of exchange was to be strictly verbal. Any physical contact was hazardous because it was too gratifying and too suggestive and could shift the relationship from the symbolic realm of words to the physical world of action. When analysts failed to behave according to these guidelines, Freud cautioned, they risked acting out with clients their childhood desires and internal conflicts. Freud called these interactions *transference enactments*, the origin of the now common expression "acting out."

Even today, some psychoanalytically inclined therapists hold to a very strict definition of boundaries. To touch the client, offer her a cup of tea, cry at her stories of childhood torment, or even express empathy with too kind a look is to gratify transference strivings or to hold out the promise of gratifying them.

## Do as I Say, Not as I Do

The considerable discrepancy between what therapists say and how they actually behave vis-à-vis boundaries also goes back to Freud. His written prescription to others was much stricter than the boundaries he observed in his own practice. On occasion Freud took a patient along on a family vacation so analysis could continue uninterrupted. He analyzed people with whom he also had social and professional relationships, the most egregious case being his own daughter, Anna. Freud assisted a few clients financially and fed at least one of the stars of his case studies, the Rat Man, a meal.

Former analysands who have written memoirs of their work with Freud do not depict him as always having been neutral or abstinent, either. He vigorously promoted his interpretations against their protests, revealed details of his own family life, and behaved like a meddling yenta in their personal affairs.

Freud's dualistic stance toward boundaries—do as I say, not as I do—set a precedent for the field that continues. Gloria, a forty-five-year-old psychiatrist, compared her demands as a patient with the code of conduct she uses as a therapist: "My therapist once hugged me when I asked him to after a particularly wrenching session. For him to have refused would have altered my ability to trust him. However, I do *not* touch my own patients."

## The Corrective Emotional Experience

Almost from the moment Freud laid out therapeutic boundaries, his contemporaries began to question them. Sándor Ferenczi, one of Freud's early followers and an affectionate man by nature, advocated that some elements of a genuine, loving relationship, such as compassion and affection, had their place in analysis. He wondered if these natural, human expressions might not even be curative in their own right.

Ferenczi acceded to his patients' requests for marathon sessions, held patients on his lap, and allowed them to kiss him. In the "mutual therapy" he devised, he switched roles with some of them and told them all about his own emotional distress, which was considerable.

Ferenczi's "experiments" culminated in a soap opera–ish romantic triangle with Gizella Pálos and her daughter, Elma; he eventually married Gizella.

Despite these complications, Ferenczi never gave up his then-heretical conviction that authenticity, warmth, and compassion were necessary elements of the therapeutic relationship. Nonetheless, his clinical diary of 1932 documents the numerous, sometimes hilarious, and exceedingly messy jams he got into as a result of his unorthodox approach. Once, in an attempt to express his authentic feelings during sessions rather than hiding behind the neutral analytic persona, he allowed his sleepiness to show:

> Instead of being offended, as I feared, [the patient] felt deeply honored that I would behave so naturally in his presence. "This shows that you have great trust in me! Next time don't exert yourself anymore, just fall asleep."

Ferenczi took his patient's advice to heart and proceeded to fall asleep on a regular basis in their sessions. His dedication to authentic expression interfered with his ability to function as a therapist, however. At a subsequent session, the patient implored him: "Please don't fall asleep today, I so badly need your presence. I am so very distraught." Ferenczi reports that at "this appeal" he awoke from his "half daze."

The loyal Freudians denounced Ferenczi, but other thinkers picked up the strand of his thought. In the mid-1940s, Franz Alexander, who had been a patient of Ferenczi, declared the curative agent in psychotherapy to be not insight, but the "corrective emotional experience" of being in a positive relationship with the therapist. The therapist need only do *exactly the opposite* of what the patient's parents had done to reverse the consequences of their faulty parenting. Where they were critical, the therapist should be approving; where they were rejecting, she should be accepting. In this way, the bond with the therapist would set up a new paradigm for intimacy.

Traditional psychoanalysts objected to the very idea of a corrective emotional experience. Trying to be a good parent figure carried too great a risk of gratifying infantile fantasies and encouraging transference enactments. The idea of therapy as a corrective emotional experience has since gone through a number of permutations. The debate over the extent to which the relationship with the therapist is corrective in its own right, and the extent to which this bond in itself can reverse the experiences of childhood, is ongoing.

# A Plea for Authenticity

Psychologist Carl Rogers, principal founder of the humanistic psychology movement in the 1940s, was a gentle, soft-spoken midwesterner. Although reserved and somewhat formal in his manner, Rogers radiated acceptance of humanity with all its flaws. Rebelling against the emotional unresponsiveness of the psychoanalysts and their intellectualized, theory-bound approach, Rogers defined the therapist not as an object for transference projections but as a real person in a genuine, human bond. He urged therapists to be "authentic" and not to adopt an artificial therapeutic persona.

Perhaps the most important curative element in his therapy was "unconditional positive regard," a selflessly motivated but nevertheless genuine form of platonic love for the client. The therapist's primary role was to assist the client in coming to her own truths and mobilizing her own innate capacity for healthy growth. The therapist should do everything possible to equalize the power inequities of the relationship and to build a supportive alliance. Although Rogers defined the psychotherapeutic relationship as "real," it was hardly just another ordinary relationship in the world. It was emblematic, far more important to the client than ordinary social engagements, and had the potential to set a new paradigm for all the client's interactions with others. Many therapists identified with Rogers's message, and for a time Rogerian therapy revolutionized therapeutic practice. Among the most popular humanistic approaches that followed were Fritz Perls's Gestalt therapy and Rollo May's Existentialist school. These therapies shared a belief that the real, authentic, supportive relationship between therapist and client served as an agent of change. They sought to equalize the power imbalance in the relationship, suggesting that absolute parity might be possible.

In the social climate of the late 1960s and 1970s, humanistic psychology's notions of "authenticity" and the "real relationship" were used to justify all manner of radically experimental therapies. The formality of psychoanalysis, in fact nearly all the rules that ever governed the psychotherapy relationship, had broken down. The "human potential" and "encounter" movements attempted to dismantle psychological defenses rapidly so that clients could have more intense emotional experiences, more "authentic" relationships with others. Therapists held twenty-four-hour group marathons in which people were encouraged to say whatever they felt or thought about the other group members without censure. Therapists berated and harangued their clients in the name of authenticity. Gestalt-inspired therapies degenerated into group gropes. Charismatic therapists were guru-ized, and they used their mystique as a license to exploit their patients.

Sexual liaisons between therapists and clients were perpetrated in the name of "liberation." To some practitioners, they were the natural outgrowth of the notion of the corrective emotional experience: If therapists could reverse their clients' childhood experiences by giving them a better experience of caretaking or love, why couldn't they also correct their sexual problems by giving them a corrective *sexual* experience? A few practitioners went so far as to write books and articles in their defense.

Perhaps because of these excesses, few therapists today identify themselves as Rogerians or even as humanists. The humanist influence endures, however, in the widespread acceptance of empathy and unconditional positive regard as important elements of the psychotherapeutic bond. Even the strictest psychoanalyst today is likely to be more emotionally responsive and authentic than his pre-humanistic revolution forebears.

# A Working Partnership

In the 1960s, behaviorism, which was based on a core of laboratory study with animals, made its way into psychotherapeutic treatment. The behaviorists rejected the notion that unconscious dynamics or instinctual sexual and aggressive drives caused human behavior. Instead, they regarded behavior as the product of environmental conditioning and thus amenable to change through similar channels. The cognitive-behaviorists of today combine some behaviorist techniques with findings from cognitive research. They focus on identifying and directly challenging the dysfunctional thoughts, be-liefs, and assumptions behind maladaptive behavior.

For the behaviorists and the cognitive-behaviorists, the relation-ship with the therapist is a collaborative partnership. The therapist functions as teacher and coach. As Lazarus explains it, the relation-ship between client and therapist in cognitive-behavioral therapies is the "soil in which techniques take root." The active agent of change is in the techniques and direct interventions the therapist employs and is not a function of being in an inherently corrective relationship.

Avoidance of transference enactments motivated Freud's delin-eation of firm boundaries. Without this belief in transference, ther-apeutic boundaries have sometimes seemed up for grabs. As theo-rists have redefined the therapist's role, the nature of the relationship between client and therapist, and the effective agent in therapy, they have also challenged the strictly drawn analytic boundaries. For the most part, however, post-Freudian therapists have *reacted* against the psychoanalytic boundaries, against what they perceive as dog-matism, without delineating specific alternatives. Even today, when therapists decide what boundaries to observe in their own practices, they may be reacting against what they see as overly authoritar-ian models. Most practitioners today would agree in principle that boundaries are necessary to structure the relationship and to protect the client from the therapist's unfair abuse of power. The problem is that they disagree about the particulars or about when a breach in the boundaries constitutes such an abuse. For example, Lazarus, a respected leader in the field, doesn't see what's wrong with play-ing a game of tennis with a client or regard a dual relationship as necessarily an abuse of power.

## The Basic Rules

When I asked leading therapists to talk to me about the boundaries they kept in their own practices, most agreed about the basics. Therapy should take place in the office, not in exotic locales. A client should be able to count on a particular appointment time, which the therapist does not change frequently or capriciously. Therapists should be on time for sessions and not extend sessions beyond their usual limits, except in extreme situations. Therapists should establish fees in advance, and the client should pay on a regular basis. Therapists should not take phone calls or allow other interruptions during sessions. They should not self-disclose casually or self-disclose particularly intimate material. Their emotional reactions to the client's material should not be so extreme as to interfere with the client's freedom to express herself. They should be consistent, reliable, and professional in their demeanor. Ongoing dual relationships, that is, clients' having any other role in their therapists' lives, are unacceptable because they carry too great a risk of exploitation. Any sexual involvement is exploitative and unethical.

Beyond these fundamental limits, however, therapists pleaded for a consideration of context. They want to be able to negotiate boundaries according to the individual client's needs; they want to consider each situation individually as it comes up. But where does this leave the client who is struggling with boundary issues in her own therapy? When boundary dilemmas have plagued psychotherapy since Breuer handfed Anna O., when therapists say one thing and do another, when they imply that when it comes to boundary considerations, therapists know best, how can a client maintain her own power and confidence that the boundaries of her therapy are appropriate?

## Thinking about Boundaries

I have come to the conclusion that if women in therapy are to preserve their own power and protect their own vulnerabilities, they need to develop their own framework for thinking about boundaries. The most perplexing boundary questions are often subtle. For example, should a client expect her therapist to extend a session when she is particularly distraught? Should a client who has worked for years in her therapy to be able to sustain a romantic relationship expect her therapist to attend her wedding? If a therapist is committed to authenticity, does that mean she should answer the client's questions about her personal life? Should she reveal or hide the effect the client's disclosures are having on her? Should she express her annoyance at the client's lack of progress? Should she acknowledge any sexual attraction to the client?

These sorts of questions, which lie outside the domain of the profession's ethics codes, fall on the cusp of ethics and technique. The individual therapist, in the sanctity of his or her office, often decides them alone. That is why some therapists drink tea with their clients during sessions and others don't; some have family photos in plain view and others don't; some will attend an occasional social function where a client is present and others will leave a party if they spot a client across the room; some will hug routinely, some will hug only if asked, and some will flinch at the client's hand when proffered for even a handshake.

I believe that a woman has a right to know her therapist's basic stance regarding therapeutic boundaries and the rationale behind that stance. For example, a woman shouldn't have to show up for a therapy session with a cup of coffee in hand and be told that she'll have to leave it outside the office because her therapist doesn't permit clients to drink beverages during sessions. She should have some idea if hugs are always (or never, or sometimes, depending on the circumstances) included among the services she is purchasing. She should be able to anticipate what will happen if she needs to talk to her therapist in between sessions and the extent to which her therapist's personal life is off limits.

Some therapists argue that there is more to be gained therapeutically in waiting to see which boundaries become an issue and only discussing them then. But this policy leaves too many women in therapy feeling as if they are moving blindly around in the dark, hoping not to bump into the sharp corners of the therapist's boundaries.

Therapeutic boundaries are critical because of the relationship's inherent power inequities and because so many aspects of the process remain unknowable. First and foremost, boundaries set limits for the therapist's expression of power and protect the client from the misuse of that power. They provide a consistent, reliable, predictable, knowable frame for a process that remains somewhat mysterious.

When there is a shift in the boundaries, a client should ask herself: Does this have the potential for an abuse of power? It seems clear that any dual relationship—going into business with your therapist, serving as your therapist's teaching assistant, babysitting your therapist's children, serving in any additional role beyond that of client—carries a tremendous potential for exploitation simply because client and therapist do not begin on even ground or have exactly the same agendas. In the secondary relationship, the therapist will have some motive other than protecting the client's therapeutic interests. There is no way for this second agenda not to jeopardize the therapy. The client depends on her therapist too much in his or her professional role to risk that relationship with a potential conflict of interest. There is no way for a therapist or any other human being to enter into these other sorts of relationships without introducing some of their own needs and interests and agendas, which are more than likely to be in conflict with the client's needs *as a client*.

Let's get back to Lazarus's example. Can he really play tennis with a client and protect the client's therapeutic interests? I can certainly imagine many things that could happen on a tennis court to endanger the therapeutic relationship. Competing with your therapist, watching him lose his temper when he fumbles a serve, colliding with him and being inadvertently responsible for his broken ankle, finding out he has a tasteless tattoo on his upper arm, observing him interact with his shallow friends on the sidelines, hearing him laugh at an offensive joke—all these real life interactions simply carry too many risks in the context of the primary therapeutic relationship. The client simply has too much at stake, too great an investment in preserving the therapist in his therapeutic role. When a woman has invested time, money, hope, and intimacy in the prospect of personal change, should she risk that investment for an afternoon's amusement? Would any competent and responsible therapist invite her to take that chance?

What may be most painful for the client about such secondary social encounters may be having to come face-to-face with the discrepancy between her own emotional investment and her therapist's. A client playing tennis with her therapist is unlikely to be able to keep it in perspective as a casual social event.

In her book *At Personal Risk*, professor of social work Marilyn Peterson defines boundary violations as "acts that breach the core intent of the therapist–client association." If an act threatens the bond created in the therapy relationship, then it is suspect, even if its exploitative potential is not obvious. The core intent of the therapist–client association is to serve the client's therapeutic needs.

When a boundary is breached, a client can also employ Peterson's criteria and ask: Is the therapist putting aside his or her needs to act in my therapeutic interest? Is the therapist using power carefully to protect my vulnerability? In the case of the tennis game, for example, it would be virtually impossible for a therapist to put aside all his own needs and desires and still play a reasonable game of tennis. The tennis court is not the therapist's office, and different rules apply. No therapist could completely protect the client's vulnerabilities and safeguard the therapy when torn by the demands of this other social engagement.

The single most important boundary to preserve in the client–therapist relationship is that between the client's needs as a client (which may differ from what the client needs in other contexts and from other relationships) and the therapist's needs. About any potential shift in the therapeutic boundaries, a client can ask, "*Who* is this for? *Whose* needs, and *which* needs, are being served? Is this likely to be in my long-term therapeutic interest?"

When the client herself longs for the boundary shift, feels honored perhaps at the prospect of getting to play tennis with her therapist, she needs to ask herself if what she is longing for is what she is going to get. When a shift in the boundaries carries the promise of providing far more than the act itself, when it has assumed undue symbolic weight, the client is likely to be at her most vulnerable.

# The Symbolic Meaning of Boundaries

Clear boundaries are important because of the disproportionate importance of small things in psychotherapy, because of the client's sometimes childlike vulnerability in the relationship. The intense feelings that surface in psychotherapy often gravitate toward these boundaries and disputes about them. It is possible for a dispute over a refused hug, for example, to become the locus for all a woman's unresolved feelings about authority, power, limits, the forbidden, deprivation, and gratification. In short, boundaries become even more crucial because they can assume symbolic meanings.

For example, Angela had rather strict and controlling parents. Her space, body, even her most private thoughts were subject to continual parental incursion. In her therapy relationship, Angela perceived the boundaries as protecting her from her therapist's incipient invasiveness. But at the same time that she cherished the safety the boundaries afforded, she also felt the need to test them. Her parents' daughter, she could not help but regard her therapist's adherence to the boundaries, his lack of invasiveness, as an absence of caring. Clearly any shift in the boundaries would have profound connotations for Angela.

Pepper, on the other hand, grew up in a very formal household where feelings were not expressed and there were many unspoken secrets. She regarded the boundaries as being like all the locked doors in her childhood home, an impediment to intimacy. She imagined that if only the rules were relaxed, if only she and her therapist could go somewhere outside of his office, she could allow herself to feel more.

The symbolic meaning of boundaries and of boundary crossings is highly idiosyncratic, but boundaries always have the potential to become disproportionately important to clients.

The stories that follow illustrate some of the idiosyncratic meanings that a shift in the boundaries can assume for women in therapy and the impact that such shifts can have on the client–therapist relationship. In the first two stories, unusual circumstances result in boundary shifts. In each case, the relationship improves because the client is able to discuss the shift and its symbolic meanings with her therapist.

### Lana's Story: Would You Like to Wear My Sweater?

Lana was in her five o'clock therapy session when the Seattle temperature took a sudden downward turn. She was wearing a lightweight cotton blouse and complained to her therapist, Ruth, that she was "freezing." Ruth turned up the heat and then offered Lana the forest green cable knit sweater that always hung on a hanger on a hook on the inside door of her office. In doing so, Ruth might argue, she was showing concern for Lana and taking care of her in a way that was well within the limits of her professional role. After all, the therapy was threatening to come to a standstill because her client was too uncomfortable to proceed. To have let her client shiver with the sweater hanging on the door might have conveyed the message that Ruth was selfish and insensitive.

If the psychotherapeutic relationship were like any other social relationship in the world, the only civil thing for Ruth to have done would have been to offer Lana her sweater. The only reasonable way for Lana to have responded would have been to accept the sweater graciously. But the approximate relationship always has another, symbolic dimension. For Lana, the sweater was not just any sweater, it was *her therapist's sweater*, and it had taken on symbolic meaning. Lana had come to associate it fondly with Ruth. Sometimes during therapy sessions, she found it easier to look at the sweater and think about Ruth fondly than to look Ruth in the eye. In relationships outside of therapy, Lana tended to "lose herself" in the other person's life. Then she would get angry at herself for her own malleability and would retreat. Lana was struggling to learn how to be close to another person and still hold on to herself.

Lana imagined that Ruth was impervious to the influence of others, that she was totally self-contained. Lana admired and feared this self-containment. Would Ruth be disgusted if she knew just how close to her Lana sometimes longed to get? The prospect of putting on Ruth's sweater made Lana nervous because it brought up all her complicated feelings about closeness and distance, and the risk of once more losing herself. To put on Ruth's sweater and have it not fit might mean having to confront the differences between them in too visceral a way. Of course, Lana was not aware of all these meanings immediately, simply of her own discomfort, which she trusted enough to take seriously. She acknowledged that this simple act had meanings beyond itself and that therapy was one place where she did not have to deny that simple acts could have complex meanings. But she didn't want to talk about her feelings initially—wouldn't that seem like a crazy overreaction to a kind offer? It was only a sweater! Lana simply thanked her therapist and declined the offer.

Ruth was astute enough to bring the episode up again later so that she and Lana could sort out its various meanings and what Lana might learn from them. Even when crossing a boundary does not seem an obvious exploitation of the therapist's power, it may still constitute an exploitation of the therapist's *symbolic power* because of the disproportionate weight the boundary holds for the client. Lana's story illustrates that if a client takes herself seriously, she can safeguard the boundaries of her own therapy even when her therapist momentarily fails to do so.

## Gina's Story: A Visit in the Hospital

Gina, a young woman in her twenties who had been in therapy for about a year, was rushed to the hospital for emergency abdominal surgery. In response to her distressed phone call, John, her therapist, visited her the next day. Gina was in a great deal of pain when John appeared in the doorway of her hospital room. Saying little, he came into the room, sat at her bedside, took her hand when she held it out to him, and offered a few reassuring words. After a short while, and after making sure that Gina had friends coming to see her, John left.

For Gina, John's visit meant that he cared about her and could endure seeing the depth of her vulnerability and pain. She recognized the visit as an exception to the therapy frame and did not expect it to be repeated. Illness was not a means by which Gina ordinarily expressed her desires to be taken care of, so she did not fantasize, as some clients might have, about getting sick in order to receive John's further ministrations. After Gina recovered from her surgery, she and John discussed the hospital visit, what it had meant to her, and its place in the context of their relationship.

It would seem that John thought carefully before deciding to visit Gina, was thoughtful and deliberate in his behavior while at the hospital, and helped Gina assess its meaning afterward. If the visit roused any fantasies of perfect love or eternal care, Gina knew that these fantasies were open to discussion. Some therapists would not have made the hospital visit because they believe it important not to take the relationship outside the confines of the office. Others might argue that the visit could hold the promise of providing more than the therapy relationship could deliver. Many therapists would make the decision as to whether to go to the hospital based on the individual relationship.

What seems most important in this case is that John was not cavalier about his behavior. He considered all its possible ramifications of meaning and later created a safe forum in which Gina could discuss those meanings with him. He did not make the mistake of thinking that his visit was equivalent to that of another friend—this was a professional visit that would have symbolic resonance.

Therapists who take their power seriously also take the boundaries of therapy seriously. When they bend the therapeutic frame, they do so carefully and explore the meaning their action has for the client. They recognize that not all meanings may emerge at first and that clients may be reluctant to acknowledge just how important a seemingly trivial exchange is to them.

## Patti's Story: Would You Like to Rescue Me?

Patti was raised by an alcoholic aunt whom she often had to take care of as a child. She had been in therapy with Meg, whom she liked very much, for a little more than a year. Some days when Patti was driving down the highway, she daydreamed that she came upon Meg's car broken down by the side of the road. Patti imagined rushing to Meg's rescue, demonstrating how competent and capable and caring she was, and that Meg would be forever grateful. Patti had tentatively disclosed these rescue fantasies to Meg without divulging just how intense and gratifying they were. Patti's childhood had taught her that to be valued in a relationship she had to be the rescuer.

Patti and Meg's lives intersected beyond the therapy room since they were both active in the feminist/lesbian community. One night Patti was a volunteer ticket-taker for a charity event. She heard someone whisper, "How would you like to rescue me?" and turned to find Meg standing before her, looking chagrined. "I'm so embarrassed, I've forgotten my ticket back at the office," Meg implored. "Can you just let me *slip* in?"

Patti had been instructed not to let anyone in without a ticket, regardless of her excuse, but how could Patti say no to her therapist? She let Meg through the door, feeling a simultaneous rush of annoyance, excitement, and guilt.

That night Patti dreamed she and Meg were in bed together and that Meg was seducing her. As Meg gently caressed Patti's shoulders and was about to kiss her, she passed wind loudly instead. Patti awoke with a start. She didn't see the connection between what had transpired at the charity ball and the dream, however, until Meg raised the topic at their next session.

"I really want to talk with you about what happened the other night," Meg began. She regretted having crossed a boundary and, in her words, "contaminating our public relationship with information from therapy." Meg's open, nondefensive admission of her mistake and her willingness to consider all of its ramifications mediated its volatile impact. She knew that boundary crossings that become unspeakable secrets between therapist and client could do ongoing damage.

Meg had unknowingly exploited her power to gain illicit access to the charity event. Worse, by asking Patti to "rescue" her, she had exploited her symbolic power by employing Patti's fantasy to serve her own needs. Simply put, she had crossed a boundary out of her own interest, while couching the crossing in terms of gratifying Patti's fantasy. Fortunately, Meg was able to limit the damages by admitting her mistake and discussing the meaning of her own impulsive action.

"Some part of me knew," Patti said, "because in my dream, Meg committed this jarring indiscretion." In her dream, Patti placed her exchange with Meg in the context of a sexual seduction, revealing that symbolically, even nonsexual boundary crossings can take on a sexual charge. They represent an illicit gratification outside the bounds of the sanctioned therapeutic relationship. And there was something seductive in the way Meg used Patti's rescue fantasy to get what she wanted. Given the therapist's greater power, most clients would find it awkward to say "no" if put in Patti's position. The added symbolic charge of Patti's secret rescue fantasy rendered her incapable of turning Meg down.

Often clients feel an exhilarating sense of specialness when a boundary bends, a thrill tinged with undercurrents of unease. The feeling may be similar regardless of whether it is the therapist or the client who bends the frame. Mia followed her therapist to a dance studio to watch her practice ballet. "I felt happy and special and uncomfortable and ashamed," she reported. Danielle's therapist repeatedly confided in her about her personal life, adding that these were facts she'd never told another patient. Of being singled out as special, Danielle said: "In a way it thrilled me, and in another way it drove me crazy!"

When the boundary slips, clients may also feel that the roles have reversed and that they are obliged to take care of the therapist. The role reversal may feel exhilarating at first with its promise of equalizing power; eventually, however, it is bound to get in the way of therapy. The client finds herself in the position of Ferenczi's patient, torn between taking care of her therapist by letting him sleep and taking care of herself by waking him up to do therapy.

## Seduction and Punishment

Psychologist Michael Kahn offers two other considerations for a client to use in assessing the impact of a boundary shift: Does it feel like some form of seduction? Does it feel like some kind of punishment? Seduction need not be overtly sexual; *any* act that stirs some kind of desire in the client for the therapist is seductive. Often when an act is seductive, the client feels lured in and led to expect more than is possible in the approximate realm of psychotherapy. She starts to want something and to imagine that the therapist is offering something beyond the usual therapeutic services. The therapist has singled her out as special: "Does he *really* love me?" "Do the rules of therapy still pertain to us?"

Punishment is anything the therapist does that hurts or damages the client in order to satisfy the therapist's needs. When a boundary shifts and a woman feels uncomfortable or special, she should ask herself, "Is there some way in which my therapist's action is serving as a form of psychological punishment or seduction for me?" And she should be able to take the question to her therapist. Of course, the therapist may disagree with the client's assessment, but a good therapist will be able to talk about the punitive or seductive connotations of her own behavior without becoming defensive.

## Arlene's Story: The Question of a Hug

Arlene is forty-nine and in training to become a therapist herself. She has been in therapy with Paul for three years. At the end of their very first session together, he asked her if she wanted a hug. After that, the hug became a regular part of each session's closing. Arlene became very attached to this ritual:

> If I only see him once a week, that's one hug a week instead of two. I'm embarrassed to admit that I think about it in those terms, but I do.
>
> The hug means caring, acceptance, validation. I was raised to feel it was wrong or bad to have any needs of my own. The hug says that it's okay to give affection, it's okay to be vulnerable, I don't have to be ashamed.

Arlene's parents divorced when she was two years old and she saw her father, whom she perceived to be withdrawn and indifferent, only on the weekends. Her mother's affection felt to her like a clingy demand. Arlene remembered her mother as taking things away from her if Arlene wanted them too much or if they made her feel too special.

One afternoon, about a year and a half into Arlene's therapy, Paul was visibly upset when he came into the waiting room to get her for their session. She looked at him sympathetically, and he said, "I think *I* need a hug." Arlene was only too happy to oblige. "I gave him a hug and I was feeling very special and really good."

At the time, Arlene was having "all sorts of fantasies" about Paul. Some of them were romantic, but mostly she imagined him as a "good daddy" who embodied everything she didn't get from her own father: "openness, affection, and respect." Arlene recalls feeling "like a little girl who couldn't bear the thought of losing Paul."

The next session, when Paul came out into the waiting room to get Arlene, she rose immediately and hugged him, institutionalizing the spontaneous gesture of the prior session. She interpreted Paul's lackluster response as tacit approval to initiate a new unspoken rule between them: Hugs were now de rigueur at the beginning as well as at the end of sessions.

Arlene wonders now if she hadn't been half-aware of taking advantage of a spontaneous breach in the boundaries—Paul did seem less than enthusiastic about the session-opening hugs. But the hugs felt so good and meant so much to Arlene that she could not help but reach for Paul each time he came into the waiting room.

Two months after the initial breach, as Arlene rose from her chair and moved toward Paul for their opening hug, he stopped her. "I'm not going to do this anymore," he said. "*You* want something from me that *I* don't want to give." Arlene recalls the rebuff as being "like a slap in the face." Paul had initiated the opening hugs and now he didn't seem "willing to own it."

Paul later acknowledged that he never should have asked Arlene for a hug in the first place and should not have allowed the hugs to continue but that now he had to put a stop to them to take care of himself. Arlene's hugs felt too "greedy," too "grabby," too "possessive," and that made him uncomfortable.

Arlene felt so devastated by Paul's remarks that she did not raise the subject of the hug again for many months. Once again, as in childhood, something good, something that made her feel special, had been taken away from her because she had been too greedy and let her needs show.

Paul's initial breach in the boundaries clearly arose out of his own need: He spontaneously used his client to comfort himself and, in doing so, failed to put his client's interests above his own. Such an occasional slip happens in many therapies. Paul was human and he'd had a bad day. Because Paul was so important to her, Arlene was exquisitely attuned to his mental state and was eager to equalize the relationship by becoming his caretaker. In a sense she also took advantage of his sadness to breach the boundaries and to get something more from him than was ordinarily permitted.

Once the initial breach occurred, Paul may have felt guilty for having used Arlene to satisfy his own needs, so he allowed the session-opening hugs to continue as an unspoken secret between therapist and client. Perhaps he was also having difficulty rationalizing the logic of his own boundaries: Why, exactly, was a hug okay at the end of sessions and not at the beginning?

When Paul terminated the session-opening hugs, he again justified his action on the basis of serving his own needs rather than Arlene's—her greediness was making him uncomfortable. In both initiating the hug and in putting a stop to it, then, Paul had put his own interests above his client's. He had not used his greater power responsibly to protect Arlene's greater vulnerability. That is not to say, of course, that continuing to hug Arlene at the beginning of sessions would have been in her long-term therapeutic interests, either.

Paul's request for the hug had seductive connotations because it lured Arlene into feeling as though she were special, not like other clients, and that Paul and she had a relationship beyond the bounds of the usual client–therapist alliance. Although it made Arlene feel temporarily powerful, it did not actually increase her power in the relationship in any way. To the contrary, she felt less able to predict or control what might happen in the therapy. She could not even talk about the hug for fear of losing it. So Paul erred further by allowing the crossing to become an unspoken secret between therapist and client.

He interpreted Arlene's hugs as being greedy because they felt greedy to him, never giving Arlene ample opportunity to explore what the hugs meant to her. Being able to give love back was as important a part of the fantasy for Arlene as was the taking of love; her withdrawn father had not only given little but had also seemed incapable of taking any pleasure or joy in her love for him. This aspect of the hug's meaning was lost on Paul, who only perceived Arlene's greed.

If Paul had set the right therapeutic context, Arlene might have been able to use Paul's perception that her hugs felt "greedy" to advance her understanding of herself. As the rationale for his rejection, the comment did more harm than good. In fact, the hug had such a heavy symbolic charge for Arlene that she could not help but seem greedy, especially when she expected anything good to be snatched away from her. When Paul halted the hugs, his behavior had punitive connotations: He withdrew his favors out of disapproval of Arlene's behavior. Arlene felt that it was the vulnerable, hurt child in her who was punished:

> The message he was giving me in therapy was it's okay to feel, to be open, to give, to let yourself be vulnerable, to have needs—you don't have to feel ashamed. But then when I got into a situation with him where I thought that's what I was doing, I was told that I was wrong because I was too grabby about it. He kicked the needy little girl part of me around.

When a boundary shifts in therapy, the client often experiences a sense of vertigo, of dislocation, the ground temporarily falling away beneath her. She does not dare to question the therapist's intent because the crossing feels like a bonus beyond the usual economy of the therapeutic exchange. Often a boundary crossing unleashes the fantasy that deep, childlike wishes and needs are finally going to be met, that she is finally going to get what she has been waiting for all her life. The floodgates are open, the rules are gone, the sky is going to rain love. She imagines that she and her therapist are going to make a leap from the approximate realm to the real world. Of course, the leap to the real world that the client imagines is often colored by fantasy. She may not think that she and the therapist will merely be lovers with all the risks and vicissitudes that such a relationship entails but that they will be soul mates for life. The imagined gratification carries a supercharge.

For Arlene, Paul's hugs were magical. They came from the person who seemed symbolically capable of rectifying all the failings of her father. His hugs were gold doled out at the end of sessions, more immediate and gratifying than the therapy itself. When Paul opened the coffers by offering a hug at the beginning of the sessions as well, implying that it was as much for him as for her, Arlene felt that she could finally get what she had always wanted, and she hung on for dear life. These were the issues that Arlene and Paul needed to address if they were ever to get beyond the boundary breach.

## To Hug or Not to Hug?

Touch, and other physical contact, may be the most controversial boundary in therapy. Most psychotherapy runs on a verbal economy; the medium of exchange is words, rather than actions, with therapists varying even in their degree of emotional expressiveness. Touch is more primal, more visceral—and more provocative. My interviewees reported that hugs had the potential to become a sort of extra-therapeutic reward system, like the pediatrician's lollipop awarded after getting a shot. Along these lines, clients also reported that hugs readily took on punitive connotations since there was always a threat that they would be withheld if the client "misbehaved" during the session.

Hugs also tended to become a taboo subject, not discussed during sessions even when they were routinely offered at the end and practically never discussed while they were happening. They became a secret between client and therapist, and as we have already seen, such secrets in the relationship are always dangerous.

Clients also tended to become inordinately invested in the therapist's hugs. Arlene was far from alone in confessing that they became more meaningful than the therapy itself; other women felt likewise. Cheryl admitted, "I looked forward through my whole session to the hug at the end."

One of the problems with touch in psychotherapy is that a hug between two people of unequal power is not the same as a hug between equals. The person with greater power, in this case the therapist, "rations" the hugs, and the client cannot "take" a hug whenever she wants one. This suggests to the client that the therapist's hugs are of tremendous value. And then there is always the possibility that a hug will stir sexual desire.

How therapists think about touch varies widely. Psychoanalytically oriented therapists are less likely to touch their clients because physical contact carries the danger of gratifying transference fantasies that need to be understood, not acted out. Therapists influenced by the humanistic movement, and, more recently, by the recovery movement, are more inclined to hug routinely at the end of sessions. Many therapists take a moderate position, offering a pat on the back or an occasional hug if the client asks for it or if a session is particularly grueling.

To believe that touch is always benign or helpful to clients ("hugs heal") seems quite a naive position, given the complexity of clients' feelings. My research suggests that touch is powerful, that it has mixed effects and far-reaching ramifications, and that it is seldom a simple social gesture.

If a client knows that a hug would mean too much or confuse her about the approximate nature of the relationship, she should draw the boundary and simply let the therapist know that she would prefer not to be hugged. If the therapist's hugs have become too important to her, she should be able to discuss their meanings with her therapist, without fear that the wrong answer will result in their being withdrawn.

## Clara's Story: Want to Be My Friend?

The boundaries began to break down in Clara's therapy when Jaye, her therapist, in the middle of a break-up from her boyfriend, started to confide in Clara during therapy sessions. She told Clara that she knew she should be talking to a colleague and not to a client, but that she also thought there was something artificial about the idea of "there being a neutral clinical person who's listening to this other person who's got all the problems, and wasn't there some level of relationship where we could just be two human beings together?"

Jaye's disclosures became a secret in Clara's therapy. Initially Clara felt excited, special, singled out. If she could be as important to Jaye as Jaye was to her, perhaps she could avoid the devastating rejection she had felt when an earlier therapy relationship terminated. And Clara's current therapy was also in danger of termination since she was approaching the maximum number of sessions her HMO allowed.

From their very first session together, Clara had felt very strong feelings for Jaye. Jaye was so caring, so accepting. Clara began to idealize Jaye, and after a few months she could scarcely think of anything besides Jaye and her therapy sessions. Clara trusted Jaye as she had never trusted anyone, allowing Jaye to see her in all her vulnerability. As Clara says, "One kind word from Jaye had a greater impact than a thousand compliments from anyone else." Whatever Jaye said, Clara believed. Their relationship became emblematic: This was the first time anyone had really heard and understood Clara; this was the relationship that would make up for all the hurts of the past.

A few weeks after Jaye began to confide her own problems in Clara, she suggested that she and Clara get together, "outside of the boundaries of the client/therapist thing." Jaye and Clara wound up taking a hike together in the mountains. Their Sunday together felt to Clara "like a dream come true."

After that, Clara couldn't wait to see Jaye again, but Jaye became ambivalent, setting dates and then canceling them at the last minute. Clara felt confused, helpless, and trapped by the duality of their relationship:

> When it's your therapist you're dealing with and you are also friends, well, sort of friends, how do you know when you're getting a therapist's response and when you're getting a friend's? . . . I try not to think about it because she's my therapist and I need her for that.

Jaye had gotten herself into a bind. Once she had allowed therapy sessions to deteriorate into two-way gabfests, how could she go back to being the therapist? Besides, she was going to have to terminate Clara's therapy soon, and termination promised to be emotionally devastating to Clara. Wouldn't it be easier to simply segue into a social relationship?

Unfortunately, Clara's perception of the Sunday afternoon she spent with Jaye as a "dream come true" revealed that the relationship carried inordinate symbolic weight and that Jaye had disproportionate power. A friendship would inevitably mean more to Clara than to Jaye because it continued to carry the symbolic weight of their emblematic, highly charged, and inadequately explored therapy relationship. And any problem in the friendship could threaten whatever gains Clara had made in therapy.

It's clear that Jaye was not acting in Clara's therapeutic interest but had allowed her own needs to intrude. Rather than using her power carefully and responsibly, she had rationalized that her power was just a pretense ("we're just two human beings") that she could drop whenever it became too great a burden. Jaye may have felt that she had too many problems of her own to be a good therapist and that her own psychological distress excused her from the responsibility she'd assumed.

If being a therapist required having no psychological problems of one's own, there would be no therapists. Good therapists use the boundaries to keep their own problems from getting in the client's way.

Clara had two dreams about Jaye that illustrate the symbolic weight of the relationship and the impact of the boundary shift. She had the first dream early in her therapy:

> I was waiting for Jaye so I tried on her dress. It was a white dress with a long flowing white skirt, almost a wedding gown. I was disappointed that it wasn't as beautiful on me as it was on Jaye. But then, in a flash, I became Jaye. I was beautiful too, wearing her beautiful white dress. She was going to a wedding with me. It meant that everything was going to be okay.

In the dream, Clara expressed a wish to become like Jaye, even to become one with Jaye, in order to achieve a greater sense of identity and well-being. The wedding represented some sort of happy merger between them. For Clara, friendship with Jaye, "a dream come true," continued to carry the same disproportionate symbolic weight as the fantasied wedding.

In the midst of worrying about the status of their relationship, Clara had quite another dream:

> I was in Jaye's office and walked out to the reception area to sign out but I couldn't figure out which kind of service to check so I just signed my name. Then I realized that I needed to go back in because I wasn't finished yet, but Jaye had walked away to do something else. When Jaye came into the room, she said, "I wasn't able to work with you last night, but I need your help today."

In the dream, Clara is supposed to sign out, probably symbolic of her termination, but she can't figure out which kind of service to check—the nature of her relationship with Jaye has become unclear. She just signs her name, realizing that her therapy isn't complete (she needs to go back in), but her therapist has disappeared. The role reversal and incursion of Jaye's needs into Clara's therapy are evident in Jaye's final declaration: "*I wasn't able to work with you last night but I need your help today.*"

Clara's relationship with Jaye was still up in the air when my contact with her ended. She was trying to convince me (and probably herself) that she was ready to have an equal relationship with Jaye, but she remained confused:

> I feel a real connection with Jaye, not just the transference. The sort of connection you feel with somebody that you have a lot in common with. I no longer feel like there is some magic going on. I mean . . . in a way . . . I still do.

Perhaps Clara and Jaye made the transition to friendship successfully, but the risks of the situation turning out otherwise seemed much greater, too great for either therapist or client to be taking the chance.

That said, good boundaries are not equivalent to good therapy. Boundaries exist to protect the therapy; they are not the therapy. It is quite possible for a therapist to keep the boundary and lose the patient by enforcing boundaries in a restrictive, legalistic, defensive manner. One of the complaints that I heard most often from women was just how bad, how invisible and impotent, their therapists' lack of emotional responsiveness could make them feel. And some therapists certainly used the boundaries to maintain this emotional distance. But a boundaried relationship does not have to be an emotionally distant relationship. Therapists can be warm, responsive, and authentic and still maintain a protective frame around the relationship.

How a therapist thinks about boundaries, talks about boundaries, with her clients can have as much impact as the actual boundaries kept. When therapists presented the boundaries as arbitrary rules, their clients were likely to resent their restrictiveness. Some therapists also played "good cop, bad cop," implying that boundaries were imposed by some anonymous outside authority (the law, the licensing board, the training institute, and so on) and that they would have a much freer relationship with the client if not for their fear of getting into trouble. They colluded in the client's fantasy that the boundaries were what was keeping her from getting what she needed from her therapist. Other therapists presented the boundaries solely in terms of their own self-protection, as if the boundaries were an electrified fence erected to protect them from their clients' incessant, infantile demands. In fact, boundaries do protect therapists' interests as well, and most good therapists acknowledge this. They protect their privacy, time, psychological integrity, relative objectivity, and ability to sustain the relationship.

Women in therapy may have an easier time with boundaries if they can recognize that therapeutic boundaries ultimately serve their best interests. Therapy is a fragile, paradoxical relationship always at risk of turning into something else—friendship, romance, the worship of devotee for guru. Boundaries prevent this from happening.

They remind client and therapist that their relationship is approximate, that in its therapeutic capacity there are things that it can never be, but that what it is can be relied upon. A client is safer and maintains more of her own power by staying inside the therapeutic frame than by attempting to alter it. Within its structure, she can allow herself to be completely vulnerable.

So where does this leave Arnold Lazarus? If we just listen to the difference in tone between Clara's agonized ruminations over the boundaries of her therapy and Lazarus's cavalier, off-the-cuff treatment of the same topic, we discover all we need to know about the disproportionate importance of boundaries to clients.

# 5

# Making Sense
# of Transference

*For they saw, standing in just the spot the screen had hidden, a little old man, with a bald head and a wrinkled face, who seemed to be as much surprised as they were. The Tin Woodman, raising his axe, rushed toward the little man and cried out, "Who are you?"*

*"I am Oz, the Great and Terrible," said the little man in a trembling voice, "but don't strike me—please don't!—and I'll do anything you want me to."*

*Our friends looked at him in surprise and dismay.*
*"I thought Oz was a great Head," said Dorothy.*
*"And I thought Oz was a lovely Lady," said the Scarecrow.*
*"And I thought Oz was a terrible Beast," said the Tin Woodman.*
*"And I thought Oz was a Ball of Fire," exclaimed the Lion.*
*"No; you are all wrong," said the little man, meekly. "I have been making believe."*

*"Making believe!" cried Dorothy. "Are you not a great Wizard?"*
*. . . "Not a bit of it, my dear; I'm just a common man."*

From *The Wonderful Wizard of Oz* (L. Frank Baum)

Imagine that three friends each went to the same therapist once and then compared their first impressions. They reached an easy consensus on the therapist's obvious traits, but beyond that, their observations were as different as if they had gone with Dorothy to see the Wizard.

Zoe, the therapist, was a tall, large-framed woman of forty-eight. She had salt and pepper hair, wore little make-up, and dressed in long Indian cotton print skirts and loose cotton blouses. Zoe kept firm therapeutic boundaries and disclosed little about her personal life, but she also believed in being authentic and empathic. She maintained eye contact, listened attentively, and spoke in a soft, soothing voice.

Of the three women, Patty liked Zoe immediately. She saw her as an earth mother who would be nurturing and kind. Amy suspected that Zoe was not as she seemed—she was hiding a lot of weight under her full skirt and a dominating personality under that soft-spoken demeanor. Charlotte noticed that Zoe was wearing a gold band and concluded that she was married—probably to a bourgeois physician or academic with whom she probably had a very conventional sex life. How would she ever be able to understand Charlotte's bisexuality and enthusiasm for group sex?

Patty, Amy, and Charlotte's first impressions were a combination of astute data-gathering and psychological projection. Given limited information, they used their prior knowledge and experience of people and relationships to draw some conclusions about Zoe. They considered what she actually told them about herself and made assumptions based on subtler cues—Zoe's clothing, her office furnishings, and, most importantly, her demeanor, body language, facial expressions, and choice of words. Inevitably, they also perceived Zoe through the filters of their own emotional histories. They may have all met the same woman, but Patty met a good mother; Amy, a duplicitous controller; Charlotte, a puritanical judge. All saw through the templates of their past experiences, beliefs, and longings.

The differences among the women's impressions suggests that projection contributed significantly to each, yet it would be nearly impossible to delineate where projection ended and "realistic" perception began. Were Patty, Amy, or Charlotte to embark on therapy with Zoe, their feelings about her might change. But we can be certain that they would never be completely freed from the influences of the past.

# The History of an Idea

The simple observation that human beings have a tendency to see the present through the emotional filters of the past is at the foundation of the notion of transference. Of course, Freud's theory went way beyond this seemingly inarguable fact. He conceptualized transference as a sort of return, a recapitulation of feelings frozen since infancy into the present:

> The most remarkable thing is this. The patient is not satisfied with regarding the analyst in the light of reality as a helper and adviser who . . . would himself be content with some such role as that of a guide on a difficult mountain climb. On the contrary, the patient sees in him the return, the reincarnation of some important figure out of his childhood . . . and consequently transfers on to him feelings and reactions which undoubtedly applied to this prototype.

Transference had a phantasmagoric quality and involved a certain transubstantiation; presto chango and the analyst took on the guise of the childhood parent. Freud emphasized the quasi-mystical nature of the phenomenon, likening transference to a "menacing illusion" and a "waking dream":

> Just as happens in dreams, the patient regards the products of the awakening of his unconscious impulses as contemporaneous and real; he seeks to put his passions into action without taking any account of the real situation.

Transference also had the potential to distort, even completely block, the light of reality. The illusion was not only unconscious; it could overwhelm all other perception.

What was transferred in transference according to Freud were remnants of aggressive and sexual drives from infancy and early childhood. These unresolved, irrational feelings could be linked to the developmental phases in which they first arose. Thus, a transference could be labeled oedipal or preoedipal, depending on the period when it first surfaced and its original object (father or mother). And these feelings could emerge in the therapeutic relationship intact, as if they had been suspended in time. All phases of the patient's childhood might be recapitulated in relationship to the analyst, who, like the Wizard of Oz, had a predilection for taking on all manner of fantastical shapes.

If the transference experience had a phantasmagoric quality, it also had an inherent therapeutic potential. Reexperiencing the past in the present, and then realizing how past experience was distorting perception, could be curative. Transference could be resolved as the patient became conscious of her transference feelings, accepted their origins in early infantile strivings that could never be satisfied, and made a new peace with what was possible in adult life. For this to occur, the analyst had to be careful not to gratify the patient's irrational, infantile longings and to offer dispassionate interpretation instead.

During the course of his career, Freud also offered a second, more commonsense notion of transference as a relationship template. According to this view, we all construct models of how relationships with significant others work based on our most important bonds in childhood. We unconsciously perceive, and even structure, later relationships to correspond to these internalized templates.

Following Freud, the psychoanalysts took possession of the idea of transference and developed an awesome and arcane body of writings on the subject. In the past one hundred years, they have directed the transference discourse down ever more convoluted and self-referential paths. Until quite recently, psychoanalytic thinkers seemed far less interested in subjecting the phenomenon to scientific scrutiny than in developing more and more complicated theoretical offshoots. They argued that no clinician who had observed transference needed any further proof of its existence and that scientific inquiry was apt to prove reductive because it simply could not capture the subtlety and power of the phenomenon.

And so, in the psychoanalytic literature, theorists argued ad infinitum as to whether particular transferences were oedipal or pre-oedipal, oral or genital, erotic or erotized. They tended to agree, however, that transference and its interpretation were at the very heart of psychoanalysis. The patient's greatest insights and growth would come through understanding her own transference wishes and fantasies.

When the humanistic school of therapy emerged in the 1940s and challenged psychoanalytic theory, it also questioned the notion of transference and its centrality in treatment. Carl Rogers and his followers argued that the "real relationship" between a humane, authentic, collegial—as opposed to cold and paternalistic—therapist would allow the client's "self-actualizing" tendencies to flourish. In reconceptualizing the therapist as less an object for transference projections and more a real person in genuine relationship to the client, they seemed compelled to disown the concept of transference altogether. As psychologist Michael Kahn explains, "Transference may have been one of the babies thrown out with the bath water in the humanistic revolution." Transference came with too much theoretical baggage: psychoanalytic mumbo-jumbo about encapsulated past-in-present and innate instinctual drives.

The humanists also argued that some of the experiences chalked up to transference, such as the client's intense and childlike feelings of vulnerability and need in relation to the therapist, might be mere side effects of the psychoanalytic treatment, created by the analyst's rejecting and inauthentic demeanor. If clients experienced childlike feelings in therapy, that might be because their paternalistic analysts treated them like children. The humanists questioned whether psychoanalytic therapy was not simply a set-up to induce certain intense feelings that might have limited relevance to a person's emotional life outside of therapy. By offering genuine support, encouragement, and emotional responsiveness, therapists would not evoke those same sorts of troublesome transference feelings.

The behaviorist school that began to gain prominence in the 1960s and 1970s seemed to agree with the humanists that transference theory was unacceptable. Extracting basic principles of behavioral change from animal studies, they asserted that they could alter behavior without delving into "unconscious" processes that could not be demonstrated in any laboratory. They relied on simpler

mechanisms that could be readily demonstrated, such as conditioning, to explain human behavior.

As behaviorism grew into cognitive-behaviorism, the focus remained on conscious processes. Believing that thoughts precede
emotions, cognitive-behavioral therapists today help clients identify
the conscious thoughts that precede and accompany feelings and
moods. They directly confront their clients' "dysfunctional" or "negative" thought patterns and attempt to replace them with more positive attitudes. According to their precepts, changing behavior does
not require uncovering "formative" childhood experiences. In fact,
dwelling on childhood experiences is usually counterproductive.
For the cognitive-behaviorists, the notion of transference is simply
besides the point.

Drew Westen, a Harvard University psychologist and leader in
the movement to integrate the various threads that make up psychotherapeutic thought, clarified the cognitive-behaviorist position. "For years," he explained, "the cognitive-behaviorists didn't
talk about transference processes and had very little to say about the
therapist–client relationship other than that you had to maintain a
positive therapeutic alliance to get the work done."

When I asked Arnold Lazarus, a pioneer of the cognitive-
behaviorist movement, to describe his own perspective on transference, he acknowledged the fundamental fact that people, like the
three women in the opening of this chapter, generalize from previous relationships to current ones. But he can explain this phenomenon in terms of simple behaviorist concepts such as "stimulus-
response generalization." As for the rest of transference theory, he
considers it "an involved notion that deals with infantile gratification and frustration and desires and distortions [that is] rather questionable from a scientific standpoint." For him the relationship with
the therapist is the "soil in which techniques take root," and the
proper emphasis is on techniques that have been demonstrated to
work, not on the relationship.

"We don't think about transference in the sense of an automatic distorted relationship," Connie Hammen, a leading cognitive-

behavioral theorist at UCLA, told me. "We certainly don't view it as a mechanism of change. We believe that people have real relationships with their therapists that might be distorted by maladaptive schemas and thoughts, and we might use that information for teaching and therapeutic purposes." As for the client's sexual desire or irrational longings directed at the therapist, Hammen said that she might help a client to articulate such feelings but wouldn't devote a lot of time and attention to them. "We want the relationship to be useful and based on reality. We are not going to spend the whole session talking about what goes on between the two of us."

This polarization between the psychoanalytic and other therapeutic schools has done nothing to promote clear thinking about the matter of transference. Instead it seems to have resulted in therapists having to choose between "believing" in transference in its quasi-mystical, psychoanalytic sense and denying its importance altogether. The psychoanalysts haven't been interested in subjecting transference to rigorous study or in reframing it in more testable terms, and the more research-oriented psychologists haven't wanted to waste their energy looking at a Freudian construct. If the psychoanalysts went too far by regarding the client as a transference-generating dreamer who projected her instincts willy-nilly onto the blank screen of the analyst, the humanists and cognitive-behaviorists may have gone too far by denying their importance as symbolic figures altogether.

## What Therapists Call Transference

With the lack of consensus in the field about transference, a number of different experiences the client may have—thoughts, feelings, reactions, biases, ideas—sometimes receive the "transference" label. The disproportionate importance the client may attribute to small things in the relationship with her therapist; idealization; attachment and dependency; love; sexual attraction; rage; holding the therapist up as a standard by which to define herself; placing the therapist in the role of a parent or experiencing childlike longings toward the therapist are some of a wide spectrum of experiences that are sometimes termed transference.

What a therapist calls transference may have as much to do with the therapist's theoretical persuasion as with the client's experiences. To call an experience transference implies a belief about its origins in an earlier relationship with a significant other, usually a parent.

There are certain feelings that therapists seem particularly inclined to label as transference, regardless of theoretical persuasion. The most intense feelings, especially love, hate, and sexual desire—in short, those feelings that make therapists the most uncomfortable when directed at them—are those most likely to be deemed transference. A therapist who has never before applied a psychoanalytic construct in a woman's therapy may be quick to shout "oedipal transference" when she announces her intention to seduce him.

For the client, accepting that a behavior, thought, or feeling derives from transference sometimes requires a leap of faith. The women I interviewed found it far easier to accept that they had learned to make certain generalizations about other people based on their early relationships than that their most profound feelings for the current people in their lives were based on transference. In other words, a woman could accept the premise that because her mother was invasive she tended to withhold information from her therapist or that because her father was overbearing she expected all men to be overbearing. She found it much harder to accept the premise that she felt attracted to her therapist because she had had unconscious sexual feelings for her father early in childhood that she had then transferred to her therapist. The woman cannot recall having ever felt sexual attraction for her father; in fact the very thought of having sex with her father is repellant. In contrast, her feelings seem very clearly, very specifically, very intensely directed toward her beloved therapist and no other.

The therapists I interviewed told me that they sometimes apply the transference label to a client's experiences so as to "normalize" those experiences. They want to let the client know that such emotions happen in therapy. But clients sometimes perceive that the term is being applied reductively, as if their therapists are hoping that by labeling the experience, they will dissipate its intensity or put the lid on any further discussion.

The effect is often to leave the woman feeling isolated and ashamed of her feelings. She wants a much clearer understanding of what is known about transference and about the prospects for working her feelings through. A woman named Sandy recalled to me how she felt when she became attracted to her therapist: "I knew it was irrational to be so attracted to her because she wasn't at all attractive." When Sandy confided her feelings to her therapist, she laughed them off dismissively by saying, "Oh, that's only transference!" Well, that explanation wasn't enough for Sandy. She spent the evening at the college library reading everything in the professional literature she could get her hands on about the subject. She emerged many hours later, exhausted and still somewhat baffled.

The story should never end when the therapist attaches the transference label. Instead, that moment should mark the beginning of an exploration and dialogue between therapist and client.

## What Clients Want to Know

Women like Sandy know the questions about transference that they'd like to see psychotherapists address. If transference derives from earlier experiences, they ask, why might a woman have strong longings to be mothered by one therapist and not by another? Is it something about that particular therapist that evokes those feelings? How much is coming from the client and how much from the therapist?

If a therapist reminds a woman of all her father's worst traits, should she stick it out with him in the hopes of finally resolving her own feelings about that earlier relationship, or should she simply find another therapist she likes more? Is being in love with your therapist inherently therapeutic, despite the painfulness of unrequited love, or should a woman who finds herself falling in love with her therapist cut the relationship off before it gets any more painful?

When I talked with women, we could also concoct some of the studies to answer these questions. How about putting twenty women into therapy with the same therapist to see how many fall in love with him? If a considerable percentage of them did, wouldn't that suggest that the therapist was being seductive? What about following a woman through nine months of therapy with each of three different therapists and documenting how her feelings varied from practitioner to practitioner? Comparing the emotional issues that became significant in each of those relationships might shed some new light on transference. The researchers could then go on to compare them with the feelings that came up most often in the woman's extra-therapeutic life. Such a study might begin to clarify those particular feelings that are stirred by the particular constraints of the approximate relationship.

The studies my respondents and I brainstormed are not very feasible and probably wouldn't get past any university human subjects' protection committee because they involve too many psychological risks. It would also be difficult to design these studies so as to isolate the individual variables that might account for a given woman's reactions.

Meanwhile, clients have been performing some of their own ad hoc experiments. Some have gone to multiple therapists of various persuasions and have kept informal therapy histories. Their "data" suggest that some women do feel the same sort of intense feelings for nearly every therapist, regardless of what he or she brings to the mix. Silvie, for example, was erotic-transference prone, falling in love and wanting to have sex with every therapist she consulted: "I fell in love with three therapists in a row. It was very painful for a number of years." Fortunately, she was "able to work it through with the last one."

The pattern is not always so intractable. Other women reported only falling in love with one therapist out of three or getting into a ticklish boundary dispute with a single practitioner. This belies Freud's notion of transference as inevitable and scarcely affected by the particulars of the actual present relationship.

These "data" suggest instead that we have a propensity to repeat certain patterns in the relationships with our therapists and also that at least part of what is sometimes attributed to transference is the product of what happens between two particular people in the context of a particular relationship.

We also have to wonder about the ways in which a therapist's thinking about transference influence the sort of feelings clients experience. Therapists have disproportionate power and clients are suggestible. If a therapist encourages her client to present her current feelings in childhood terms, might the client not begin to think about them this way? Clients of therapists who conceptualize themselves as parental stand-ins may have more "transference" experiences. So, too, cognitive-behavioral therapists who are all business, who never talk about transference and discourage their clients from dwelling too long on their feelings, might actually reduce the number of intense feelings their clients direct at them. They will certainly reduce the number of feelings their clients tell them about. A therapist who acts like a buddy and self-discloses all her failings may nip idealization in the bud. An analyst who is very depriving and unresponsive may cause his patients to feel especially lonely and needy. And a therapist who is subtly seductive is bound to evoke sexual feelings in clients. Precisely how therapist behaviors influence their clients' feelings has never been the subject of serious inquiry. We are left with our speculations.

## Scientific Scrutiny of Transference

In recent years there has been a rapprochement in psychotherapy circles. Enlightened integrationists like Harvard University's Drew Westen strive to merge psychoanalytic theory with the most significant findings from laboratory psychology. Westen believes in transference because he's seen it time and again in his own psychoanalytically oriented clinical practice, but he's also a scientist who feels that the concept needs to be demystified and its individual processes delineated. What some therapists label as transference may actually constitute several different phenomena, and only careful study will be able to differentiate them.

So far transference has proven a slippery concept for scientific study. To begin with, there's no consensus in the field as to the definition of the term and thus no consensus as to whether what's being observed is truly transference. Any careful study must methodically parse out all the different aspects of the phenomenon (or phenomena) and identify the multiple variables involved.

Researchers have been best able to document transference as a template applied from one relationship to another. The cognitive aspects of the phenomenon—ideas, biases, expectations, attitudes that are learned—have been easier to isolate than feelings and desires. As Westen explains, "So far the cognitive people have focused on the less emotional side of transference. That's now starting to change, but I suspect it will be a while before we see more in cognitive literature on the way people's wishes, fears and conflicts play out in their relationships." Love and erotic desire in therapy may well be the last aspect of transference that researchers will be able to tackle in the laboratory. It is much easier to demonstrate transference as a bias about one person displaced to another than as a displaced longing for love. Even more difficult to demonstrate would be the psychoanalytic concept that transference might contain not only a longing for love but also a fear of receiving it, a belief that it is undeserved, and an ongoing internal conflict among these motives. And it would seem nearly impossible for a study to prove that this sort of internal bind originated in particular childhood experiences.

At least as far as the cognitive side of the phenomenon goes, research psychologists who were disdainful of transference for so long have begun to reframe it in their own language and to subject it to controlled study. In a chapter entitled "Social-Cognitive and Narrative Perspectives on Transference," psychologists Jefferson Singer and Jerome Singer offered this reframing of transference: "a social-cognitive phenomenon that imposes previously held knowledge structures, images of self or other, and sequences of behavioral responses upon new interactions and situations."

One way that researchers studying transference in the laboratory have explained it is in terms of information processing. From this perspective, transference operates in the service of efficiency. It is more efficient to assume that the future will largely resemble the past and to categorize experiences and relationships based on that assumption than to have to process every experience or relationship as entirely novel. For example, a woman will face fewer surprises if she imagines that all authority figures will behave as did authority figures in the past. To have to characterize each authority figure from scratch would require a far greater expenditure of mental energy. Of course, there is particular information about particular authority figures that she might miss with her generalizations. And if her past experiences with authority figures were particularly harsh, she might be less able to perceive the full range of behaviors that authority figures are capable of demonstrating.

When part of what psychoanalysts call transference is recast in terms of information processing, the process seems less pathological. If psychoanalytic theory deems that we are driven by a "repetition compulsion" to repeat the past, information processing theory explains that we are simply inclined by make-up to repeat the same assumptions over and over again.

According to leading transference researcher Susan M. Andersen of New York University (NYU), the information-processing model recasts transference as "part of the basic human meaning-making process." What information-processing theory may not yet be able to explain is the complexity of feelings and motivations that accompany this repetition of assumptions, or why it is so difficult for new experience to penetrate our patterns. For example, a woman who expects every man she becomes involved with to behave as her authoritarian and dismissive father did may at the same time be wishing for someone to break her father's mold, and yet may seem to sabotage every attempt by a man to do so. The information-processing model cannot yet add much to our understanding of this typically human and confounded scenario.

Over the past five years, Andersen and her team of associates at NYU have devised a series of ingenious, elaborately designed studies to document empirically some of the processes by which transference occurs. These studies conceptualize what is transferred in transference as an internalized "representation of a significant other."

Researchers tell subjects that they are about to meet a stranger seated in a room next door. In preparation, they read a description of the stranger comprised of a number of different traits and characteristics. Unbeknownst to them, the list includes some of the characteristics they used to describe a significant other several weeks earlier when they participated in what they believed was a completely unrelated study. When the stranger is described in some of the terms derived from their own significant-other description, subjects assume, without conscious awareness, that the new person will have other traits they associate with their significant other. A new person who resembles a known person in even a minimal way will be perceived to be more like the known person than the evidence would warrant.

According to Andersen, people tend to "go beyond the information given" and to fill in the blanks with what is most familiar. Andersen explains that we all hold mental schemas, representations of our significant others. Any piece of this representation may be enough to evoke the entire gestalt. So, if someone has black hair and a great sense of humor like our Uncle Fred, we may well assume that he also eats too much and drives a sports car as does Uncle Fred. Any resemblance evokes the whole representation.

Going beyond cognitive processes for the first time, Andersen has also begun to establish that feelings and desires about the significant other are linked to this representation. Once a subject assumes that the stranger she is about to meet resembles a significant other that she likes, she looks forward to meeting the stranger and getting to know her. She is predisposed to like her. If she assumes that the stranger resembles a significant other whom she does not like, she transfers her aversion as well. And all of this takes place very quickly, outside of conscious awareness, on the basis of very little information, without the subject realizing that she has made a connection between her significant other and the stranger.

Anderson has also demonstrated that how a person feels *about herself* in the presence of another person is linked to her mental representation of that person. By triggering a significant-other representation, a particular self-image may also be triggered. In other words, the way a woman feels about herself in the presence of her mother may be very different than the way she feels about herself when with her father, or a sibling, or someone else. If the woman believes that she is about to spend time with someone who resembles her mother, she may begin to feel *about herself* the way she does in her mother's presence. And this process is also unconscious. The woman need not consciously recognize the resemblance between the stranger and her mother to begin to feel as she does when with her mother.

Andersen's ever-growing body of transference research suggests that representations of significant others are linked in what cognitive researchers call an "associational network" with feelings, desires, and images of the self. What does it take to cue these representations? Andersen suspects that some cues may be more potent than others in evoking these representations but that "a whole variety of cues may provoke transference." Andersen is also beginning to suspect that in some situations it may not take much to evoke our significant-other representations because these representations are "chronically accessible."

By the time my interviewee Dr. V. collapsed at my feet, by the time I had begun to associate his fall with my father's stroke, I was already "primed" to put Dr. V. in a paternal category and to feel about him accordingly. Andersen's research suggests that people may be primed to apply their significant other representations broadly, even to encounters where they are not especially appropriate.

In Andersen's transference studies, subjects describe a significant other who need not be a parent. Since Andersen has not studied parental representations in particular, she cannot yet say how mental representations of parents might differ from other representations of significant others or how representations formed early in childhood might differ from those formed later. Andersen suspects that some early experiences are more formative of significant-other schemas than others and that parental representations may well serve as the framework, the "meta" structures from which all later representations are drawn.

Anderson's studies posit at least some of the experiences chalked up to transference as normal, predominantly cognitive processes. They suggest that transference may only become maladaptive when we apply our internalized representations of others too broadly and too strenuously and when we cannot correct our misperceptions even when confronted by contradictory evidence.

## Living by a Script

First developed by therapist Silvan Tomkins in the 1960s, script theory isolates at least one aspect of what is transferred in transference in the form of "scripts," condensed narratives for how to respond emotionally in relationships. Researchers analyze a subject's life story and transcripts of her therapy sessions to break the subject's life story down into scenes. These are small units of experience that contain an emotion and an object of the emotion. According to script theory, from childhood onward, people unconsciously organize their own significant scenes to derive idiosyncratic scripts.

Tomkins gave this example of how a script forms: A little girl is separated from her parents and hospitalized. In the hospital nurses put her in a strange crib where various medical practitioners examine her and a photographer videotapes her. Later, when her parents leave her in a crib at a childcare facility and a stranger takes her picture, she begins to cry. She interprets this benign event through her traumatic hospital experience script. Without being able to verbalize the process, the little girl concludes, unconsciously of course, that, in Tomkins's words, "situations of being examined by strangers should be interpreted as dangerous."

In 1992, researchers Amy P. Demorest of Amherst College and Irving Alexander of Duke University gave ten subjects three hours in which to write their life stories, asking them to be sure to include their most significant memories. Trained raters then extracted scenes from these histories, each of which featured an interaction with another person and an emotion tied to that interaction. From each subject's body of scenes, the raters derived the subjects' scripts.

The researchers then showed the same subjects provocative photographs in which people's expressions were ambiguous and conveyed mixed emotional states, such as sadness–anger. The subjects looked at the pictures and made up fictional stories about the people. The researchers then gave raters who hadn't met the subjects the life story scripts and the fictional stories to see if they could match them.

Demorest and Irving found that although the stories featured fictional plot lines and characters, the scripts extracted from them matched those in the subjects' life stories in striking ways. For example, one woman included as an important life event her mother's becoming ill with multiple sclerosis. As she coped with her mother's illness, she turned to her father for emotional support. She was profoundly disappointed when he could neither express his own feelings nor help her to express hers. When shown a photograph of a woman expressing sadness–anger and asked to make up a narrative that would tell the story behind the picture, the subject wrote that the woman had just attempted to elicit support for a cancer charity from the manager of a business. The manager was aloof, the woman in the picture could not reach him, and she left feeling defeated. The autobiography and story share the script of a woman seeking support from an emotionally distant authority to deal with a serious illness and being unable to make the desired emotional connection.

In general, subjects told fictional stories that strongly reflected the scripts derived from their own life experiences. This study and others of script theory suggest that part of what is transferred in transference is a script for relationships with a significant other.

# When None of the Scripts Apply

Script theory may also serve to explain why some of the intense experiences sometimes attributed to transference can be so unsettling.

The psychotherapy relationship does not quite fit any other pattern: It's not friendship, it's not romance, it's not familial, and yet in some respects it resembles these other relationships. None of the scripts apply perfectly.

Nor does the therapist respond as a script might predict. Instead of reacting to the client's behavior, the therapist interprets it, intervenes in order to change it, or endures it empathically. So, in the psychotherapy relationship, a client may find herself running through multiple scripts of significant-other relationships, none of which come out as expected. Dr. V. had told me that transference was like standing on the corner of 42nd Street and Times Square—every imaginable feeling was likely to come by. In the language of script theory, being in a relationship with such high stakes that is at the same time so ambiguous may evoke all of a client's most primary and emotionally charged scripts.

## The Core Conflictual Relationship Theme

If the script is one way of abstracting the content of what is transferred in transference, the core conflictual relationship theme (CCRT) is another. Psychologists Lester Luborsky and Paul Crits-Christoph of the Center for Psychotherapy Research at the University of Pennsylvania have developed a large body of research based on this concept. After analyzing hours of transcripts of actual therapy sessions, they isolated recurring themes that contain a wish, need, or intention directed toward another person, the other person's response to it, and the subject's reaction to the other's response. An example of a theme might be, "I wish to be understood and empathized with but others misunderstand me, and then I feel hopeless."

With a reasonable degree of consistency, researchers were able to identify idiosyncratic and recurrent themes in the stories individuals told about their interactions with others. They were also able to demonstrate that these themes recurred in all the significant relationships people discussed in therapy. Further, the same themes that characterized an individual's personal relationships tended to occur in the client's relationship with the therapist.

Models like the CCRT or script are useful not only because they represent the content of transference in a concise and measurable form but also because they provide an instrument for monitoring the progress of therapy. During the course of successful therapy, Luborsky and Crits-Christoph suggest, the client's themes become less constrained and allow for a more open-ended and less negative range of outcomes. For example, the theme offered earlier might change to "I wish to be understood and empathized with, and if I express my needs clearly, I will sometimes be understood."

## What Do We Really Know?

What the empirical research on transference has shown is rather modest compared to the scope of women's questions. What's been proven in many different studies, using different models—significant-other representation, script, CCRT, and others—is that people tend to have dominant interpersonal themes that characterize their relationships. Those themes encompass thoughts, emotions, expectations, and reactions. The themes that are significant in the client's outside relationships are also apt to become important in her relationship with the therapist.

This is a critical finding because the feelings that clients develop for their therapists are only useful as tools for change if they mirror what goes on in the client's other relationships, not if they are anomalies owing to the unusual stresses of the approximate relationship. Perhaps these themes express themselves in more extreme forms in the relationship with the therapist because of the approximate relationship's unique constraints.

For example, a woman in the throes of the golden fantasy may find herself wishing that her therapist would take perfect care of her forever. She may not harbor such an extreme form of this wish in her relationship with her boyfriend. However, she may have an underlying dissatisfaction that no matter what her boyfriend does, it does not feel as if he is taking good enough care of her. By looking at the exaggerated form of the wish in her relationship with her therapist, she may come to understand the origins of the wish in its more modulated form and be able to reconsider what it is reasonable and unreasonable to expect from a romantic relationship.

Susan Andersen's research makes a strong case for the fact that we tend to perceive new people in our lives based on prototypes from the past and that we do so without conscious awareness. She has also begun to demonstrate that thoughts and feelings about the other person and ourselves are inextricably bound up in these prototypes. Although Andersen's research is a long way from demonstrating how we develop our recurrent and complex emotional responses, it does suggest that if a woman perceives her therapist to be judgmental like her father, she is likely to feel the same combination of rage at his judgments and longing for his unconditional love that she felt for her father.

The research cannot yet explain why some experiences in childhood seem particularly determinative, how these experiences translate into recurrent patterns, or why these patterns can be so resistant even when confronted again and again by input that should discredit them. It cannot yet recommend the best therapeutic approach for altering these patterns.

So clients and therapists continue to struggle with and resist the very notion of transference. After all, we want to believe that we are capable of responding to people for themselves, that every relationship begins as a clean slate, that our actions are guided by reason and accurate perception, that we are neither slaves to the past nor actors in a play whose script we have not consciously written.

Often the experiences of childhood serve as background watercolor tints, so subtle that we hardly notice them. But some experiences, particularly certain kinds of childhood trauma, are not subtle in their influences at all. Instead of background tints, they are like spray paint in the hands of an angry graffitist—they blight our field of view. This sort of transference insists that every story is the same story, every relationship the same relationship.

## *Jo's Story: Therapy and Torture*

Jo, a woman in her late twenties, is in training to be a therapist herself. She has a great deal of insight about her past and tremendous compassion for her clients. Still, the past is too present in her day-to-day experience of the world. In early childhood through adolescence, Jo's mother seemed obsessed with her daughter's most private bodily functions. She characterized Jo's body as gross and bad, requiring constant vigilance and hygiene, subject to invasion from without. Her female sexuality harbored particular dangers:

> When I was a child, my mother only allowed me to pee once a day. She said, "Big girls, big-bladder big girls only need to pee once a day." I learned to hold it in. I learned how to suppress the urge until it went away. In the fourth grade I spent the night at a friend's house. She told her mother that I was only allowed to pee once a day. Her mother was shocked. I thought they had wimpy bladders.
>
> Right after I got my period for the first time, my mother decided that I had head lice. We would have these multi-hour rituals every day after school in which I'd be in my underwear and she'd pick at my hair and scalp trying to get rid of the lice that only she could see.
>
> She broke the locks on the bathroom door. She was always bursting into my room. She was always saying, "You're dirty, you're gross, you smell bad. Nobody will ever want you."

Jo is now in therapy with Max, an empathic and patient man who impresses her as a nice person who "would try to do the right thing." Max encourages her to express what she is feeling rather than to intellectualize, which is her wont. Intellectualization served the very useful purpose in childhood of distancing her from her daily torment.

But now, through the filter of the past, therapy threatens to turn into another form of torture. When Max suggests to Jo that she intellectualize less and express more feeling instead, his suggestion feels like one of her mother's attempts to control her. As her mother demanded that she hold in her urine and deny the natural urges of her body, Max seems to be demanding that she bring something forth out of herself, something that might be "dirty and gross," and present it for his critical examination.

Sometimes Jo imagines that Max is a good father-figure, someone who would have intervened to stop her mother's bizarre behavior. Other times, she imagines that Max is her lover: "In my sexual fantasies he's a nice torturer. He's a spy trying to get information out of me. If I don't give him the right information, he doesn't let me urinate."

Jo's experiences with her mother have invaded her sexuality. Desire, pleasure, need, and humiliation have become intertwined. Jo's feelings about her therapist express her actual experiences with her mother: her mother's controlling invasiveness and her injunction against urination.

They also reflect Jo's attempts to master the past by controlling childhood events in fantasy. She has had to wrest sexual pleasure out of a landscape of torture. In her sexual fantasies about Max, she both relinquishes her body to the mother who provides the only form of love she knows (by imagining that her lover would also demand she hold in her urine) and takes her body back from her (by having pleasure).

Despite Jo's seemingly automatic tendency to conceptualize her interactions with her therapist in terms of his coerciveness, she can also cite the many ways in which her therapist's behavior does not fit this pattern. Patiently and consistently, he shows her over and over again through their interactions that he is not a torturer and that he does not finds her unattractive, gross, or dirty: "He doesn't treat me like I have lice. Even when I told him that I had sexual fantasies about him, he didn't seem grossed out."

With the weight of new evidence contradicting her expectations, Jo begins to have sexual fantasies about her therapist that are less reliant on the past: "We go to an island and it is really nice and I don't feel tortured. It is a loving relationship. That's scary to even imagine, though." In terms of the scientific research on transference, we might say that her script is slowly changing or that her

CCRT is becoming less rigid. She is no longer applying her mother-representation to everyone else who tries to get close to her. She is beginning to free that internalized representation of her mother from her own self-image so that she can begin to conceive of feeling love and connection for another, of feeling loved by another, without also feeling dirty and gross.

To imagine a relationship that is not based on her mother's rules of engagement, in which pleasure need not be snatched from the jaws of pain, is a frightening prospect for Jo. The emotionally novel experience, even the positive emotionally novel experience, can be more unsettling to imagine than a repetition of the reliable past. In therapy, Jo projects the model for intimate relationships that she has known onto her relationship with Max, but she also tentatively asserts her wish for something better. In attempting to understand the influence of past and present, it is important that she and her therapist see both: the relentless draw of the bond with her mother and the tenuous reaching for a tortureless love.

## CCRT versus Waking Dream

While research has begun to demonstrate some aspects of the transference phenomenon, terms like significant-other representation, script, and CCRT simply do not do justice to the emotional power of transference experiences. Freud's more poetic concept of waking dream, of past-in-present illusion may overly mystify the psychological mechanisms involved, yet it may come closer to describing what some transference experiences *feel* like. There is no experience that can make you believe in transference in its more mystical sense than being in a therapy session and feeling again as if you are three years old and the therapist is your mother.

The neutral language of the laboratory can scarcely begin to describe Jo's brave struggle to separate her therapist's image from her mother's, to redraw herself as a woman in relation to him, to redefine the very terms of love.

## Summing It Up

When I asked Drew Westen to sum up the ramifications of the transference research to date, he suggested that we need to retain a very broad definition of transference as "a whole host of ways in which thoughts, feelings, motives, conflicts between motives, and behavioral scripts are activated in relationships, including the therapy relationship," but that we not see transference as a unitary phenomenon. In other words, different behaviors and aspects of the therapist and the therapeutic situation may cue different transferences at different times. And the very nature of the approximate relationship is apt to evoke only certain sorts of transference, those "associated with asymmetrical attachment relationships," usually parental relationships. Further, it seems clear to Westen that the individual therapist, and the specific vicissitudes of the relationship between that therapist and a particular client, will have a tremendous impact on the transferences evoked.

If cognitive researchers and psychoanalytic therapists still disagree as to exactly what is transferred in transference, how transference patterns originate, and why some experiences have the power to create such indelible and relentlessly recurring patterns, they do agree on this: Human beings have a propensity to see the world through the filters of past experience, but they also have the capacity to recognize the limitations of this view. If the experiences that we call transference can feel mystical, an even more profound feeling may come at the moment when a woman like Jo recognizes her pattern and, perhaps for the first time in her life, also sees beyond it. If the past is ever present in the therapist's office, so too is the prospect of a more freely chosen future.

# 6

# The Gaslighting Bind

In the final act of the 1944 film *Gaslight*, which is set at the turn of the century, Paula, who is played by Ingrid Bergman, has just received a visit from the Scotland Yard detective who is beginning to catch on to her husband Gregory's criminal activities. Gregory, played by Charles Boyer, is desperate to convince her that the visit was only a delusion:

> *Paula* [her strength waning]: He was here—he was here. I know it—he was here. I couldn't have dreamed it—or did I? Did I dream it?
> [Gregory remains standing. His eyes follow Paula as she walks across the room.]
> *Gregory* [very quietly]: You dreamed it. You dream all day long—
> *Paula*: Are you really saying I have dreamed?
> Gregory [with uncanny calm]: Everything.
> *Paula*: All that happened?
> *Gregory*: All that did not happen.
> *Paula*: Then it's true? My mind is going—
> *Gregory*: Haven't I told you?
> *Paula*: It was a dream ... a dream ... a dream.

Gregory, a dashing psychopath, schemes to convince his naive young wife Paula that she is going mad so that he can commit her to an institution and gain control of her fortune. By making Paula question her own senses, Gregory nearly drives her mad for real.

To convince her that she is hallucinating, he denies the dimming of the gaslights that she observes in her bedroom every evening. By far Gregory's most damaging deception is his pretense of love. Once Gregory has feigned love and Paula has reciprocated, she cannot bear to imagine that he might not adore her after all. It is preferable to believe that she is truly loved—but insane.

The film *Gaslight* gave birth to the verb "to gaslight," meaning to intentionally drive someone crazy by making her mistrust her own perception of reality. The term soon made its way into descriptions of what therapists can do to their clients. In fact, the film's Svengali-like male authority figure and trusting young ingenue are reminiscent of the therapist–patient dyad in psychotherapy's early days. Although the archetype no longer applies—most women today are not in therapy with older men, but with other women—the gaslight scenario continues to exemplify a client's worst fear: becoming dependent on a master of psychological manipulation who, in the name of concern, undermines her belief in herself and renders her crazy.

The notion of transference lends itself to gaslighting because it can be used to disempower clients and protect therapists' authority. As Gregory told Paula that her reality was only a dream, Freud described the transference of his patients as a kind of "dream." He wrote, "The analysand, in a *waking dream*, fights for direct gratification of instinctual needs while the analyst fights on the side of reason."

Freud had dual motives when he came up with the concept of transference. He was acting as a scientist, describing a phenomenon he had observed, first in Josef Breuer's patient, Anna O., and subsequently in his own patients. But he was also an ideologue, scrambling to defend his fledgling discipline from attack. Distinguishing the strong emotions that went on in therapy from those that occurred in other social interactions, deeming them transference, made analysis a privileged space where the ordinary social prohibitions did not apply. Had Freud not come up with the idea of transference, his new discipline might have met with even greater public condemnation; the Viennese society of the time simply could not tolerate two strangers of the opposite sex alone in a room together discussing forbidden feelings, many of them sexual, unless the encounter was sterilized by clinical intent. Transference was the sterilizing agent, proof that what went on in the analyst's office was not a "real" intimate encounter between two people.

In an effort to isolate transference as a biologist might a bacterium on a slide, Freud downplayed the contribution of the therapist's individual personality. He argued, for example, that a patient so inclined by her unresolved childhood issues would develop transference-love for *any* analyst; the "personal charms" of the particular practitioner had nothing to do with it. Freud exaggerated the distinction between transference and "real" feelings while also acknowledging that transference was ubiquitous in real life relationships. From the beginning he seemed to be saying two things at once: Transference was both real and unreal. It was something distinctive that happened in the therapist's office, and it was something that happened in every human encounter. Transference-love was an entity unto itself, and all love had its roots in transference.

This seeming contradiction has spawned ongoing debate among therapists. It continues to plague our attempts to think clearly about transference. Clients and therapists continue to ask, "How is transference real and how is it unreal? How are the feelings that go on in therapy the same as the feelings that go on in every other relationship and how are they different?" The two motives that gave birth to the concept—one descriptive and the other defensive—also continue to influence the way therapists today work with transference. When therapists use the concept of transference defensively, they risk gaslighting their clients.

## The Transference Bind

The transference bind goes something like this: A woman perceives something about her therapist, perhaps that he is inattentive or that he has a bias against women. Or perhaps she suspects that the therapist is thinking or feeling something about her—whether hostility, boredom, or sexual arousal. She conveys her suspicions to her therapist, who promptly attributes them to transference. In effect the therapist says, "This is about you and your past." That leaves the client with virtually unanswerable questions: "Are my feelings real, or are they transference? And what about you?" the client thinks. "Isn't some part of what I am feeling about you?"

For a dizzying moment the therapist's office turns into a house of mirrors, with the client unable to tell which surfaces offer accurate reflections and which distort. She's in the same bind as Paula, *Gaslight's* heroine—if she can't trust her own perceptions she must be crazy, and if she can't trust the person she's relying on to take care of her, then she has been abandoned.

Johanna, a woman in my survey, stayed in therapy a few months with an older male therapist who used the concept of transference this way. "If I argued with my therapist he would get really defensive and it was always just about me," she reported. "He had no insight into his contribution to my reactions."

It's all too easy for a therapist to label a client's feelings "transference" to avoid feeling responsible for them and to remove himself psychologically from the fray of a true person-to-person encounter. As psychiatry critic Thomas Szasz explains, if the analyst can view the client's love or hate as transference, he can convince himself that the patient does not have these feelings and dispositions toward *him*. Meanwhile, the client finds herself in a maddening dilemma: Some part of what she is experiencing in therapy has been labeled "transference" so cannot be wholly trusted, and yet she knows what she is feeling . . . or does she? Doubt creeps in. To believe in the validity of her own feelings is to jeopardize the relationship with the professional upon whom she depends for care. She can discredit herself or distrust her therapist; there seems to be no middle ground.

Darlene told me about having become entangled in just such a bind about ten years before. Then in her mid-twenties, she had been seeing the same therapist for several years but had never completely trusted him. "My therapist's personality was like my father's," she said, "and when I would go into his office and see empty cases of beer bottles, I'd accuse him of being an alcoholic—just like my father. And he'd say, 'Can't you see that this is your transference? I'm not your father.' I should have said, 'Who are you trying to kid?' At the time, I kept thinking, maybe it *is* me."

When a woman like Darlene observes similarities between her therapist and a significant other, in this case her father, three possible explanations come to mind: (1) My therapist seems to be just like my father but he really isn't—my transference is coloring my view; (2) I have had the incredible misfortune of finding a therapist who *is* just like my father; or (3) I am doing something to trigger my therapist to behave just like my father. Both the first and third alternatives offer ample room for a woman to blame herself.

With a therapist less inclined to use transference as a defense, a woman in therapy can find her way to the gray zones between these three hypotheses. In Darlene's case, the therapist resembled her father in some significant ways—like his drinking—but even that did not mean that he necessarily possessed all her father's worst traits. She also may have had a heightened sensitivity to certain behaviors that resembled her father's, causing her to generalize and invoke the whole father-gestalt. By doing so, she may have missed seeing important differences between her therapist and her father. As for the third alternative, even if Darlene's actions triggered the therapist to behave as her father had, he should have had the skill to call her attention to what she was doing rather than reacting. That might have enabled Darlene to understand just how her behaviors triggered certain behaviors in others. Although she never confronted her therapist directly about his defensive use of the notion of transference, eventually Darlene left him and made her way to someone more adept at seeing the gray zones.

## Andi's Story: The Somnolent Dr. S.

Andi entered therapy because of depression and problems in her marriage. She had been in therapy for eight months with Dr. S., a weathered therapist who had been kind, focused, and level-headed during their twice-weekly sessions. Andi had come to rely on him. Then, in one late afternoon session, something untoward happened.

Andi recounted: "He fell asleep. Just for a minute his head nodded off, and I got so angry. It felt like the ultimate form of discounting me." Andi couldn't believe her own eyes. Was she paying this man exorbitant fees to sleep? Nevertheless, she couldn't bring herself to raise the subject out of the fear of finding out that she was so boring she put even her therapist to sleep. But after Dr. S. fell asleep again a few weeks later, Andi was so enraged she had no choice but to confront him. He apologized first with a simple explanation: He was exhausted. As they discussed the topic further, he offered a more complicated rationalization. He had fallen asleep because Andi was presenting a "false self," and not being fully herself in the therapy.

Andi's dilemma presents a slight variation on the usual transference bind. She had not simply observed something in Dr. S. that he could deny—he had *undeniably* fallen asleep. However, he chose to blame his falling asleep on something *unreal* about Andi; if she had been more genuine, he would have felt less sleepy. The incident had tremendous gaslighting potential in that it caused Andi to question her own sense of reality. Had she been putting on a false front to avoid her feelings? Was Dr. S. seeing something in her that she could not see in herself? Was it her fault that he couldn't do his job?

The shared reality of therapist and client slipped. Andi wondered if Dr. S. was intentionally trying to drive her crazy. She considered leaving the therapy. But she already felt a strong bond with Dr. S. and had found his perspective on her problems helpful, so she decided to persevere. In the next session, she held nothing back, expressing all her anger about his falling asleep and abandoning her and then turning around and blaming her for his failings! She described the confrontation:

> Expressing my anger to him opened the door. I hadn't dealt with my anger at all before that in therapy, and truth was I felt it about everything; angry that I had to work and take care of myself. Angry that I had to have feelings. . . . A lot of anger at everything finally got expressed.

Of course, it goes without saying that Dr. S. should not have fallen asleep in Andi's sessions. But therapists are human and lose concentration, even nod off during sessions, more times than they would probably like to admit. Once a therapist has made this kind of mistake, how can therapist and client recover from it?

In Andi's case, what began in a transference bind ended in therapeutic gains because Andi took the chance of fully expressing what she felt and Dr. S. was willing finally to hear her. They were able to use the impasse to open up the therapy rather than shut it down. When Andi expressed her feelings in all their vehemence, Dr. S. did not discount their legitimacy; he could tolerate her rage and was willing and eager to hear more. And he was as curious about her anger as he was about any of her other feelings. Andi recalled, "No matter what I did, I could see that he wasn't going to react in the way that people in my previous family relationships had reacted."

Without being fully aware of it, Andi had expected her therapist to respond to her anger as her parents had—with greater anger and further blame. When he did not, when the script did not turn out the way that she had anticipated, the incident gave her an opportunity to explore the way her past had colored her expectations of other people. While Andi never believed that her "false self" had put her therapist to sleep, their discussion of the subject enlivened their relationship and freed Andi to express more of her genuine feelings. Andi saw that, despite his gaffe, Dr. S. would take responsibility for his own feelings and not let them intrude on her therapy.

## Getting Out of the Transference Bind

In recent years, psychoanalytically oriented therapists have revised the way they conceptualize transference. The tendency in the past was to portray the client as an indiscriminate projector of transference distortions onto the blank screen of the neutral therapist. Only the therapist had the objectivity to distinguish the client's transference from accurate perception.

In current thinking, neither party in the therapist—client relationship has an exclusive franchise on reality. Neither has the authority to definitively label the other's perceptions as "transference," and transference can never be isolated completely from the context in which it occurs. That context is the current relationship with the therapist. Certainly the client's history, experience, and unresolved longings contribute powerfully to how she experiences her therapist, but how the therapist actually behaves in the here and now, the subtle back-and-forth of their interactions are equally important. Although good therapists attempt to keep their history, experience, and wishes from getting in the client's way, those factors are never entirely absent from the encounter, either. The good therapist is simply aware of them and repeatedly questions how they may be influencing the present.

As Michael Kahn says, "There are always two unconsciouses in the room in complex interaction with each other." Freud's notion of the absolutely neutral and objective therapist able to extract the client's transference and keep his or her feelings completely out of the equation is now recognized as merely another illusion.

Analyst Merton Gill was instrumental in this new way of thinking. In the 1970s, he analyzed numerous transcripts of therapy sessions, looking in particular at interactions that involved transference issues. He came to see clients as having a wide range of possible reactions to their therapists determined partly by their pasts and partly by the present encounter. Without access to the usual social information about the therapist, the client can only formulate hypotheses to explain some of her perceptions of her therapist. The therapist's task is not to act as the arbiter of reality by ruling on the accuracy of these hypotheses but simply to point out recurrent patterns and alternate ways to make sense of the same information.

For example, when a client perceives her therapist's bland "uh-huh" to convey disapproval, the therapist's job might be to help the client recognize the full range of connotations that an "uh-huh" can convey. Are there reasons why the client might be predisposed to interpret it in terms of disapproval? According to Gill, the therapist cannot discount the possibility that the client is picking up something in his or her "uh-huh" to which the therapist is blind. The therapist is not the only one in the room with the power to see what is hidden or to hear what is unsaid.

To avoid gaslighting the client, Gill suggests that therapist and client begin by looking closely at what the client perceives to be going on in their relationship. Together they might explore the evidence for the client's point of view in a nondefensive fashion. The therapist welcomes all of the client's perceptions, assumptions, concerns, fantasies, and thoughts with equanimity. After coming to some tentative consensus, the therapist and client may then proceed to look at other situations that the client experienced in the same way. The therapist might say, for instance, "You tend to experience my 'uh-huhs' as disapproving. Do you think that you might be interpreting your boss's silences the same way?" If the client detects a recurrent pattern, she may choose to look backward to childhood for the formative events. With her therapist she might consider how her mother's vaguely disapproving, but never fully articulated, comments led her to read any ambiguous gesture as an expression of disapproval.

As psychiatrist Arnold Cooper pointed out in his article "Changes in Psychoanalytic Ideas: Transference Interpretation," the therapist may well be the object of the client's transference projections from the past, but the therapist's more important role is as provider of a safe haven for the client to explore these projections. The therapist who becomes authoritarian or dogmatic, who blames the client, who insists on an all-or-nothing, real-or-transference world, threatens this safe haven. That the client feel safe to examine and experiment with changing her behavior is far more important than that she accept any of the therapist's interpretations. After all, these are limited by the therapist's own perceptual filters.

Norman D. Schaffer, a psychologist who studied with Gill at the University of Illinois, believes that it is essential for the therapist to work both sides of the relationship, the interpersonal—what is going on between the two people in the here and now—and the intrapsychic—what the client is thinking and feeling, which may be influenced by the past. For example, when a woman confronts her therapist with his behaving "just like my judgmental father did," he can deny the resemblance and end the discussion. It will be far more useful to the client, however, if he can demonstrate the distinction in the very way he responds to the accusation, says Schaffer. By not being judgmental and by being open-minded to the client's viewpoint, he can show the client just how much *unlike* her father he is. The therapist's flexibility, his willingness to see the gray areas counters the transference, which is by definition closed, black-and-white, and repetitive. If human beings are sometimes inclined to see every relationship as the same relationship, every story as having the same inevitable outcome, good therapists reveal that every relationship has the potential to follow multiple narrative lines.

If we think of transference as being like a filter that colors all the experience that passes through it, becoming aware of one's own transference can mean seeing without the filter, if only for an instant. That little hint of unfiltered perception may be enough to make the client aware of the filter's existence. The therapist is not the Great All-Knowing One who can see without filters, but simply someone who has greater knowledge of their working principles and awareness of where his or her own filters lie.

In the best outcome, a therapist and client in a bind negotiate their way back to a shared reality that is gracious enough to hold the intrapsychic and interpersonal hypotheses in suspension at the same time. The client can think, yes, this feeling does harken back to my mother, but it also has meaning in my current relationship with my therapist.

Despite the popularity of these more enlightened ways of thinking about transference, my research suggests that therapists still, often unwittingly, use the notion of transference to gaslight their clients.

## Rhonda's Story: Rustling Behind the Couch

Rhonda, a fifty-six-year-old therapist who has seen her analyst four times a week for the past two years, provided an illustrative story. Like Andi, she was able to negotiate her way through a transference bind and learn an important lesson as a result. To do so, she also needed to confront her therapist directly.

Rhonda was in traditional psychoanalysis, with her analyst June sitting behind her as she lay on the couch. As Rhonda poured out her heart during sessions, she could often hear June picking at her nails and brushing lint off her clothing. These seemingly minute distractions began to drive Rhonda "insane." Was June trying to "brush her off?" Was Rhonda making June nervous?

Finally, there came a session when, as soon as the rustling began, Rhonda bolted upright and inquired loudly: "What's going on back there?"

June calmly explained Rhonda's seemingly disproportionate reaction: Her mother had been distracted and indifferent when Rhonda was growing up. June's nail-picking and lint-brushing reminded Rhonda of her mother. In effect, June said, "You are responding disproportionately because this behavior reminds you of a far more significant behavior in your mother that occurred at a time when you were dependent on her for your care. My very trivial behavior is symbolic of that earlier neglect and that is why it bothers you so much." In short, she laid the blame for Rhonda's overblown emotional reaction on her maternal transference. End of story.

Rhonda listened patiently and then rejected June's conclusion. "No," Rhonda said. "This is about our relationship and what I need from you." Granted, June was right about Rhonda's past relationship with her mother; her difficulty in capturing her overburdened mother's attention probably heightened her sensitivity to any suggestion of inattention in other important people in her life. Another client might have been impervious to June's nail-picking or have had an altogether different response. But when June chose to interpret Rhonda's reaction strictly in terms of Rhonda's past she did not do justice to their present relationship.

Rhonda reacted strongly not only because of her experience with her mother but also because she expected June to provide complete and undivided attention during their sessions. Was this an unreasonable expectation? It might have been in an ordinary social relationship, but given the added weight of the approximate relationship, it was not. Given that Rhonda was revealing very painful material in the hope that she might change her life, given that her time with June was limited and costly, given the considerable emotional investment she had made over the course of her analysis, her expectation starts to seem more reasonable. Freud once said that an analyst should be like a surgeon. If a patient learned that her surgeon stopped in the middle of a life-and-death procedure to pick lint off his scrubs, she might be more than a little upset. Rhonda felt like that patient:

> She tried to interpret her behavior away, and I said, "No, this is a problem you have." My feeling was that she wasn't present enough. It was ultimately about her capacity to take care of me. This was my life, this was not, "Oh, let's just play therapy."

Her relationship with June had become the paradigmatic relationship in Rhonda's life, the relationship that would prove whether *anyone* had the capacity to take care of her or if everyone would fail her as her mother had failed her.

For several weeks, Rhonda and June negotiated their way through the impasse. Rhonda began to realize how quickly she had generalized a more global assessment of her therapist's capacity for caretaking from her isolated habit of picking lint. That generalization and the intensity of her wish to be taken care of derived partly from her childhood relationship with her mother. In turn, June acknowledged that her habit was distracting and that Rhonda had every right to expect her full attention. But Rhonda also had to accept that June might not always be able to provide Rhonda's idealized representation of what that attentiveness should look (and sound) like. June assured Rhonda that she would do everything in her power to "take care of her" to the extent possible within the limits of the approximate relationship. And Rhonda began to reconsider her feelings about the limits to which one adult could take care of another. She emerged with an appreciation of June's strengths as a therapist: "She wasn't defensive and she was willing to take responsibility and look at herself. If she had had to discount my reactions, that would have just killed me."

When June was willing to own her own behavior, Rhonda was able to see the many ways in which her therapist was unlike her mother. Now, whenever Rhonda encounters someone who is distracted or indifferent, she is less likely to assume that the whole mother package automatically comes with it. By becoming more aware of her own perceptual filters, she has become less prone to dismissing other people outright.

## Faith's Story: A Broken Promise

What happens when a therapist seems incapable of taking responsibility for her own failings and when those failings go beyond inattentiveness to what the client considers betrayal? In Faith's story, a transference impasse nearly destroyed the therapy. By the time client and therapist salvaged the relationship, damage had been done to the client's capacity to trust.

Faith was twenty-four when she began to see Carole for individual therapy and joined her incest survivors' group. Faith and her three sisters had endured years of sexual and physical abuse by their stepfather. Their mother, addicted to sleeping pills, had wandered through Faith's childhood in a daze, never intervening to protect her daughters. One day, a situation arose in group therapy that reminded Faith all too well of how it felt to grow up in her family. "After group, we members started to go out to dinner together so that we could wind down, be supportive of one another if somebody needed to cry."

Faith and Carole's impasse began with a breach in the boundaries. When Carole found out about what she called the "subgroup," she objected but failed to reinstate the boundaries definitively. She never explained to the members why she believed the "subgroup" might threaten the cohesiveness, safety, and integrity of the group. Faith attributed Carole's upset to her "loss of control." Through the filter of her childhood, Faith perceived Carole as a powerful and potentially abusive "parent." She and her "sisters" in the group were vulnerable children who had to rely on each other for care and surreptitiously resist the intrusions of their controlling therapist-parent.

Soon after the conflict over the subgroup, Carole informed the group that she was going to bring in a new member because she needed the additional income. The members resisted and agreed to pay for any sessions they missed so that Carole wouldn't act out of financial need, and Carole promised not to bring in anyone new. Despite this agreement, within a few months, Carole brought up the issue of expanding the group again. Faith recalls, "We were all so beaten down that we just said 'Bring her in.'"

The woman Carole invited to attend the next group session was an alcoholic with bipolar disorder. She was physically threatening and verbally attacked some of the other members.

Faith was terrified and enraged. She concluded that Carole had brought the woman in to punish the group for not being obedient children and forming the subgroup. The new member and therapist recreated a couple reminiscent of Faith's childhood: one out-of-control person and another who failed to protect her from that person.

Whatever her motives, Carole had behaved inconsistently and irresponsibly, beginning with her reaction to the formation of the subgroup. When she initially formed the group, she failed to establish clear and reliable boundaries. She should have set rules for what could and could not occur inside and outside of the group and should have established consistent policies about fees, missed sessions, criteria for the admission of new members, and socializing outside of the larger meetings. By focusing so much of her clients' attention on her own financial problems, Carole reversed the roles and made the members feel as if they had to take care of her. She promised not to bring anyone else into the group and then wavered and brought someone in who threatened their safety.

In her first individual therapy session after the disastrous group session, Faith railed that Carole had used her to satisfy her own needs in the same way that Faith's stepfather had used her as an object to satisfy his needs. According to Faith, Carole had not protected her and could no longer be trusted.

Carole chalked Faith's rage up to transference. It was Faith's mother who had failed to protect her, not Carole. Faith's childhood experiences were causing her to "overreact." As Faith recalls, "Carole was convinced that my anger had to do with my mother and she didn't deserve it at all. I felt that she deserved every ounce of it."

Faith and Carole had reached a serious impasse with each assuming an all-or-nothing, black-and-white position. Carole attributed the problem solely to Faith's intrapsychic struggles, while Faith argued that the problem lay in their interpersonal relationship. Faith found herself in a classic gaslighting bind: To be true to herself was to lose her therapist. Most disturbing to Faith was the feeling that she was finally glimpsing the *real* Carole, the vengeful, controlling monster who had been hiding under the concerned therapeutic persona.

Week after week in her individual sessions, Faith raged and Carole denied any culpability. Finally, Faith told Carole that she was leaving therapy. Only then did Carole soften and admit that she might have made a mistake by letting the new member into the group without more careful screening. Once she made this concession, she and Faith were able to put her mistake into the broader context of their work together. They negotiated their way back to a consensual reality that could accommodate both the interpersonal and intrapsychic aspects of their dispute. Faith reflects:

> What I think now is that Carole owned part of it. She brought in someone who ought not to have been there. But I can see that my anger towards her was so big that it went beyond the situation. What she did was very similar to what my own mother did to me, which was not keep me safe. But it turned out all right because I kept talking to Carole about what was going on and we were able to resolve it.

Faith realized that she had a tendency to see things in terms of black or white, all or nothing. As she sorted out the influences of past and present, she began to allow herself a wider range of emotions, "a multitude of contradictory feelings" about Carole. She began to realize that when she fell into an "all-or-nothing" mode with her, she lost sight of the complexity of their relationship.

Seeing the world in terms of all or nothing was one consequence of Faith's abusive childhood. How could she reconcile the images of the daytime stepfather who took care of her with those of the nighttime stepfather who sexually abused her? She split the good and bad as if the father she needed were not the same person who hurt her. In the dangerous world of her childhood, subtlety and ambivalence were luxuries she could not afford. Now she was trying to achieve a more mature, more modulated view of human relationships.

Eventually, Carole could tolerate Faith's rage without having to attribute it immediately to transference. Once Carole could acknowledge the legitimacy of Faith's anger, client and therapist could negotiate their way through the impasse. When Faith saw that Carole could tolerate her feelings without blaming her, punishing her, abandoning her, or being irreparably damaged herself, there was a subtle shift in Faith's internal world.

Nevertheless, what Faith had seen in Carole had shaken the foundation of their relationship. Faith wondered if she would always have to maintain a certain vigilance to protect herself from Carole's blind spots. Reading Faith's story, we might ask if it would have helped for Carole to have been more forthcoming, to have confessed more of her own emotional motivations.

## The Dilemma of Self-Disclosure

The question of self-disclosure may be the most difficult boundary issue in psychotherapy. How much and what does a therapist, such as Carole, need to disclose about her own life? When in a transference bind, the client may feel that the only way out is for the therapist to self-disclose fully. As long as there is ambiguity, how is the client to know what is real? How can she trust her therapist if she doesn't know with whom she is dealing? For the therapist to refuse to tell can seem an act of gaslighting in itself, yet total self-disclosure may not be the best course of action, especially in the long run.

Psychiatrist and author Keith Ablow of Boston addressed this dilemma by describing his work with a woman who was sexually abused in childhood. Her family had denied the reality of her experience from early childhood on. "With her," Ablow says, "I would acknowledge my true feelings if she hit home because I didn't want to appear dishonest in any way. I didn't want to fall into the trap of saying, 'Well, it's *your* problem.'" With other patients, however, Ablow might not divulge the same information. For a therapist to acknowledge that a client has accurately read his immediate emotional response is very different from a therapist's volunteering information or sharing deeper motivations, memories, fantasies, or life experiences.

I asked a number of expert therapists about the self-disclosure issues raised by the case of Carole and Faith. They agreed that Carole needed to "own" her part in evoking Faith's feelings. It was appropriate for her to apologize for failing to adequately screen the new member. She needed to validate the legitimacy of Faith's anger toward her because Faith had every right to be angry regardless of her childhood, regardless of her transference.

The therapists did not believe, however, that Carole should have confided her deeper motives. Even if she were aware of bringing in the new member so as to regain control or even to punish the group, disclosing these motives to Faith would not have served any therapeutic purpose. Carole might have conceded to Faith that she had been upset about the subgroup and that her own feelings had clouded her judgment. More importantly, she could pledge to consider her feelings more carefully in the future.

To ensure that her reactions did not interfere with her future therapeutic work, Carole should have sought consultation with another therapist. Divulging the full extent of her feelings to Faith may have proved more of a burden than a relief. In the end, words would only go so far anyway. Repair of the relationship would depend on Carole's ability to act consistently in Faith's best interest.

Congruence, like authenticity, is a term that therapists use when describing how much the therapist should reveal of his or her self in therapy. To be congruent is to maintain some essential match between the person one is outside of the therapy room and the person one is as therapist. Alice Brand-Bartlett, an analyst with the Menninger Foundation, is an advocate of congruence: "I try to stay fairly congruent. I may not say everything, but I really feel strongly that one should never lie to a patient." Brand–Bartlett would not deny feelings that became apparent to her clients. According to her, clients can read between the lines just as therapists can, and to be told that they are *not perceiving* what they *are perceiving* is to risk inadvertent gaslighting.

Richard Fox, analyst and former education director of the Los Angeles Psychoanalytic Institute, takes a "don't deny, but don't confess" position. "I might apologize for a manifestation of anger," he says. "but I wouldn't say to a patient, 'some of the things you were talking about were making me anxious,' because it's *my* job to take care of my own feelings. That does not mean to deny them or to push them back on the patient."

## The "Realness" of the Therapist

When there is a transference impasse, the question of who the therapist "really" is can become the client's central concern. When shared reality falls apart in the therapy room, everything the client thought she knew about the therapist may suddenly come into question. Nearly everyone fears being taken in by a gaslighting Gregory pretending to be someone he is not, and the risk is always present in therapy because there is so much the client does not know about the therapist, so much that the client needs from the therapist, and so much that remains enigmatic. Therapists who disclose too much, who reveal every emotion and impulse they feel, who tell their clients their own life stories and recount their own childhood traumas shift the focus of the therapy to themselves. Often they inhibit their clients' free expression and make them feel as if they must be the caretakers. At the other extreme, the therapist who is calculatedly playing a part, saying one thing and feeling another, is not operating in good faith.

The hours that I have spent talking to clients and expert therapists have led me to believe that the best practitioners, regardless of their theoretical bent, succeed at being authentic and congruent without burdening the client with too much information about their personal lives. Even so, the question of the therapist's authenticity is apt to come up repeatedly in many therapies. It can become a problem when the therapist starts to feel something that he does not think that he should be feeling and is torn between revealing that feeling or hiding it from the client.

## Emma's Story: The Poet and the Nihilist

In this story, Emma, a published poet and literature teacher, and her therapist, David, failed to work their way out of a transference bind that hinged on David's disclosure of feelings. The therapeutic relationship exploded, undermining the progress Emma had made and leaving her to wonder what really happened in the therapy room. The ultimate problem may have been a discrepancy between the way Emma needed to see David and the way he wanted to see himself.

For Emma, the story begins with her father, who was chronically ill and then died when she was seven:

> I remember my father mostly through pictures. There's a picture of us together when I was three and I look just thrilled to be with him. He was already sick. He had a rare illness and tumors that didn't appear to be malignant but were.
>
> I always felt that I could hurt him just by touching him. One time I was playing and I saw him coming and I ran and jumped up into his arms. My head hit his chin and he bit his tongue and I was so upset. I thought, "Oh my God, I caused this. Just by loving somebody I hurt him."

As a young child, Emma spent many days at home, in the quiet confinement of the living room, alone with her father. When he died, Emma felt guilty, as if she should have been able to prevent it. She wondered if somehow her feelings were responsible. Maybe her love, maybe the very intensity of her love for him, had "brought this on." If love had killed her father, what was its lethal component, Emma wondered.

When Emma turned thirty-six, the same age her father was when he died, and her daughter was seven, the same age she had been when she lost him, her best friend died of AIDS. Old feelings resurfaced. She had a vivid memory of being in her father's hospital room the last time she saw him alive. She remembered, "He looked so strange, swollen up with tumors. I felt myself being pushed toward him and not wanting to—I was afraid. I was scared of my own feelings and I didn't know what to do."

Emma went into therapy with David, a man in his late fifties. He had a very traditional office with an oversized mahogany desk and an antique clock that bonged on the hour. David was somewhat formal in his demeanor and always wore a suit and tie. His office smelled faintly of pipe tobacco. Emma's father had been a pipe smoker. In her first session, feelings that had seemed frozen for some time surfaced, and, out of character with her usual reserve, Emma cried. From that day on, whenever she was in David's office, she felt, "I'm where I'm supposed to be finally."

Part of Emma's comfort came from David's constancy, the ritualistic reliability of their routine. At the beginning of each session, David took Emma's coat and hung it on a hanger on the back of his door. He never touched her, only her coat, and yet the considerate, deliberate way he took it from her communicated caring. Every time Emma left David, she "felt torn away." In her car after her sessions, she would wail, the sense of loss and grief washing over her "in waves." Her pain seemed so old, so deep, that Emma felt almost as if she had gotten her father back from the dead. And when she left each session, she grieved as deeply as if she were losing her father over and over again. Here was the grief, she thought, that her mother had never allowed her to express in childhood.

David offered something even more precious than constancy: He understood Emma as no other person ever had. "David got me," Emma says. "He got who I was right down to the core." And David was also the first person to challenge many of Emma's longest held secret beliefs. As a kid, she thought she should have been able to save her dad, and when she couldn't, she saw it as her failure. The guilt remained, and thirty years later Emma still had "a distorted sense of [her] own power." David helped her to understand that every child goes through a period of feeling that she is at the center of the world, that her behaviors, even her thoughts and wishes and fantasies can determine the outcome of events. The price of feeling that powerful is guilt. David taught her that "no one has that much power," and "took [her] off the hook."

Emma had also preserved something valuable from her feeling of childhood omnipotence; the act of writing poetry still had near-magical power for her. David helped Emma relish her creative power but distinguish it from responsibility for events that were beyond her control.

After about a year of treatment, while Emma still felt extremely attached to David, he began to "wean" her from the therapy, first by cutting the frequency of her sessions. David said that he wanted to discourage Emma's "overdependency." As Emma felt pushed away, her feelings for David only intensified. She had fantasies of being held, protected, and kept safe, a young child in David's arms. She could almost feel what it would be like to merge with him. When she was away from him she'd think about how good it would feel to be in his office with him, "not even having to talk."

At the beginning of the therapy, David and Emma had talked about her fear that all deep, loving relationships end, as her relationship with her father ended, in monstrous transformation and death. They had discussed the ways in which being with David reminded her of being with her father. Once David became intent on wrapping the therapy up, however, he cut Emma off whenever she began to talk about her paternal transference. Emma's more profound feelings had become a topic that was off bounds. In the void, Emma began to speculate about David's motivations even though his feelings were not available for discussion either. There were too many unspoken secrets between them.

Emma imagined two possible reasons why David seemed intent on pushing her out: Either he didn't like her, or he liked her too much. If she had shared her speculations with a skillful therapist such as analyst Richard Fox, he would have taken them each up in turn, he says, exploring the fantasies, wishes, and presuppositions behind each. To do so would require that he have a handle on his own feelings, of course. He would have to have been willing to consider how liking Emma too little or too much might be motivating his own actions. A therapist aware of his own feelings and motivations would also have given Emma more control over the staging of her own termination so as not to repeat her childhood experience of traumatic loss.

For a therapist to keep a handle on his own feelings when a client's feelings are as intense as Emma's can be challenging. A thoughtful therapist would have been analyzing his own behavior and monitoring his own responses all along the way.

Was Emma right—did David dislike her or like her too much? We are left with conjecture. What we do know is that the symbolic side of the relationship was forced to go underground as David seemed to become increasingly uncomfortable with Emma's regarding him as the idealized father of early childhood. It's not hard to imagine that being put in the place of the weak, soft, sickly father on his death bed, coupled with Emma's longings for a closeness akin to merger, might have been uncomfortable for a man David's age, rousing his own fears of physical deterioration and mortality. Perhaps Emma's image was too discordant with the idealized image David held of himself as a virile, still energetic man.

Mixed with Emma's childlike feelings for David were more adult sexual longings. She was afraid to talk too much about these feelings with David, afraid to repeat history. She had an old pattern of falling into sexual relationships with powerful, older men. These alliances always ended badly. Emma blamed herself for having "sexualized" these relationships and wondered perhaps if sexuality wasn't the lethal component of love.

Knowing about her past and her fear of repeating it, David should have explored Emma's sexual feelings, reassuring her that, whatever she felt or wished or tried to enact in their own relationship, he could handle it within the confines of the therapy. As analyst Janet Hadda says, "The patient's job is to repeat in the therapy all the stuff that has been disastrous before. So Emma's job was to sexualize the relationship, to set the therapist up. And his job was to not let it happen, but to point out how it was happening."

Instead, David turned Emma's fear of her own sexual powers against her in a session that began rather innocuously. Emma was telling David about some student evaluations she had received. David said that he had "stopped believing" in what students reported about him. "Even when students say you are wonderful that doesn't mean you are wonderful," he said. Emma saw a connection to their own relationship. She said,

> There's something I've noticed about you. You reject positive feelings that come your way. That makes me wonder about who you are and what you want from other people. I never know how you feel about me.

The room suddenly grew very quiet. Emma remembers the intensity with which David leaned in closer and looked into her eyes, and exactly what he said:

> "You know how I feel," he said. But I didn't. I had been confused by his behavior. "No, I don't," I said. He repeated the words several times, "You know how I feel." And then he said, still looking very intently at me, "But we are not going to repeat the old pattern."

What had Emma been hoping to hear? David seemed to want Emma to know exactly how he felt and yet he seemed in a quandary about telling her. The intensity, the eye contact communicated one thing, and yet his words were ambiguous. What did he mean about the pattern—was he blaming Emma for "sexualizing" yet another relationship? Emma left the session agonizing and continued to agonize for a solid week.

At her next session, Emma questioned David about what he had intimated in the previous session. He bristled. "Well, I thought you might have misunderstood what I meant. I was trying to say that you are okay with me. You are just okay." Emma recalls that his entire demeanor was different. He had withdrawn emotionally. In a defensive tone he told Emma that the problem was *her* recurrent pattern of sexualizing relationships with father figures. "This is what *you* do," David said. "You sexualize relationships out of boredom."

Emma could not recall having ever been bored in therapy. What was David talking about? Why did he want to hurt her?

David moved on and they were talking about Emma's poetry. He asked her why she brought her poems to him to read. "What makes you think I understand anything you write?" David said. "I'm not literary." Emma felt devastated. David had renounced everything important to her—teaching was meaningless, what she wrote was meaningless, and their relationship, her sense that David had really "gotten her" had been an illusion:

> I felt dead. Killed. I was thrown back to little kid-dish questions. Did I do this? What did I do bad? What did I feel that was bad? How did I make this happen? The transference had been so big and intense and complete that when this happened, everything shattered inside.

The catastrophic final session of Emma's therapy began with David's refusal to address what had happened in the prior session; instead, he harshly denied that he had any deep feelings for her. Their conversation about student evaluations seemed to be a coded communication about their own relationship, with David saying, "*You* may think that I'm wonderful but I'm not; don't confuse your illusions about me with the real me; I'm not your good father." David hinted that there was something beneath his good teacher facade that his students could not perceive, something beneath the good father persona that Emma refused to see. Emma's response, "Why can't you accept good feelings?", may have been a coded way of saying, "Why can't you accept my love?" And David's comment, "We're not going to repeat the old pattern," was half invitation, half warning.

Therapist Michael Kahn suggests that there are two ways that therapists damage clients: by seducing them and punishing them. David did both, seducing Emma with his provocative but unexplained "You know how I feel" remark and then punishing her for *his* unacknowledged feelings. Apparently, David did not know how to manage the feelings he had for Emma without acting on them, so he had to deny them instead. In the process, he had to deny and denounce everything of meaning to Emma.

Whose repetitive pattern was David really afraid of—Emma's or his own? He had excluded from therapy all discussion of Emma's deeper feelings toward him, and now he blamed the downfall of her therapy on her recurrent pattern of sexualizing relationships. In effect, David gaslighted Emma by killing off the good father of her transference in one fell swoop. He fulfilled Emma's worst fear that love ends in the beloved's ugly transformation and death.

It would seem that David had been operating under the premise that therapists should not feel strong feelings for their patients. The therapists I talked to about this case agree that David should have sought supervision as soon as he began to feel unmanageable feelings about Emma. That does not mean that such feelings are abnormal or unusual among therapists. On the contrary, strong feelings are the medium of therapy and can go both ways. The difference between competent and less competent therapists is not whether they have those feelings; it's what they do with them.

"Thinking you're not supposed to have the feelings creates the problem," says analyst Richard Fox. "That's our ideal: no tears, no erections. But we are human beings. People do stir things up in us." What do good therapists do with the strong feelings clients stir up? First, they struggle to distinguish their own feelings from the client's. They subject them to the same rigorous process of therapeutic examination to which they subject the client's feelings. If they can't do it alone they seek consultation with another therapist. They distinguish judiciously between having feelings, acknowledging those feelings to themselves, disclosing them to the client, and acting on them. They don't blame their clients for making them feel something they do not want to feel.

After many months and an exchange of letters, Emma asked to see David again to discuss the breach. She remembers being so nervous in the waiting room that she almost "barfed on the *Time* magazine" before her session. She remembers very clearly what David said when he first saw her: "I can't believe you're here. My worst fear was that you'd never come back."

And then he explained that the very emotions he had expressed, the "anger and the rejection were the opposite of what [he] had felt." David went on to explain that in trying to protect Emma, he had "fallen into another trap." He told her that he didn't understand yet how his own psychological dynamics contributed to their abrupt break-up but that he could no longer serve as her therapist.

Emma has come to her own tentative and painful conclusion: "The problem wasn't the sexual feelings between us; it was the love. The more he pushed his loving feelings away, the more angry he became, and then he had to blame it all on me." In denying their own feelings, therapists can gaslight their clients. When they own and understand them, they do not have to treat the client as the one with all the feelings—the one with all the transference—the client is simply the one whose turn it is to get the therapy.

When client and therapist are trapped in a bind, it is easy for the client to believe that the only way out is to determine definitively: Is it real or is it transference? The stories in this chapter have shown that the answer is always that it's both: It's real *and* it's transference. The relationship between therapist and client is a fine balance of the symbolic and the real, and the way out of a bind is through an appreciation of the subtle complexities of that balance. The shared reality that client and therapist create is fragile; it lacks the trappings of day-to-day life and social support to sustain it. Client and therapist may need to negotiate and renegotiate this reality over and over again throughout the course of therapy.

# 7

# Dreams of
# the Perfect Mother

A riel has a secret dream. Now twenty-seven, she can't remember how long she's had it. She only knows that she's not yet willing to let it go. Ariel dreams of getting a mother, not just any mother, but the perfect mother who could take care of all her needs completely forever. This is how she describes it:

> I am on a chronic search for a mother—and I don't even know where it comes from. All I know is that I have this terrible mother-yearning, like being homesick for a home that has been destroyed.
>
> I see every therapist as someone who is going to adopt me, take care of me for the rest of my life, and never leave me. Some of my therapists have suggested that for me to feel this way my own mother must have failed me, that she must not have been a good mother. That's such a mean way to think about her—I have to push those thoughts aside.

Ariel has gone from one therapist to another in her quest but has never gotten very far in her therapy. She has regarded each of her therapists as holding out the promise of a homecoming, and when each has disappointed her, she has turned to the next candidate for the maternal post. Her intent to get a mother has competed with her therapists' agendas. They have thought that she should take more responsibility for her own actions so that her life would have more of an adult direction. The course that she charts for herself veers backward—to childhood and what she feels has been lost and must be recovered.

Ariel's longings for a mother are so literal and extreme that they shine like a searchlight in her therapy. Perhaps Ariel is unique only in the degree of her desire to be mothered, in her refusal to recognize the futility of her search. A number of the women that I talked to described moments in therapy when they wished that their therapists could be their mothers—or at least mother them temporarily before sending them back out into the world. For many women, the therapist did become a safe mother-home to which they felt they could always return for sanctuary.

Psychoanalytic theorist Margaret Mahler described the way that toddlers "emotionally refuel" by going back to mother over and over again for reassurance as they broaden their excursions into the world. Kris expressed a similar impulse toward her therapist:

> There were times when I would get nervous at home, convinced I was going to lose my connection with her . . . afraid that she would forget me. I felt as if I were swimming and needed to keep coming back for a minute to hang on to the side of the pool before getting back out into the water.

Women who fully recognize the impossibility of the therapist's actually mothering them may still have a fleeting fantasy of being nurtured in a fashion usually reserved for young children. As Joan recounted, "I fantasize that she is my mother and holds me in her arms." Another fantasy women commonly reported involved the nearly archetypal childhood scene of being rescued following injury or defeat. Mother arrives at the scene and scoops the child up in her arms, offering supreme solace. Brianna described her personal version of this scenario:

> I would dream about breaking my leg or being hurt. Though an adult in the dream, I would be feeling very childlike feelings. And my therapist would be the one to tell me it was going to be okay and to comfort me.

Other women described feelings harkening back to the preverbal rapport of infant and caregiver. They longed to be in the presence of the therapist without having to speak; they longed to be understood without having to explain themselves. To her clients, a therapist's performance as a mother may become the most salient piece of information about her extra-therapeutic life, as if good mothers automatically made good therapists. "I imagine she's a warm and patient mother," Amy said. Seeing her therapist as simply another ordinary mother was not enough for Georgia. She imagined her therapist as the consummate mother: "I dreamed that she introduced me to a sea of her children." Perhaps the other clients with whom Georgia had to share her therapist's attention accounted for that sea.

A woman's wish to see the therapist not only as a mother but as the mother of a young child could defy reason: "Even though she is too old to have a baby, in my dream she was sitting on her office floor with a little baby in her arms, and I knew that it was hers." Some women recounted times in therapy when the comparison between their therapists and their own mothers became a principal concern. They would struggle with the specific terms of this mother–therapist equation. When they compared their therapists to their own mothers, it was often to their mothers' detriment. Judy said, "I wished my mother had been more like her. Strong, attractive, straightforward." It seems easy for a therapist to become the idealized embodiment of everything one's own mother was not. Of course, the therapist may also become the locus for projection of all of a mother's traits. "I dreamed about her mixed up with both good and bad aspects of my mother," Pam related. Women fear that their therapists may turn out to be more like their own mothers than they recognized at first. Gina, a woman in her twenties, recounted a dream that expressed the mother–therapist equivalence in graphically physical terms:

My therapist and I went to the beach. We were lying on our stomachs across from each other, face to face, looking at a book together, probably my journal. She went to adjust her bathing suit and her breast fell out. I immediately recognized it as the breast of my mother. I went into physical convulsions in my dream and woke up!

Janet struggled to enjoy her therapist as a positive mother figure without projecting her own mother's negative traits onto her:

> For a long time I was really afraid to let her become somebody important to me like a mother. I didn't want to contaminate her with what mothering meant to me . . . not being nurtured, not being cared for, even though being nurtured and cared for was exactly what I yearned for. I kept thinking, "Oh, God, if I make her into a mother image, I'm going to draw further away from her."

Janet was not the only one with ambivalent feelings about being mothered. In Ruth's dream, succor turned into suffocation: "My therapist was holding me, my back was to her, and she had many arms wrapped around me, octopus-like, and I was smothering." A daughter's need to be mothered can turn her into an octopus as well. As Sam reported,

> When I feel needy I see myself taking on the monstrous appearance of a giant sucker, an octopus with all of these tentacles, and each tentacle is covered with these little suckers, and I am afraid that I will suck my therapist dry, and in order for her to remain alive, she will have to disentangle herself from me.

Nor are the feelings women have about being mothered reserved for female therapists. Clients have fantasies of perfect mothering—that is, perfectly attuned, acutely responsive, and all-loving early caretaking—about their male therapists as well. These feelings sometimes take on more of a romantic cast, perhaps because they seem more acceptable, more adult somehow, to therapist and client when shaped in that direction. A therapist comfortable with seeing himself in a "maternal" role might recognize maternal longings for what they are, without having to recast them in sexual terms or in another way more consonant with his male identity. Maria, a thirty-two-year-old woman, had feelings for her male therapist that certainly sound maternal: "I had the sense of being in a nest; he was so attuned to me that he could read my mind." The therapist here encompasses traits of an ideal caregiver—he is a safe home, and he reads and understands Maria's innermost needs.

In the women I surveyed, such childlike longings to be mothered by their therapists were common. Just how typical they are among women in therapy in general is unknown because no one has really asked women about these feelings in any sort of systematic way. It's possible that women have more of these sorts of feelings when their therapists conceptualize themselves as mother figures. On the other hand, it's possible that clients with less receptive therapists have the feelings but don't disclose them because there seems to be no room for them in the therapy.

Too often in the psychotherapeutic literature, these longings have been written about from the standpoint of the unwilling (usually male) therapist-recipient. The client who wants her therapist to mother her has been depicted in such disparaging terms as "greedy," "needy," "clingy," "manipulative," "primitive," "enmeshed," "regressed," or "overdependent."

Feminist critics such as Jean Baker Miller and her clinician-colleagues at the Stone Center at Wellesley College argue that theorists have established psychological norms on the basis of what is considered normal for males in this culture. The measure of a man's maturity has been his differentiation and separation from his mother. In this culture, a healthy man is an autonomous man who doesn't admit to too many "childlike" feelings. In a culture that values individuality and competitive striving, longings for closeness with a mother figure, or for passive merger with something larger than the self, have been characterized as pathological.

According to the Stone Center theorists, female psychology is different. Women continue to identify with their mothers in order to assume female identities, and women traditionally derive their self-definition from their relationship to others. Mothering is a socially endorsed female activity. Thus, the urge to mother and be mothered may be quite normal in adult women. Of course, there are significant differences in degree between Ariel's impossible quest to find a new mother and a woman who functions independently in her daily life but has fleeting fantasies of maternal comfort or self-less merger.

Ariel's wish, and the more modulated longings of these other women, raise an important question about the relationship between client and therapist: How much of a good mother should a therapist be? What sort of mothering can a therapist provide? Should the therapist behave like the mother of an adult, of an adolescent, of a three-year-old, or of an infant?

## The Urge to Go Back

If Ariel fantasizes about getting a perfect mother, she has her counterparts in those therapists who imagine that they can cure their clients by embodying some aspects of the perfect mother for them. When taken most literally, the reparenting mission constitutes the most extreme form of "corrective emotional experience," an attempt to go back and redo childhood.

That is exactly what British therapist Jacqui Schiff did in the 1960s. She offered "reparenting therapy" as a radical treatment for schizophrenia and other severe forms of mental illness. Like many innovations in psychotherapy, reparenting was soon co-opted as a cure-all for all manner of psychological maladies and misadjustments. And as with many other new schools of therapy, patients became converts and then treaters so that they could pass the legacy on to others.

Schiff reparented Mame, and Mame sought to return the favor by devoting her life to reparenting others. When Ann, who is now in her forties, contacted Mame in the 1970s, she was a young woman desperate for help:

> The main message I had gotten from my own mom was, "Don't be alive. Kill yourself." My father had killed himself and the urge was so powerful that I felt it would take something very powerful to counteract it. I came to the conclusion that if I didn't have a new healthy mom I might not make it.

Driven by extreme need, Ann chose an extreme form of treatment. A few hours of chatting every week in a therapist's office seemed as if it would be completely impotent against all those years of accumulated childhood lessons. To counter the life-negating messages of her own mom, Ann would need a life-affirming counter-mom who would be just as persuasive. Mame promised to be that person.

Some of Mame's patients actually moved in with her; others, like Ann, maintained separate residences. The concept behind re-parenting was that patients would regress to infancy and then progress again through the various stages of childhood, with a good parent at the helm. Twenty years later, Ann still has mixed feelings about the experience. She emerged from the therapy with a greater sense of herself and her own potential. She has gone on to have a good life and become a therapist herself. Some of her "siblings" actually did seem to "grow up" while under "mom's" care, but the approach harmed others. Ann never gave herself up completely to the process and does not feel that she suffered any damages, although the mothering part of the treatment was ultimately confusing. She continues to love the woman who, with what seemed the best of intentions, signed a contract promising to be her new mom for life. And it pains her to say anything bad about "mom." Nevertheless, when Ann describes a group therapy session where patients "got little," she cannot help but reveal some of the logistical absurdities of adults attempting to go back to childhood:

> People would curl up by Mame as if she were a mother dog with her puppies. Their heads would be on her lap and the rest of their bodies would be on the floor. She was very knowledgeable about child development and babies' cries and could pinpoint how old everybody was by their cries. After a certain point of their crying, she would give them a bottle. At the beginning of the group, people would prepare each other's bottles. The idea was that a baby shouldn't have to fix her own bottle.

Ann stayed in the therapy for several years, but she began to find the "mom" part of the contract problematic:

Getting a new mom was fraught with problems. The bound-aries got more and more confused. My mom didn't take very good care of herself so wasn't a good role model in that regard, and then she started getting more and more of her needs met by her clients. The children wound up taking care of mom.

When I needed to ventilate my anger I couldn't express it against mom, I had to go somewhere else. . . . I guess I don't believe anymore that it's possible to get a new mom.

To attempt to literally reparent an adult constitutes a futile mis-sion. In attempting to administer to the three-year-old, the therapist may deny the needs and capabilities of the thirty-year-old invest-ment banker sitting across from her in the room. In taking care of the infant, the therapist may actually abandon the client—at least the adult part of the client capable of understanding and observing and processing the insights of therapy.

Let's suppose that a woman's mother was depressed over the course of several years when the woman was an infant and young child. The woman's therapist believes that the experience of living through her mother's depression is one reason why she now has an exaggerated vulnerability to rejection and a predisposition to be-coming depressed. Can the therapist now simply give the woman the nurturance she missed as a child, and so reverse the past?

It may be more helpful for the client to use her adult capacities to understand the subtleties of her interactions with her mother, how her mother's depression felt like rejection, and the way that she may have internalized her rejecting mother as a critical voice in her head. Without this understanding, the woman may be incapable of taking in "mother's love," even when it is offered. A woman whose mother loved her through a veil of depression is apt to feel more than longing for what she missed; she is also apt to feel rage and grief over the past. The therapist who presumes to simply replace what was lost may be denying the woman her complexity and the right to express all that she feels besides longing. As Ann described, when she felt anger, she had to take it somewhere outside of her therapy. There wasn't room in the therapy to be angry at Mom.

It's naive to assume that any adult's fantasy of perfect mothering is a simple wish. Whatever happened in childhood, whatever the child internalized, has been confounded by the years of feelings and experiences that have occurred since. Beneath the surface of the client's plea for a good mother may reside a complex of irreconcilable wishes. To try to fulfill any one of them is to deny the woman's history and to deprive her of the right to grieve what was lost and to own the ways she has compensated for her losses.

The boundary dilemmas are also insurmountable. The therapist immediately finds herself in a dual relationship. She is mother and she is therapist. But mothers have different needs and interests in their children than do competent therapists. No one can maintain the neutrality and perspective required of a therapist when emotionally engaged as a parent. And no one can parent well without deep emotional engagement.

Aside from the dual relationship problem, it is nearly impossible to maintain a therapeutic frame when a therapist is living, or nearly living, with her clients. What is the therapist to do with her own needs? As the boundaries become more confused, the therapist's personal needs are apt to get in the way of therapy. This is complicated by the fact that therapists who imagine they can cure their clients by reparenting them perfectly are often driven by the secret wish to be reparented themselves. Their clients often wind up as Mame's did, mothering them.

That is not to say that they are not also driven by a sincere desire to help. The therapists that I interviewed told me that the draw to give the client what she asks for, be it perfect mother, tireless lover, or even their opposites—is a very powerful draw. Every therapist wishes from time to time that she could magically cure her clients by crawling into their fantasies with them.

Boston psychiatrist and author Keith Ablow recalled a time early in his career when he was treating an elderly woman. She had been depressed ever since her son had died suddenly earlier that year. During the course of the therapy she began to cheer up but only as she began to attribute more and more of her son's traits to Ablow.

She was also attempting to nudge Ablow into fulfilling her son's role. She wasn't getting better because she was acknowledging and grieving the loss of her son; she was attempting a magical shortcut by which she could replace her lost son via Ablow.

"I had the impulse to become her son," Ablow says, "and thought maybe that would cure her, if she could just get back the son who died." Ablow now recognizes the futility of such an undertaking: "It's a fantasy that you could replace some other person; you would be imperfect in the role and you would be abandoning the one of therapist that you promised to play to begin with." As a therapist, his job was to help the woman to grieve her loss and survive it, not to pretend that he could save her from the necessity of grieving by magically replacing what she had lost.

The impulse behind reparenting, the belief that it might be possible to somehow go back and fix the mistakes of childhood by becoming a new and improved version of the parent for the client, is a very old one in psychotherapy. Freud cautioned that any attempt to reparent the client was to make concrete what had to remain completely symbolic. What clients longed for was unrealistic; what they needed was to understand why they wanted what they wanted and why getting it was now impossible. Ferenczi saw himself more as a loving mother than a stern father. Franz Alexander also took a more moderate view, believing that the therapeutic relationship could provide some sort of corrective emotional experience and so reverse the past.

Since that time, therapists have considered and reconsidered the extent to which they could "reparent" their clients. The notion of a corrective emotional experience through some kind of reparenting continues to live to varying degrees and in a variety of forms in different psychotherapies. If most therapists would agree that literally reparenting a client is not a viable option, they would probably disagree as to when other more modulated interventions leave the realm of the symbolic or presume to promise too much. There are therapists who offer direct advice to their clients about how to live their lives, in the way that a good parent might counsel his or her adult child. Some consider their setting of limits as providing some of the discipline that the parent of an adolescent might use to help the youngster develop self-discipline. And some therapists perform functions that we associate with taking care of an infant or young child. What should a therapist do for clients like Ariel or Ann, who insist that their only hope lies in getting a mother? What could Ariel do to make her therapy more effective?

## Kohut's Compromise

One answer may lie in the work of Heinz Kohut. For psychologist Michael Kahn, Kohut's approach constitutes a new synthesis between the psychoanalysts and the humanists. His "self-psychology" represents one particular compromise on the continuum between the strict Freudian analyst who would interpret the client's wishes dispassionately out of fear of providing any measure of "infantile gratification" and the humanist who would strive to cure by providing a corrective emotional experience. With its emphasis on empathy, self-psychology is representative of a middle ground that many therapies try to maintain.

According to Kohut, children rely on adults to satisfy certain psychological needs. A young child may view her parents more as objects capable of satisfying her needs than as people with needs of their own. As a child grows up, she assumes some of the psychological functions provided by others, and so internalizes the parent. By doing so, she not only becomes capable of taking care of her own emotional needs, but she also comes to recognize other people as having needs and identities of their own. According to Kohut, when a child's fundamental developmental needs are not satisfied fully, she may get stuck at some point on the developmental continuum.

For Kohut, Ariel's wish to be mothered, her passivity and seeming refusal to take charge of her own life, reflect a stalling on the path to adult development. But needs that were inadequately satisfied during childhood cannot be satisfied literally anymore. The therapist cannot love the client as a parent would love a child. The client cannot go back and complete the developmental process of childhood. However, the therapist's profound empathy can substitute emotionally for the direct fulfillment of the client's needs. Client and therapist together can complete a new growth process that is *analogous* to the thwarted process of development.

Empathy, "the capacity to think and feel oneself into the inner life of another person," is the most important gift that the therapist can offer. The therapist effecting Kohut's compromise says in effect, "I cannot give you what you did not get in childhood, but I can give you supremely empathic understanding—understanding without judging you, shaming you, rejecting you. This understanding will satisfy to some degree the unrequited developmental need behind your request and, along with a fuller comprehension of the experiences that led to your current state, will allow you to complete a maturation process that was disturbed in childhood."

The therapist cannot provide perfect mothering, but can create an atmosphere that is nurturing and empathic, that resembles good mothering in some limited respects. There may be resonances in the therapist's behavior of the parent a two-year-old needs, but the therapist always addresses the adult the client has become. To hold the client on her lap and rock her to sleep may be too provocative, may be too great a denial of the past. To do so would be to hold out the promise of providing what no therapist can provide. But the therapist can talk to the client empathically about the fantasy of being held, while holding the client symbolically with her soft voice and unwavering tolerance of her client's feelings.

## Ariel's Story: The Mother-Pill

With this therapeutic approach in mind, let's return to Ariel. Ironically, despite the fact that she has spent years sitting in therapists' offices hoping that they would adopt her, Ariel has kept her wish something of a secret from her therapists. She has never said straightforwardly to any one of them: "Look, I wish that you could just be my mother and take care of me." She has always felt too ashamed and too afraid that her therapist's rejection would destroy her dream.

I'm afraid that the therapist will just tell me it's some stupid fantasy based on something that happened long ago. As soon as I told her I wanted to be mothered, she would become reject-ing and judgmental. She would think that my wanting to be mothered makes me unlovable.

Instead, Ariel has sought in more covert ways to get them to mother her. She has hoped against hope that she would happen onto a therapist who would want to mother her as much as she wants to be mothered.

Ariel not only carries the impossible wish for a perfect mother, but she also believes that by merely having the wish she becomes unmotherable. She has placed herself in an unresolvable trap: The more she wants to be mothered, the more unmotherable she be-comes. A therapist taking an approach akin to Kohut's would em-pathize with Ariel until she felt safe enough to state the fantasy directly. By simply giving the fantasy voice, "I dream of getting a perfect mother and I believe that wanting this makes me unlov-able," Ariel might begin to gain a sense of greater self-possession. The dream would lose some of the charge and potential for shame it gets by remaining underground. She and her therapist could then acknowledge the depth of her longing and the unresolvable bind that her desire and her belief about that desire create. For it is the bind that probably causes Ariel the greatest pain.

A good therapist would be as curious as Ariel to fully grasp the fantasy: What exactly would it feel like, look like, to be taken care of perfectly forever? What would Ariel do every day with her per-fect mother? Would being mothered that way mean giving up all autonomy? Wouldn't that create other problems? What has been the impact on Ariel's life of keeping this wish so secret for so long?

To help Ariel understand the origins of the bind—to want to be loved is to be unlovable—a good therapist would help Ariel turn her attention precisely to where she is most reluctant to look: her real mother and the relationship they had during Ariel's childhood. By keeping her quest for the perfect mother alive, by acting as if it is possible for an adult to get a perfect mother, Ariel puts off looking at that relationship and having to feel angry or sad about what happened:

> The first memory that comes to mind when I talk about my wish for a mother is of having a splinter in my foot. My father was taking it out and I was crying because it hurt. My mother kept telling me to shut up and not cry. When I think of being hurt and wanting to be taken care of, I hear my mother saying, "Shut up. Who the hell are *you* to be whining and crying and *wanting* to be taken care of?"

Ariel recalls her father's ministrations after she stepped on a splinter. Her mother disapproved, particularly of Ariel's wanting, expecting, or taking pleasure in being taken care of. The message Ariel received was that physical injury and suffering might merit a caretaking response, while the desire to be cared for, or any pleasure taken in being cared for ("Who are you to want to be taken care of?"), would result in rejection. Hence it is easy to see why the very wish to be mothered became equated for Ariel with rejection.

Unable to disentangle the wish to hurt herself from the wish to solicit caretaking, Ariel has repeatedly wounded herself and attempted suicide, beginning in adolescence. Death at her own hand seems to mean the ultimate abnegation of desire. To have no desire promises to bring reunion with a mother who could not love her as long as she asked to be loved.

Alice Brand-Bartlett, an analyst at the Menninger Institute, believes that it's very important for a client like Ariel to be able to express her maternal longings freely in therapy without being shamed. By expressing them, she will learn that they do not necessarily elicit rejection. Ariel's desire will be extricated from its bind.

"It's an important part of the treatment for these longings to come out, and for the client to be able to accept them, and to see that both client and therapist can survive them," Brand-Bartlett explains. "Then the client will feel less inclined to act out self-destructively in an effort to get her longings met."

Psychologist Judith Armstrong, who specializes in treating child-hood trauma, would help Ariel to see her alternate-mother fantasy as a coping device that she created, probably while still a young child, to comfort herself. In doing so, Armstrong would shift the locus of control to Ariel so that she could begin to reconceptualize herself as an adult still employing a fantasy she made up as a child, not as a passive child who must continue to wait for something to happen.

In fact, Ariel acknowledges that she does use the fantasy of a perfect mother in an active way to comfort herself when she is feel-ing upset. In a sense, the fantasy replaces the state of ideal caretak-ing it describes and is a substitute mother that Ariel herself controls.

Ariel's wish is another version of the golden fantasy. Psychoan-alyst Sydney Smith, who first coined the term, traces the golden fantasy's roots to the infant's earliest relationship with the mother, particularly the period of separation-individuation that occurs at about twelve to eighteen months. It is then when the child learns that she is distinct from the mother and must forge her own iden-tity. The golden fantasy implicitly contains within it an Edenic nar-rative: "Such a blissful state was actual but now has been lost." As Ariel laments, "In therapy once I found myself crying, 'Where did she go? Where did she go?' I guess I was thinking about my mother. Somewhere along the line I feel like I lost her." According to Smith, holding on to the golden fantasy can be a way of protecting the image of one's own mother as having once been perfect. A mother whose perfect love was somehow lost is preferable to a mother whose love was inevitably disappointing. Immersion in the fantasy is a way of denying the actual experiences of one's childhood and of putting off the mourning that comes with accepting that what was lost cannot be recaptured. Ariel's childhood is never really over as long as she can maintain her search. Paradoxically, Ariel uses the fantasy of some other perfect mother not to criticize her own mother, but to protect her mother's image:

> Some of my therapists have suggested that for me to feel this
> way my mother must have failed me, that she must not have

been a good mother. That's such a mean way to think about her—I have to push those thoughts aside.

As unbearable as unrequited longing, for Ariel at least, the longing is preferable to expressing any hostility against her mother. It is preferable to mourning.

The golden fantasy is universal, according to Smith, and people are extremely reluctant to confess the hold it has on them. To do so is to jeopardize its survival. The dream of a perfect mother flourishes in darkness and secrecy. To expose it is to begin to see it as a fantasy that must be examined in the context of one's real life history. As Ariel says, "There's a magical feeling about the fantasy, as if it represents the real me, and if I talk about it too much, it will lose its power. It will never come true." A good therapist would help Ariel to see that the fantasy is one way that she holds on to some semblance of a good mother, and a good motherable self inside. To give it up—and exposing it is to risk giving it up—is to feel the full measure of her motherlessness.

Ariel's wish bathes her therapists—she often speaks of them as if they are standing together in a group portrait—in a blinding maternal haze. They are faceless, nameless, indistinguishable objects of her need, "Stepford" moms without any needs of their own. In Kohut's terms, Ariel still needs her significant others to function as "self-objects" to help her complete her development and cannot yet recognize them as people with needs of their own.

There's a further irony. Although Ariel craves perfect mothering in the abstract, she finds it difficult to take any pleasure in the nurturance her therapists do provide. According to Brand-Bartlett, this is another area of conflict and contradiction to which Ariel and her therapist need to turn. Brand-Bartlett would look empathically with Ariel at her inability to recognize and enjoy the maternal element in what her therapists do give her. "She may have a problem with taking it in, even when she does get it, because it still never feels quite right," Brand-Bartlett explains.

When Ariel is in her therapist's office and a certain intimacy is possible, it does not feel "quite right":

I want to see my therapist as all-compassionate, all-nurturing. Just thinking about it is comforting. But when I am actually in her office and think about her being perfect, I don't feel good, I feel threatened. If I let go of the fantasy, there will be nothing but isolated nothingness out there. At the same time, I'm really very afraid of the intimacy in being close to her.

Sydney Smith writes about the terror of merger that is the underside of the golden fantasy. She traces it to the toddler's conflict over autonomy versus her wish to return to the "symbiosis" of her infantile life with mother. Smith's belief about the origin of this conflict is highly theoretical. What's clear, however, is that in Ariel's case, at least, her fantasy is far more complicated than her initial statement of her wish for perfect mothering might suggest. She feels good imagining closeness, but she feels bad when it actually starts to happen. She feels good imagining that her therapist is perfect when at a distance from her but bad when she thinks of her that way while in her presence.

This complexity is one more reason why a therapist cannot simply cure Ariel or other clients with mock mother-love and is one more reason why reparenting is such an impossible mission. Ariel is not a starved person desperate for food. Even if the initial cause of her problem were simply maternal deprivation, what Ariel has eaten in the absence of adequate nourishment has altered her digestive tract. The therapist who makes the mistake of attempting to satisfy Ariel's longing literally may discover an abundance of rage at what was lost in childhood. Behind the white haze of abstract, impersonal, idealized longing, there are ambivalence, anger, and grief. Ariel's fear of closeness is at least as powerful as her drive toward it.

Being the target of this sort of intense and annihilating longing can set off powerful feelings in therapists as well. Ariel's wish may feel like a demand, her refusal to state it directly a form of manipulation, the incipient threat that she will harm herself a sort of blackmail, her desire to be mothered perfectly and anonymously an aggressive invasion of the therapist's skin. Her refusal to think anything "mean" about her mother—in effect, her inability to own her own aggression and hostility—can make Ariel emotionally dangerous to other people. To her therapists, Ariel may seem like a Great Dane that thinks it's a Maltese—too big and heavy to climb up on the therapist's lap and apt to hurt the therapist if she does. If the therapist reacts defensively and pushes her off, she will only confirm Ariel's worst fear that her desire to be mothered makes her unmotherable.

The therapist must struggle to maintain empathy, continually weighing what to gratify and what to deny. She must draw clear boundaries without becoming a rejecting mother, take care of her client without promising to rescue her or to deliver more than can be delivered within the constraints of the approximate relationship.

Therapists like Armstrong or Brand-Bartlett know that becoming Ariel's perfect mother is impossible and that much of the work lies instead in looking at Ariel's relationship with her own mother:

> My mother was an alcoholic with extremely angry outbursts that came out of nowhere. I was very lonely. I worried a lot about my mother's not coming home, not being there when I got home—probably typical childhood fears.
>
> I had a dream about her once when I was very little. She was going up the stairs with my kindergarten teacher and I couldn't keep up with them. She kept on going farther and farther away. I was screaming and screaming for her and when I woke up, I was still screaming because I'd lost her.

Ariel doesn't remember much of her first twelve or thirteen years. She idealizes those years, even though the few memories she has are of being frightened and lonely. A good therapist would help Ariel look at this contradiction.

Ariel expresses little anger toward her mother; a child frequently under attack by an unpredictably rageful mother may have found the environment too dangerous for expressing any anger of her own. When the bond between them seemed so fragile, any expression of anger threatened to hasten rejection. Maintaining a state of perpetual longing now protects Ariel from feeling the full force of her own anger.

Ariel recounts another memory of being hurt and receiving care:

When I was little I fell in the swimming pool once and my mother saved me. I was crying and trying to get my breath. But she immediately put me in my cousin Sara's arms. She was the one who held me—not my mother. My cousin was a wonderful woman and I used to imagine that if anything happened to my mother, my father would marry cousin Sara.

Whether Ariel's memories are of running after her mother, of having a splinter in her foot removed, or of nearly drowning, her mother always disappoints and betrays her. In each, there is a moment primed to elicit caretaking behavior and her mother responds by turning away. When Ariel nearly drowns in the family pool, there is one crystalline moment when she is carried from the pool, fighting for breath, in which her mother's love seems unambiguous. Perhaps there were other isolated moments like this in which Ariel perceived her mother's unequivocal caring. But what was required to solicit it was woundedness, passivity, helplessness, even the threat of death.

The golden period in which Ariel fantasizes having had perfect caretaking may not have existed in a block of time at all, but in mere moments when her need for caring and her mother's willingness to care for her were in synchrony. Perhaps Ariel's loss came not once, but over and over again, each time that she and her mother failed to connect. In none of her memories or dreams is Ariel ever alone with her mother; there are always other people in the picture, often another woman or group of women. It would seem that even from a young age Ariel was looking for alternate mothers, as if one mother were not enough—or her own mother was too much.

If Ariel keeps trying to turn her therapists into Stepford moms, depersonalized figures able to take perfect care of her, behind the fantasy is Ariel's wish to impossibly transform herself into a Stepford baby that would be capable of accepting mother's love without fear, anger, or ambivalence. On some level, Ariel already knows that her dreams of the perfect mother and of the perfect Ariel-baby cannot come true: "It's a yearning for the impossible. I wish my therapist could just give me a mother-pill that I could take and not feel this terrible mother-sickness anymore."

Good therapists help their clients understand that the dream of a perfect mother is a normal human wish, a wish shared to some degree by everyone. We all long for comfort and solace, for unconditional acceptance, for the perfect synchrony between need and its fulfillment that only an all-loving parent could provide. By meeting this wish with empathy, the therapist can help the client reconcile herself to what it is possible to get from the limited love of mortal human beings.

# 8

# Mothers Lost and Found

Empathy is one way therapists provide some semblance of maternal nurturance without making the mistake of attempting to reparent their clients. But empathy is only one tact. There are a number of other aspects of the good mother that therapists may embody in their mission to restore or repair the past. Owing to a conviction in the field that many later problems result from development veering off course in the first three years of life, the mother that therapists emulate is often the good mother of infancy and early childhood.

The women I interviewed for this book described myriad ways in which their therapists were motherly or evoked a maternal atmosphere. Some spoke in dulcet tones that provided reassurance and comfort or decorated their offices in pastels that smacked of the nursery, and furnished them with overstuffed chairs that made their clients feel small and enveloped and safe when they sat in them. There were therapists who offered cups of herbal tea and other healing brews and those who wore soft, formless Mother Hubbard clothing that made their bodies seem accommodating, marshmallowy, and asexual.

Others ventured perilously closer to reparenting territory by talking baby talk and play-acting, "I'll be the mommy and you be the baby" sort of games. Therapists offered stuffed animals for clients to use as transitional objects to reenact the process by which an infant becomes attached to a piece of blanket or favorite stuffed toy. "Use this when you're away from me to feel close," one therapist said. Another went so far as to provide the stuffed animal with a cute falsetto voice: "teddy bear promises to love you and never leave you," she offered, assuming that the client could differentiate the bear's promises from her own and would not come to expect more than the approximate relationship could deliver.

A family therapist who asked to remain anonymous told me that she had been distressed to learn that some of her colleagues were mock breast-feeding their clients during sessions as a form of corrective emotional experience.

These approaches become risky when they seem to offer a level of love and concern that exceeds the bounds of the approximate relationship, when they suggest to clients that things are black and white and that it is possible to be children again and to redo the past. They become dangerous when therapists lose sight of the adult part of the client and speak only to the child. That makes it altogether too easy for the client to also lose touch with her adult self.

## Good Mothers

A massive body of research establishing the significance of infant–early caregiver bonds has led therapists in their quests to evoke the good early mother. One classic study is illustrative. In the visual bridge experiment, researchers lure a one-year-old baby to crawl forward across a pane of glass that covers a drop-off beneath it. The infant inevitably hesitates at the divide, uncertain and fearful. She looks to her mother's face for signs as to whether or not to proceed. If the mother smiles reassuringly, the infant continues, any conflicting perception of danger insubstantial in comparison to her mother's emotional cues. If the mother expresses anxiety or uncertainty herself, the infant halts her advance and cries. The emotional temperature the mother sets is more important than any other indicator in establishing the safety of the world. It is this mother, the mother of the visual bridge experiment who has the capacity to set the child's emotional temperature and deem the world good or dangerous, that many therapists see themselves replacing.

In addition to infant research, certain theoretical constructs traditionally have carried great weight in therapists' thinking about motherhood. Some of the most influential have come from reading backward from observations of adult symptoms to assumptions about their origins in childhood. Therapists have found similarities between certain adult symptoms and certain cognitive and emotional stages of childhood and have made the leap that the adult's problem is caused by having becoming "fixated" or "stuck" at that stage of development. They have then sought to somehow go back and redo that stage in psychotherapy. Not every therapist has swallowed these theories whole, but they do seem to provide a shared working vocabulary.

## The Mother Inside

British psychoanalyst Melanie Klein was the first theorist to turn her attention to the infant's earliest relationship with her mother. She began with the Freudian view: Human beings are driven by instincts and internal conflict. Inside even the youngest baby, Klein imagined a battle being waged between instinctual drives—aggressive and sexual—and defenses against those drives. The baby had strong and conflicting feelings about the breast, which represented the mother. A baby beset by the oral aggression of appetite wished not only to feed from the breast but to consume it—and the mother—completely in the process. Frightened by the ferocity of her own wishes and of the potential force of her mother's retaliation, the baby disavowed these impulses. Using a defense Klein called "projective identification," she projected her own aggression back onto her mother. An aggressive baby became a baby afraid of an aggressive mother. Then the guilt-ridden baby internalized this projected image of the bad mother and used it to punish herself.

Some of Klein's concepts seem wildly improbable. Nevertheless, she spawned a school of object relations therapists who have elaborated ever more sophisticated theories of how people "project," "introject," and "re-introject" one another's psychological material. Their contribution has been in getting therapists to think more about the ways in which we internalize our relationships with others, beginning in infancy. For surely others do exist for us as much as the people inside our heads as the people we actually encounter in the world. They are both real people in relationships with us and the versions of them that we use to comfort ourselves, blame ourselves, define ourselves. A woman of fifty has a relationship not only with her infirm seventy-five-year-old mother of the present but also with the mother she remembers and internalized at earlier stages of her life.

The mothers we keep inside may be different from our mothers' vision of themselves, different from the way others, even our own siblings, experience them. For example, a woman who felt guilty as a child about her father's doting on her at the same time that he abused her mother may have turned her guilt and confusion into an angrier, more punitive mother inside than her actual childhood mother was in relation to her.

Long after their deaths, our mothers continue to exist for us as voices and images in our heads, indistinguishable sometimes from conscience. For some of us, there will always be a mother in the doorway of our bedroom watching over us, or a mother waiting for us with an abundant lap, or a mother who is drunk and cannot be relied on. For the object relationists, part of the therapist's job is to make the client aware of these introjects and to help her internalize new ones based on taking in the experience of being with a "good mother" therapist.

## Separation-Individuation

According to Margaret Mahler, an object relationist whose theories have shaped therapists' thinking about the vicissitudes of the baby–mother bond, babies begin life in a state of *symbiosis*, psychologically merged with their mothers. They cannot differentiate the boundaries of self, other, and the external world. This symbiosis protects the baby from the terror inherent in being small and helpless and allows her to identify instead with her mother's seeming omnipotence. Only through a painful, multistep process of separation-individuation that begins at about four months and culminates at two years of age do babies achieve psychological separation from mother and a clear notion of themselves.

As Mahler would have it, separation-individuation is a passage fraught with as many perils as any dark woods in Grimms' fairy tales. The baby's instinctual drives—oral, anal, and genital—each rise up in turn to pound away at the psyche. Innate aggression threatens to overturn the prospects for more benign connection. The infant is torn between the wish to stay with her mother in an idyllic state of symbiotic merger and the thrilling prospect of independence. At the same time, the infant is terrified of being swallowed up in symbiosis and of losing her newfound autonomy.

If the mother holds the baby too close or pushes the baby away too soon, she can set the journey dangerously off course. She must be steadfast and true, attuned and responsive, in love with her child yet invested in her becoming independent. She must convey the message that the loss of her love will not be the price the infant will pay for growing up. Any failure can lead to the child's becoming stuck at a particular stage, condemned to feel a toddler's conflicts for life.

As the theory goes, by the end of separation-individuation, the child has not only begun to define herself as a distinctive human being, she has also internalized her mother as a multidimensional being, capable of a range of behaviors. The ability to internalize mother as a unified being—to recognize that the mother who brings pleasure, the mother who frustrates, the mother who may even cause pain is the same person—is called "emotional object constancy." The baby who achieves emotional object constancy can tolerate her mother's absences without unbearable distress because she has become able to hold an experience of a good mother inside. She can perform some of the soothing her mother used to provide. She is more able to mother herself.

# Scientific Facts and Satisfying Stories

Daniel Stern and other contemporary infant development researchers have questioned separation–individuation theory. It simply does not jibe with the facts as gleaned from infant study. Even
very young babies have more sophisticated cognitive faculties, better memories, and more refined sensory abilities than previously assumed. It is doubtful that babies ever perceive themselves as merged
with their mothers. According to Stern, to begin to perceive the self
at all is to perceive its separateness.

It is true of course that human beings are attracted to and also
frightened by the fantasy of entering into a state of merger with
something bigger and more powerful than themselves. Many pursue moments of such oceanic bliss during lovemaking, meditation,
or other experiences that play at the edges of merger. But symbiosis probably exists more as a universal human fantasy that first arises
later in childhood than as a half-remembered reality.

Whether separation–individuation theory is an accurate depiction of development or not, it makes for a satisfying story. It begins
in an Edenic period of oceanic merger and proceeds through a dangerous voyage. It provides a period of childhood upon which therapists can focus their search for the climactic moments of loss or
failure that set the ground for everything to follow. It neatly explains
why a woman like Ariel seems psychologically frozen at the moment of separation from her mother. She still fears and craves symbiosis with an idealized mother figure because she failed to negotiate the milestones of separation–individuation. Other clients, such
as those who are unable to hold a comforting image of the therapist in mind from session to session, those who polarize other people into categories of all-good and all-bad, are also easily conceptualized as being stuck somewhere on that separation–individuation
road. They never made it to emotional object constancy. Other
clients seem confused about the boundaries between self and other,
between self and the world.

The mere fact that an adult's issues resemble those of Mahler's infant in the throes of separation–individuation does not prove that

those issues actually originated then or that the therapist can reenact processes that should have occurred then to correct them. Barring trauma, it is more likely that children are shaped by ongoing patterns of interaction than by a single dramatic breach during a critical period. Nevertheless, it would seem that when therapists place themselves in the role of early mother, they are apt to rely on theories based on questionable facts but with high metaphorical applicability.

## Traits of the Good Mother

Based partly on research and partly on theory, then, some therapists attempt to emulate particular traits of the good early mother. The good mother is *reliable*. She can be depended upon to respond to the baby's needs in a consistent fashion. This responsiveness orders the world, deems it benign, and makes the baby feel at home in it. Thus, therapists strive to be *reliable* and *consistent* in their interactions with clients, although they may not be able to actually satisfy their clients' physical or emotional needs.

Daniel Stern and other infant researchers have established that one of the most important tasks of the early caretaker is to help the baby to *regulate* her own emotional and physiological states so that they seem less unpredictable and overwhelming. The caregiver who is attuned and responsive to these shifts in states but does not seem perturbed by them makes them more tolerable for the infant. The good mother regulates a baby's internal states by calming her when she becomes too excited, by stimulating her when she needs contact, by relieving distress when she is hungry or cold. A therapist may attempt to regulate the client's emotional states by naming them, by helping her circumscribe them, by showing her that they can begin and end without permanently altering either her, her therapist, or the relationship between them.

In the words of object relations theorist D. W. Winnicott, the good mother becomes a container for those feelings that threaten to overwhelm the baby's equilibrium. The baby comes to rely on the caregiver's psychological stability. She learns that the mother is able to tolerate her reactions, take the terror out of her experience, and not be destroyed by it. For Winnicott, physical holding creates safety and boundedness, delineating the baby's internal and external worlds.

Winnicott suggests that the therapist can symbolically *hold* the client in the way that a good mother physically holds a baby. The therapist can do so by holding the client's emotional states, by making sense of the client's often initially disorganized narrative, by providing a reliable frame in which the client–therapist relationship unfolds.

The good mother gives the baby's needs primacy and does not expect the baby to take care of her or other adults. But she also draws boundaries so that the child has a realistic sense of the limits of her own power. The good therapist gives her client's needs primacy, does not expect her clients to take care of her, but maintains boundaries so that clients understand the limits of self and other, and of the relationship.

In emulating the good early mother, therapists strive to be reliable, consistent, steadfast, calm, contained, attuned, and empathic. They see themselves as holding, organizing, and neutralizing what is too painful and disorganizing for clients to keep inside. Some therapists see themselves as taking their clients symbolically through the process of separation-individuation again, as helping them to achieve emotional object constancy and to incorporate a different kind of mother figure.

Therapists continue to debate the extent to which these approximations of early mothering are curative. Is being responsive, empathic, and consistent enough to effect change in another adult human being? Can an adult client internalize a therapist in the same way a two-year-old internalizes her mother?

## Marjorie's Story: The Music Mothers Make

Some therapists reading Marjorie's story would answer yes to these questions. Marjorie, a woman in her mid-twenties, used the relationship with her therapist to work through what could not be resolved in her relationship with her own mother. In the process she revised the voices and images of the mother she held inside. Paradoxically, Marjorie had to lose a mother in order to gain one.

Marjorie's childhood could have come out of the bleakest Dickens novel. She has been told that when she was an infant, her aunt came over to visit and found her lying in a cardboard box in her mother's dresser drawer. In the middle of the living room Marjorie's schizophrenic mother was stretched out catatonically across two folding chairs. She was hospitalized sixteen times over the course of Marjorie's childhood. Marjorie's father left when Marjorie was born and returned only sporadically for visits.

Marjorie and her four siblings were left in the care of her maternal grandmother, an often cruel woman whose behavior was mysterious to her charges. Marjorie believes now that her grandmother was also psychotic. She beat her grandchildren capriciously, withheld food, and often forbade them from using the bathroom. Marjorie remembers being sent home from kindergarten for being dirty and disheveled and wandering the neighborhood trying to charm or beg food from strangers.

Marjorie entered therapy after "yet another failed relationship." Her pattern was to cater to the other person's needs at the expense of her own. When she could tolerate her own submersion no longer, she would end the relationship. Marjorie felt as if she were "not quite human," lacking the fundamental knowledge of "how to do life." A talented pianist, Marjorie felt shy about performing.

Marjorie characterizes her relationship with her mother this way:

All I knew when I was growing up was that my mother would appear out of nowhere and then disappear again. I was six and taking a bath. Suddenly, she just appeared in the bathroom. She had been gone forever. I started sobbing, "Mommy, I missed you." That was always my response to seeing her, I would just cry. She started crying too and said, "Why are you crying?" I said, "I've missed you so much." She wrapped me in a towel and hugged me, and said, "I've missed you so much too." Then she was gone.

On her tenth birthday, Marjorie's mother appeared magically again.

I went home for lunch and there was a surprise party—all the kids from my class were there with hats on. My mother was at the piano in a blue and black dress—I'll never forget that dress—playing the birthday song. I couldn't believe she was there. I ran over to her and started to cry, and then she did, too, and then my grandmother got really mad and told me to go into the bedroom and get a grip on myself. I made myself stop crying. When I came out it was time to go back to school.

"Mom, will you be here when I get back?" I asked.

"Of course, honey," she said. "I'll be right here waiting for you."

And of course when I got home from school she was gone. I was sure it was my fault—if I hadn't cried and upset her she would have stayed with me. My grandmother told us that my mother just couldn't cope with children. I thought if I could just grow up faster, my mother would be okay.

For much of Marjorie's childhood, her mother existed as a phantom. When she disappeared as if by magic, Marjorie felt broken. She perceived her mother as fragile and prone to breaking as well. Yet when present, she and Marjorie had moments of deep emotional attunement. Marjorie suspected that it was her own strong feelings, appetites, and needs that drove her mother away.

One of the few things they shared was music:

As long as I can remember, the piano was my mother, my mother was the piano. When she'd sit down and play, the whole world was her. After she was gone, the piano remained in my grandmother's house. In our small living room, it held a big place. I played around it, crawling over and under it. Deep inside me, I felt I was communing with my mother whenever I played the piano, but I couldn't show that on the surface because I was convinced my grandmother would lock me up or punish me for it.

I lived in absolute agony, pining away for my mother every moment I can think of, just to see her face or to hold her hand.

My mother was the best thing in my life, as bad as she was, because she loved me and there was a way in which I really understood that.

Despite her mother's long and inexplicable absences, Marjorie
managed to feel loved and to internalize her mother as something
good. However, the mother Marjorie internalized was in fragmented and fleeting images: the light of her face, her fingers on the
keyboard, her cool palm against Marjorie's forehead. Inadequately
nourished by reality and hidden away from Marjorie's grandmother,
these pieces of mother became nearly indistinguishable from Marjorie's internal sensations.

When Marjorie's mother disappeared, she left her music. Perhaps like the mother of early infancy, music was powerful, comforting, all-encompassing, larger than the self. But music was distinct
from Marjorie's experience of her mother in an important way:
Marjorie could keep it and control it. Marjorie could listen to the
same piece of music over and over again; it was predictable and
repeatable.

For Marjorie, the piano itself stood in for her mother's body. Im-
mense and substantial, it was the one safe base to which she could
always return. If we think about music and the piano in terms of
Margaret Mahler's separation-individuation theory, we might consider it as fulfilling one function that Marjorie's mother failed to
provide—a safe, reliable base to which the toddler could return for
reassurance. Music and the piano also were transitional objects—
associated with mother, possessing some of her soothing attributes,
and yet under Marjorie's own control. According to D. W. Winnicott, the first theorist to look seriously at a child's "boo-boo" or
"blankie," these transitional objects function almost like training
wheels, shoring up the self as the child learns to comfort herself.
After a few years, the child divests the object of its special powers
and moves into the larger world.

For Marjorie, these transitional objects were all the mother she
had, forcing her to rely too much, too soon, on too little. The mother
inside never consolidated into a reliable source of self-definition and
support. From the standpoint of Mahler's theory, Marjorie could not

fully separate and individuate from a mother who was so absent and insubstantial. Ironically, it may be more difficult to separate psychologically from an absent mother than from a mother who is present all the time. For Marjorie, the psychic boundaries between mother and self remained murky. Her mother was conceptualized mostly in terms of what was missing, as a hole in the self.

Some therapists would think about Marjorie as remaining in Mahler's state of symbiosis—unsure when she entered therapy as to where mother, self, and world left off and began.

When Marjorie came into therapy she felt a strong identification with her mother and her mother's music. But hanging on to her mother had come to mean being *like* her mother, and that meant being crazy, too. In retrospect, Marjorie says,

> I needed for my own sanity and survival, to get to the place where I could see that there was a difference between my mother and me. But I wanted it to be a very thin difference. I didn't want to lose what little mother I had.

The challenge of Marjorie's therapy was to help her to see her mother as a more defined and separate person. In the process, Marjorie would also define herself as separate, whole, and distinct. She recalls her first therapy session with Kay:

> I arrived an hour early and threw up in the Arby's next door. I was sitting in the waiting room, when finally a door opened and a very tall, very beautiful woman with longish dark hair and big dark eyes emerged. She said my name softly, "Marjorie?" She had only the briefest smile on her face. I noticed how gracefully, how slowly she walked into her office.

When Marjorie got inside Kay's office and looked around the room, she saw some familiar signs of comfort:

> Everything was the shape and color of a piano—the legs of the table and all the polished curved wood in the room. Her desk had curved legs, piano legs with little claw feet. She had notepads with a keyboard design at the top. Everything was

black and white. She must play the piano, I thought, but was afraid to ask. Maybe there was something we could talk about.

In the beginning, music was a way of getting at how I felt. I'd begin a session by telling Kay what piece I'd heard on the way to therapy and we'd imagine the piece together.

In her first session, Marjorie found a tenuous link between the good mother she had experienced through music and her therapist. Desperate for any sense of connection with Kay, for proof that therapy could help her, she took the piano motifs in Kay's office as a sign. Later, she and Kay experienced the familiar communion in music. There was a distinction, however: Rather than as a medium of nonverbal connection, Kay used music as a vehicle for delineating and naming feelings and for making distinctions among them. In a sense, she was performing the early caregiver's function of regulating, delineating, and naming the baby's internal states.

Marjorie began to feel close to Kay, who sometimes seemed in danger of becoming another phantom:

> On bad days, I wasn't even sure Kay existed. I thought maybe I had made her up like my little personal friend. After all, no one else I knew had ever seen her. I had a dream that I was with some friends and ran into Kay in public. She disguised herself as my travel agent and assumed a clipped British accent. That way I got to keep her all to myself.

Marjorie's mother had existed for so much of the time only in Marjorie's imagination that she wondered if Kay were not also something that she had conjured up. Conversely, Marjorie wasn't sure if she really wanted Kay to exist in the outside world; if Kay existed only for her, she could be hidden away and protected, as Marjorie had hidden away and protected the mother inside from her grandmother's critical eyes. But Marjorie also needed Kay to be real, their relationship more than a fantasy.

We've seen in several other stories how crucial the issue of the therapist's realness can become to clients. In Marjorie's therapy, questions about the realness of Kay occupied many sessions. Kay was reluctant to self-disclose or reveal much initially in the way of emotion. This reticence didn't make her seem any more real to Marjorie: "I struggled and struggled over becoming attached to Kay. I'd say, 'This isn't a real relationship. This doesn't occur in nature. Maybe you're only doing this because it's your job.'" During the early period of her therapy, Marjorie would have a strange experience before each session as she waited for Kay:

> For a long time, I never had a working watch because I hated knowing what time it was. So when I'd be waiting for my sessions, I'd be convinced that I'd gotten the wrong day and wrong hour. Until Kay opened the door, I was never quite sure. When she did, I'd breathe a sigh of relief.

Marjorie's childhood had a discontinuous quality, marked by inexplicable loss and return and the transformation of mother and grandmother. As an adult Marjorie felt as if she could not quite join the real, continuous, linear world. She resisted an awareness of time, perhaps because the passage of time had meant only loss, perhaps because its structure seemed foreign to her, perhaps because Marjorie half-preferred the timeless internal world of merger in her mother's music. Yet never knowing what time it was impaired her ability to function in the real world.

Marjorie's conviction before each session that she'd gotten the time wrong may have been one way in which she expressed her conflict about joining the real world. Each time Kay opened the door, she rescued Marjorie from her confusion, as if to say, "Yes, this is the right time, you are in the right place, you are the right one." If Marjorie could not bring herself to wear a watch, she also could not bear to ask Kay for reassurance directly. Without being asked, Kay let Marjorie know repeatedly that she belonged in the world, that she had a place with Kay, and that Kay was pleased to see her. Kay addressed what Kohut called a child's mirroring needs. A good parent lets a child know, over and over again, "You belong in this world and with me," and "I am happy you are here."

This is the message a toddler seeks every time she leaves mother's safe side and returns. "Look at me," she says. "Are you happy to have me back with you?" The mother, by her excitement and acceptance, says, "Yes. I am happy you are competent to go out and I am happy that you chose to come back." The child learns that she has the power to leave and come back, that mother is there to be returned to. Marjorie seldom had the luxury of this experience in childhood; if she dared to leave her mother's side, her mother might be gone or transformed by madness by the time Marjorie returned.

Soon Marjorie moved from asking Kay for reassurance indirectly by not wearing a watch into the realm of stating her feelings directly and working them through with Kay. Unlike Ariel, who could never bring herself to say what she really wanted from her therapists, Marjorie made the leap of faith and spoke the words:

> Kay always wanted me to feel something, to have a genuine emotion while I sat there with her. At first it was awful; my emotions would come and go right away. What was hardest for me was to be vulnerable in front of somebody, to let someone know I cared about something. My grandmother had taught me that if I showed that I cared about anything I wouldn't get to keep it.

At first Marjorie's feelings were as phantom-like as her mother. She had learned to turn them off quickly to protect her mother, to protect herself from her grandmother's wrath, and to stay intact. No one had ever shown her how to contain or regulate them for herself. At bedrock was grief for the childhood she had lost and the mother she would never have:

> When my mother died I was convinced that I would die too but I never grieved. I was scared the pain would be so great that it would kill me. When I would talk about my mother, Kay would say, "That's your reporter's voice—just the facts."
>
> I remember vividly the session where I began to grieve. I was learning to rely on Kay to begin the session and to end it. I was starting to see that we could get through something. I

questioned her endlessly about how we would get through things—"What if I start crying?" I'd ask. "What will you do?"

"What do you mean what will I do?" she'd ask.

"What if I can't stop?" I'd say.

"Can't stop *ever*?" she'd say.

"No, what if I can't stop in fifty minutes and then you'd have to call an ambulance to take me away."

"I'm here," she'd say. "This is what I know how to do."

When her mother died, Marjorie withdrew into her identification with her: "This means that I'll die too," she thought, as a defense against feeling the separation from her mother, which was now final. Before Marjorie could negotiate this final separation and experience her grief, she had to feel strong enough to survive it. At first, her grief threatened to make her disappear through the mother-hole at her center.

Marjorie had never had a parent to help her regulate her own feelings, to show her that they would start and end, that they would not permanently alter her, that they could be endured by another person, even the very person to whom they were directed. Kay acted as a regulator of feeling for Marjorie, reassuring her over and over again that her feelings could be safely contained in the therapy, that Kay knew how to work with them, that they would not destroy Marjorie, Kay, or the relationship growing between them.

As Marjorie began to experience Kay as predictable, stable, and consistent, as someone who could be trusted to start and stop the session and provide a predictable frame in which to be together, as someone who could traverse the darkness, she felt safer to explore the dangerous and unbounded within. Still, feelings had a disorganizing pull. In one session, Kay asked Marjorie to recount what she remembered most vividly about being with her mother.

I was remembering the time we lived with my mother when I was twelve. She was having another psychotic break from reality. The ambulance arrived with the sirens blaring and all the neighbors came out and my mother was running around the house naked. The attendants grabbed her and put a straitjacket on her and she was crying, "Marjy, help me! Help me! Don't let them take me away!"

By the time I'd recounted this story to Kay, I wasn't reporting anymore. I began to cry and the whole world fell apart. I was crying so hard and so long there wasn't anything but the sound of my own sobs. I didn't even know where I was; I had crawled into a fetal position in the chair. Then I heard Kay's voice saying, "Talk to me. Talk to me. . . ." She wanted me to share it with her. She was pulling me out.

"My heart is breaking," I said. She didn't want me to be alone with it, to go away with my sadness. She wanted me to share it with her.

Under the pressure of feeling, Marjorie's sense of a cohesive self dissolved. There was nothing but fragments, sensations, "the sound of my own sobs." Then the bond with Kay pulled Marjorie out of this disorganization. Kay's empathy, and her attempt to help Marjorie understand and verbalize her feelings, was an organizing experience.

It is an infant's mother who facilitates and regulates shifts in the baby's internal states. The mother feeds the baby and transforms hunger to satiety, puts the baby to bed and transforms fatigue to rest, picks up the baby and turns fear and panic at separation to succor and security. She also shares the infant's states, naming them, circumscribing them, and giving them a reality outside the self. She lets the child know that human beings are sad together, hungry together, sleepy together, and survive. Naming those states and not being alone with them reduces their disorganizing power.

It is mother who teaches us that there is a self that is the same regardless of the strong states it undergoes. A sick self is still the same self; a hungry self is still the same self; a sleepy self is still the same self. Infant research suggests that this continuity of experience, of selfhood, appears to be something that only fully develops through a consistent relationship with another person. While infants are likely to begin with an innate sense of self, intense feelings and traumatic experiences can shake this nascent self's security.

Winnicott contended that infants and young children, in the throes of intense and shifting physiological and psychological states, were prone to "unthinkable anxieties." According to Winnicott, they fear "(1)going to pieces; (2) having no relation to the body; (3) having no orientation; (4) falling forever; and (5) being completely isolated with no means of communication." This description may make infancy sound like a movie directed by David Lynch, and of course, a baby's experience of such extreme states of mind cannot be proved. But adults do experience similar fears in therapy. Whether an adult's "unthinkable anxieties" are reprises of infantile states or not, it is clear that they can be terrifying.

In the throes of grief, Marjorie experienced something akin to Winnicott's primitive fears of going to pieces, having no relation to her body, and becoming completely isolated with no means of communication. Marjorie had few memories of any caretaker helping her regulate or name internal states or of reassuring her that they were normal. She had never been able to rely on any parental figure to consistently transform distress or need into gratification or comfort. On the contrary, the expression of so simple a need as hunger or the impulse to defecate was apt to result in household chaos or her grandmother's transformation into rage.

Eventually, Marjorie experienced Kay inside, as a continuous, not fragmented, presence:

> Kay became my significant other. Of course, we never saw each other outside of therapy, but paradoxically it felt like the first real relationship I'd ever had with another person. Everything I did Kay was there, in my mind, in my heart. Every accomplishment she was there. Every conflict she was there.
>
> Whenever I think about my past now, I think of Kay. I'm not alone in it anymore. There was nowhere in me we couldn't go. . . . I loved her.

Marjorie internalized Kay as more than fleeting fragments of mother-comfort. Kay became the "other" to address in her head—the other that was always with her wherever she went, the other in relation to whom she could define herself. Unlike Marjorie's mother, whenever Kay left, she returned as promised. Some therapists might say that Marjorie achieved a new level of emotional object constancy when she could visualize where Kay was when she was gone and feel assured that she would come back. Marjorie learned what children with less difficult childhoods presumably learn during separation–individuation: how to bear the coming and going of mother and keep her intact and safe inside.

Three years into her therapy, Marjorie had a terrible nightmare. If she had begun to relish her own humanity, she still feared the power of her own needs and experienced primitive fears of disintegration. She saw the dream as the ultimate test of her relationship with Kay. Only several weeks after it occurred could Marjorie muster the courage to tell the dream to Kay:

> I was this deformed thing that had been born and all there was, was a big, gaping mouth. I was just a mouth, a hungry, hungry mouth. I was horrible, horrifying to look at. In this institution where I had been hatched, they didn't know what to do with me. They were going to just throw me away. Then this other sort of monster said it would take me and have sex with me until it was time to throw me away.

To Melanie Klein or a therapist influenced by Klein's theories, Marjorie's dream would suggest an infant's early oral experiences and fantasies. A Kleinian might interpret it as the dream of the hungry baby who fears her hunger is so big, so aggressive, and so limitless that it can swallow up mother and self. As an infant, Marjorie's hunger probably went unabated; that hunger may have seemed to comprise her whole being. Marjorie recalls spending much of her childhood hungry, unable to feel anything but the gnawing emptiness inside. She could only scheme and strategize to convince her psychotic grandmother—or anybody else she could find—to feed her. For Marjorie, the hungry mouth, the ruthlessness of appetite, was equated with the bad self: "I carried the belief that my desires, my hunger and sadness, were bad for the people I loved. If I could keep them in check, people would be okay and they would stay with me."

In telling Kay the dream Marjorie asked, "What am I?" According to Kohut, children have an innate developmental need not only for mirroring experiences but also for twinning experiences in which they recognize a reassuring resemblance between themselves and other people. The prototypical twinning experience is the child's performing an activity in tandem with an adult, often in silence. A little girl and her mother bake bread; the little girl kneads a small piece of dough while her mother kneads a larger piece beside her. Twinning experiences allow the child to feel that she is part of a world of like human beings, that her needs and feelings are normal and can be understood by others. If a woman did not have satisfactory twinning experiences in childhood, she may long for an unreasonable degree of resemblance between herself and her therapist and may fantasize about the two of them performing the same activities side by side. By asking, "Who am I? Am I normal?" Marjorie was expressing mirroring and twinning needs that had never been met in childhood.

Of course, Marjorie had had some twinning experiences with her mother. But to identify with her was to be crazy. Now she needed a twinning experience with someone who could help her join the world. When she told Kay the dream she needed to hear what a child needs to hear in response to her mirroring and twinning needs: "You are my child and I love you. You are made of the same stuff as me."

Marjorie feared that Kay would say something else:

> The risk was that Kay would say, the monsters in the dream are right, that is what you are—a horrifying, deformed thing. When I told her the dream, Kay cried. It was with great restraint, but she cried for me. Her tears told me, "No, you're not this horrible, deformed thing. You're human—just like me."

By her tears, Kay showed Marjorie the normal human response to her dream, to her childhood. There are situations in therapy in which a therapist's tears might be out of place, in which they might interfere with the primacy of the client's needs and thus constitute a boundary crossing. In this instance, the therapist's tears sealed the bond of humanity between Marjorie and Kay. They made Kay's empathy palpable. They satisfied Marjorie's mirroring and twinning needs. As Marjorie found herself empathizing with Kay's sorrow, she developed a new empathy for herself. Her "marginalized" childhood, her appetites that had seemed monstrous, came into human perspective.

As Marjorie acknowledged the true impact of her childhood, she struggled to understand finally who her mother had been and to picture where she had been during her long disappearances. Marjorie obtained twenty years of her mother's medical records from the state mental hospital. For weeks the records sat in a pile on the floor between Marjorie and Kay during Marjorie's sessions. They were proof that Marjorie's mother had existed during her absences, had existed outside of Marjorie's fantasies, but Marjorie was too afraid to look at them. When she was finally ready, she and Kay read them together.

Marjorie began to grasp the extent of her mother's mental illness and to recognize that no matter how quiet a child she had been, no matter how minimal her appetites, she could not have saved her mother from psychosis.

The final challenge for the therapeutic relationship came when Kay moved her office. She was only moving two floors up in the same building but because of the multiple dislocations of her childhood, Marjorie dreaded moving. Nevertheless, in her adult life before therapy she had moved thirty times. Apparently, she had been trying to work through her conflict and pain about moving by reenacting. One move when Marjorie was a teenager had been particularly traumatic:

> The day of the move was the first time I had been alone with my mother since early childhood. I was so happy. We were at the old place waiting for my sisters and stepfather to take a load over to the new house. My mother brought her chair into the middle of the living room, and she was sitting with her feet together and her hands on her lap. She was sitting up very straight, her back straight as an arrow, very still. She started to stare off into space. "Mom, are you okay?" I said. She started babbling nonsense.

After all this time of praying to God to give my mother back to me, here she was and I was afraid of her.

Marjorie feared that she and Kay would not survive the move, that an external change would catastrophically alter the internal terrain. Moving had always meant to Marjorie that "someone was going to disappear and that I didn't know who I might end up with."

Kay and Marjorie made the most of the move therapeutically. Some therapists might have been too quick to minimize Marjorie's reaction or to reassure her by immediately putting the move into its realistic perspective. Kay worked with the deeper, symbolic meaning of the move in which two flights up could mean disappearing forever.

At the same time, Kay addressed Marjorie as an adult and reinforced her adult coping skills: "Kay treated me as if I were tender but not fragile. She walked that thin line with me really well." When Marjorie arrived at Kay's new office for the first time she was bearing a gift. It was a bonsai tree that was exactly the same age as their relationship. When Kay opened the door, she looked pleased and set the tree down on the table next to her. The next time Marjorie came to therapy, the tree was still there. Marjorie recalls how good it felt to see the tree in its place:

> It felt magical that she would actually let something of me stay with her. I asked her if it was really true that she kept it there every day because I was afraid to find out that she kept the tree in the back and only pulled it out when I came in.
>
> Kay looked at me like I was crazy. "What are you saying?" she asked.
>
> "Well, you don't leave it here all the time, do you?"
>
> "Marjorie, the tree has been in its place since the day you brought it. Why would I lie to you?"
>
> Why would she lie to me? I thought. A light went on in my head; the four years of our relationship passed before my eyes. Was it possible she had always been telling me the truth, always truly been there, not just doing her job? I separated Kay from all the people I had ever known whose motivation I'd had

to rationalize or excuse or explain. She was telling me the truth. All the time that I'd been with her I suddenly *got*. I had actually been with her all that time; she had actually been with me all that time.

All those years in therapy, I'd been lonely. Not as lonely as before but still lonely. Suddenly I wasn't lonely anymore. Kay had been there with me all along.

The bonsai tree represented Marjorie's relationship with Kay. In giving the tree to Kay, Marjorie was saying, "Take me with you when you go somewhere; don't leave me." It was the same message that Marjorie tried to give her mother so many times. Having a mother who disappeared without warning, who was mentally inconsistent, not only meant that Marjorie had difficulty internalizing her, but also that Marjorie never felt that her mother had internalized her.

Perhaps part of what allows a child to internalize the mother, to achieve emotional object constancy, is knowing that the mother is holding her inside; is thinking about her in her absence, is imagining what she is doing while she is away at school or playing at a friend's. Being held in the encompassing mind of the mother is in some ways indistinguishable from being held in the mother's surrounding arms. Knowing that the mother is holding her inside allows the child to hold the mother inside. But one cannot be held safely in a mind that keeps disintegrating. By keeping the tree in her office, Kay let Marjorie know that she was holding her in mind, even when they were not together.

The bonsai tree was proof that her relationship with Kay happened in the world, not in Marjorie's head. Kay was not a secret travel agent—she and Marjorie were traveling in the larger world together.

Kay might have done Marjorie some damage if she had considered all gifts boundary violations and refused the tree. On the other hand, a therapist who just accepted it as a nice housewarming present without appreciating its symbolic significance might have also done Marjorie an injustice.

In her moment of epiphany, Marjorie had what some therapists call a "new experience." If her expectations and assumptions (Kay will lie to me and keep the tree in the back, deceiving me by only bringing it out for my benefit) were based on the past, her epiphany was based on a new experience with Kay. Marjorie realized that the other in a relationship need not always disappear or break apart under the weight of love.

Today Marjorie considers her therapy a great success:

> For me, therapy worked. It changed my life. I learned that I have losses and they are real losses and they are gone forever. I will always be sad about them. But I don't have to relive them over and over again. Kay gave me back my mother by letting me miss her. I don't have to look for her in every relationship because I know that she's gone. But as long as I'm here with me . . . gee, that's something.
>
> I play the songs my mother played on the piano and my hands on the piano look just like her hands. It's a way of feeling myself holding myself, and of not being alone.
>
> Sadness is human; it's something I can allow myself to experience. I did not grow up in my family. I only stayed alive. I grew up in therapy.

In therapy, Marjorie lost the phantom mother of fragments and fantasy and gained a better understanding of who her mother really had been in the world. Then she was able to grieve her. As a result of her bond with Kay, Marjorie internalized a more substantial other and built a more consistent, reliable self. After five years of therapy, Marjorie was able to make part of her living as a pianist. She still felt more comfortable living alone and loving another from afar than she did in an intimate relationship.

Kay never made the mistake of attempting to become a substitute mother to Marjorie. But she did provide resonances of motherliness that, some therapists would argue, allowed Marjorie to complete a developmental process stalled in childhood.

# 9

# I'm in Love with My Therapist

Since Anna O., a woman's falling in love with her therapist has seemed so common an event as to constitute a cliché. But how much do therapists really know about why this happens and what a woman in love with her therapist should do? After observing Anna O., and then a succession of his own patients declare their love, Freud came to believe that a woman's becoming smitten with her analyst was not only usual but de rigueur for successful treatment. The patient had to express her unresolved oedipal conflict in her transference if she was ever to work it through in her analysis.

One of Freud's famous patients in the 1930s was poet Hilda Doolittle (known as H. D.), who referred to Freud fondly as the "Professor." In the memoir she wrote about her treatment, she recounted this episode in which she unknowingly refused to comply with this tenet of Freudian theory. H. D. was forty-eight, Freud was seventy-seven and approaching the end of his career:

> The Professor . . . is beating with his hand, with his fist, on the head-piece of the old-fashioned horsehair sofa. . . . I was not aware of having said anything that might account for the Professor's outburst. And even as I veered around, facing him, my mind was detached enough to wonder if this was some idea of his for speeding up the analytic content or redirecting the flow

of associated images. The Professor said, "The trouble is—I am an old man—you do not think it worth your while to love me."

Not only did Freud think it necessary for his patients to fall in love with him, when one did not, he became enraged. Few, if any, therapists today, even psychoanalysts, would say categorically that a client's falling in love is prerequisite to good therapy, or that it is always an expression of oedipal issues. But they have not reached any alternate consensus about the role of romantic love and sexual attraction in psychotherapy.

Women in therapy, particularly women who have experienced any glimmering of therapy-love, have questions for which the professional literature does not have answers. When does romantic love hinder and when does it advance the therapy? If a woman is in love with her therapist, should she leave the treatment or stick it out in hopes of resolving her feelings and learning something from them?

The profession has collected no statistics on the incidence of love in therapy. Under pressure to rein in the behavior of sexually transgressing therapists, researchers have begun to collect data on the prevalence of sexual relations between therapists and clients, and there are a few studies on therapists' sexual attraction to their clients. But no one has looked in any systematic way at clients' romantic or erotic feelings for their therapists or, for that matter, at the full spectrum of loving feelings in psychotherapy. No one can say for sure whether romantic love occurs more often with some therapists or in some sorts of therapy, and there is only a little information available on how well most therapists manage love in therapy.

I asked the women I surveyed if they had ever felt feelings of love, attachment, or dependency for any therapist and gave them the opportunity to describe those feelings. I also asked them to recount any erotic dreams or fantasies they had ever had about a therapist. The majority of women who completed only my written questionnaire did not report having ever fallen in love with a therapist. Instead, they reported a range of fond feelings—attachment, connection, warmth, affection, and gratitude. Respondents took great care to discriminate fraternal and platonic forms of love from erotic demands, which tended to be more distressing. As Mandy wrote,

"The admiration I have for my therapist has bordered on infatuation, and I feel *uncomfortable* about that."

When I interviewed women in greater depth, something curious happened: A far greater percentage confessed to having had romantic or sexual feelings for some therapist at some time in their lives. Often they denied having such feelings for their current practitioner, placing them in a closer-to-adolescence past. Charlotte said, "When I was younger, I was definitely in love with one therapist who was so kind and loving that I wanted to curl up in his lap and stay there for good." Jean reported, "I fell in love with my first therapist when I was twenty-three. . . . My pattern was to be a seductive little girl type. I had a compulsive need to keep offering myself. Fortunately, my ethical male therapists did not exploit it."

My respondents knew that falling in love with one's therapist was a cliché, and when it happened they were chagrined and felt out of control. They wrestled with the notion of transference—perhaps it made sense as an intellectual abstraction, but on an emotional level, their love felt genuine.

On my questionnaire, I asked only *if* a woman had ever had a romantic fantasy or dream and made no attempt to measure the intensity of a woman's sexual or erotic feelings or their overall impact on her therapy or her life. Of course, there is a significant difference between a woman who occasionally imagines what her therapist might be like in bed and the woman who becomes obsessed with getting her therapist there. Fleeting sexual fantasies were reported far more commonly than was obsessive love.

More than half of the women (148) denied ever having had a sexual fantasy or dream about a therapist. In fact, some of my respondents described the conscious efforts they went through to "desexualize" their feelings to avoid the humiliation of unrequitable longings. As Danielle reported, "I made an effort *not* to fall in love with her. It seemed useless to let myself slip into that mode." Shelly also resisted:

> I knew about this sexual transference thing going into it and perceived it as something that was almost inevitable, and I didn't want to do the thing that everybody else does. When I saw what

he looked like, I went, Oh, no. Here we go! Because so much of the power in therapy was his, the idea of getting some of the power back by getting him to want me was appealing.

## Romantic Fantasies

The romantic fantasies women told me about their therapists share some common elements. They often focus on the moment of reciprocation, the instant when the therapist declares his love. These fantasies isolate that electrified instant when the relationship shifts from being therapeutic to romantic, when the therapist kisses—touches—enters—the woman for the first time. The therapist's verbal declaration of love is also very significant for some women. In other fantasies eroticism is enhanced by the absence of words; the therapist silently rushes across the room and takes the woman into his or her arms, unable to bear her leaving at the end of her session.

The therapist's office was usually the setting for at least the first fantasied romantic encounter. When clients imagined the relationship progressing beyond the office, it seldom simply moved into the client's currently mundane world. Instead, the romance often had an idealized quality. As Tania described, "We go off to different countries in Europe. We eat, drink, he brings me flowers—it's very nice."

If some women resisted having sexual fantasies, at least one woman consciously attempted to have them, having heard that such feelings were a requisite part of successful therapy. Angela wrote, "I tried to have a sexual fantasy about my therapist once, but I couldn't do it. He is short, has a beard and mustache, and reminds me of Jiminy Cricket, the voice of conscience."

In my admittedly small sample, lesbians seemed more likely to admit to sexual fantasies than were heterosexual women. It was more usual for a heterosexual woman to have sexual fantasies for a female therapist than for a lesbian to fantasize about a man, but with only a handful of lesbians in my survey in therapy with male therapists, it's impossible to draw any conclusions.

Knowing or suspecting that her male therapist was homosexual precluded sexual heterosexual women in my sample from fantasizing sexually about their therapists. Perhaps a woman has to feel capable of evoking desire in the other before developing full-blown desire of her own. Perhaps those therapists identified as gay simply didn't communicate the subtle cues—verbal and nonverbal, conscious and unconscious—that passed between some clients and their heterosexual therapists to spur sexual attraction. I wouldn't presume to reach any conclusions, but the finding is provocative. Knowing that a therapist was married or in a committed relationship did not seem to prevent women from fantasizing, but knowing that a therapist was single and looking sometimes served as an added inducement.

When a woman's therapist was less physically attractive or was clearly an unsuitable partner (many years older, for example), like Dr. Jiminy Cricket, a woman might find it easier to attribute her romantic feelings to some irrational, therapy-specific phenomenon, like transference. After all, she knew she would never find Dr. Cricket attractive in any other setting. Perhaps women have the most trouble making sense of their feelings when their therapists are men they would find attractive in any context. Lara, a twenty-eight-year-old anthropology student and lover of opera whose story is told later in this chapter, felt that her therapist Dr. D. was "just too good-looking to be in this business." When a woman's therapist looks more like Tom Cruise than Jiminy Cricket, it's a little harder to chalk up her arousal to transference.

The most important finding of my research was that many women did not feel that they could discuss their romantic and sexual feelings for their therapists freely in their therapy. Ironically, women enter therapy with the hope of being able to confide all, and then, as for Anna O., one hundred years ago, their feelings for their therapists become the biggest secret of the therapy. As Sharon said,

> I fell in love with C. I wanted to seduce her. This was a mystery to me because I was in a long-term relationship. I wish C. had told me that my sexual desire was a natural part of transference. I think that would have helped.

And Alexis wrote, "I felt a kind of tormented need mixed with attraction. I was devastated when we could not deal with those feelings in therapy."

Those women who were able to discuss their romantic feelings openly with their therapists were usually grateful for the experience. As Marilyn wrote, "Barb let me love her but never used me. We openly dealt with my feelings of attraction to her." And Elena described what it was like to fall in love with one therapist after another: "I fell in love with all three of my therapists and this was very painful over many years. I finally worked it through with the last one." In many cases, however, a woman never worked through her romantic feelings for her therapist with any sense of neat closure. But at least among the women I interviewed, when romantic feelings were empathically addressed within the therapy, when the therapist did not become too invested in being loved or give out mixed signals, romantic and sexual feelings did not become obsessive and destructive. That is not to say that a woman could not become sexually obsessed with a therapist who did everything right in terms of handling her feelings, but it would seem that a therapist's mishandling a woman's feelings vastly increases her risk of getting stuck.

## Other Kinds of Love

Less sexualized forms of love may flourish in therapy without overt declaration, the word "love" never spoken. With these forms of love, a woman may long for reciprocation, but reciprocation does not become the overriding concern of her therapy. The conventional wisdom among therapists seems to be that they should leave this "positive transference" alone because it contributes to the bond and motivates the client to succeed in her therapy. Without using the word "love" a skillful therapist may be able to communicate empathy and acknowledge the client's loving feelings indirectly.

Myra, a twenty-four-year-old education student, was recounting her experiences as a nursery school student teacher to her analyst. Suddenly, she began to hear Barney the Dinosaur's theme song playing in her head—"I love you, you love me, we're a happy family." Myra recalls,     .

> I started chattering about the Barney song and asking my analyst if he knew the words. He said, "Why don't you sing it for me?" I definitely love my analyst, but I never would tell him that right out. I muttered that he should ask the first four-year-old he ran into and changed the subject.

The analyst's gentle response suggests that he may well have perceived Myra's intention, without her having had to sing the words to the song. In another example, Mildred, a sociology professor in her sixties, was smitten by her therapist, Anne. Week after week, she noticed that Anne had a beautiful floral arrangement in her office. Mildred grew roses. Mildred remembers a day about a year into her therapy:

> I look back on this and think that I must have been insane. I brought her enough roses to fill twenty therapists' offices—red roses, yellow roses, coral roses, white roses—she opened the door and there I was, my arms overflowing with roses.

Initially Anne was rattled, one of the few times that Mildred ever saw her seem less than self-possessed. Then she and Mildred went to work, side by side, finding vases, cutting stems, and getting the roses into water. Mildred goes on, "I never used the word 'love' that day, I didn't have to. This was so obvious a display of my affection." Anne never used the word either, but in the care she took with Mildred's roses, she acknowledged and accepted Mildred's love.

## Lara's Story, Part I: The Most Intense Love

A woman may declare her love in words, only when its demands have come to compete with the mission of the therapy. Lara arrived at just such an impasse.

An unusually beautiful woman, tall with a strong body, Lara attracts everyone's eyes when she enters a room. Her gestures are

dramatic and she has a cultivated, melodic voice. Lara entered therapy because of recurrent bouts of depression and disappointing romantic relationships. Now, to make matters worse, Lara has fallen
madly in love with Dr. D. "I am in love, and my feelings are more
intense than in any other romantic relationship I've ever had," she
tells me. She behaves as any woman who has just fallen in love
might, doing the "foolish things you'd expect of a teenager." She has
lingered beside Dr. D.'s car in the underground garage, memorizing
its license plate. She has made excuses to frequent stores in his part
of town, hoping for and dreading the moment that he might appear.
What she wants is not so much to see him as for him to see her, to
be imprinted somehow on his "other," extra-therapeutic life. For
Lara sometimes it seems as if her love is more real than the artifi-
cially drawn therapeutic boundaries that seem to be the only things
standing in its way.

The object of Lara's affections, Dr. D., is about twenty-five years
older than she. Influenced by the Gestalt and humanistic approaches
that were popular at the time he began his career in the 1970s, Dr.
D. appears to place a high value on the "real relationship" and on
the therapist's authenticity. He has been engaged and steadfast during the course of Lara's therapy, seemingly committed to helping her.

When a few months into her therapy, Lara first realized that she
was feeling attracted to Dr. D., she tried to play by the therapeutic
rules by telling him about her feelings. She explained that she was
"going through too much of a ritual in preparing to see him." It had
become too important to her that he find her attractive. Dr. D. responded by reassuring her that her feelings were normal and commonly occurred in therapy. He attributed them to transference: "He
made it quite clear that my feelings were about my father," Lara says.
Dr. D.'s explanation, of course, goes all the way back to Anna O.
According to Freud, the analyst was a stand-in for the father, and
transference-love was an unconscious remnant of an unresolved
oedipal conflict.

The professional literature continues to discuss erotic feelings in
therapy largely in terms of this psychoanalytic theory of transference. Even non-psychoanalytically oriented therapists resort to the

oedipal equivalence when confronted by their clients' romantic or erotic feelings. Over and over again, women told me that their therapists responded to their declarations of love with these words: "It's transference"; "It's about your father"; "It's oedipal." They sometimes sounded as though they were holding garlic up in the face of a ravenous vampire, as if they expected the mere uttering of the word "transference" to magically dissolve their clients' love. Perhaps they hoped that at the least it would protect them from having to discuss it any further. Once many therapists made this oedipal equivalence, they didn't seem to know where to go from there. They didn't know how to make this equivalence emotionally credible or personal. They didn't seem to know how to explain a woman's feelings any further or to help her understand them in a way that might lessen their painfulness.

Relabeling Lara's feelings as transference did little to dispel them. It has led her to conduct an ongoing debate in her own mind between what I like to call the "transference" and the "true love" hypotheses. Behind the debate, two mythos compete for her allegiance: the mythos of love and the mythos of transference. The mythos of love upon which women are raised teaches that love is irreducible, inarguable, a force of nature requiring action. Love belongs to the particular, special object who inspires it—there is no one else. The mythos of transference teaches that therapy-love is a product of earlier experiences, a phenomenon that can be dissected; it isn't really about the therapist, it's about earlier bonds projected onto the therapist. Lara finds herself stuck and torn between these two poles: Either her feelings are true love, irreducible, fated, irrevocable and Dr. D. is her soul mate; or her feelings are transference, a means to understanding the past perhaps, but also an illusion not to be pursued.

Lara describes her dilemma:

When I ask myself why I find Dr. D. so very attractive, I think, oh, the transference, but it's confusing. He has thick wavy black hair, a large firm jaw, green eyes, and a big, bright smile. Oh, that smile. If I were walking down the street and saw Dr. D. I would still be taken aback by how attractive he is. . . . To call my feelings transference seems somehow artificial.

From the first time Lara saw Dr. D., she felt "a kind of physical rhyming." He seemed her match, familiar somehow. "Oh, it's you," she remembers saying, only half out loud, feeling as if she had known him all her life. In the mythos of love, this feeling suggests a fated link. And if she and Dr. D. are really fated to be together, she wonders, should the mere fact that she met him as her therapist stand in their way? In the mythos of transference, of course, Dr. D.'s familiarity might suggest that Dr. D. has some resemblance to Lara's father or other family members, that he is enough like them to stimulate old feelings of love and longing.

Even Freud struggled with therapy-love and acknowledged that it was a complicated phenomenon. Although he made a strong case for treating romantic love in therapy as unreal, he also argued with his own depiction. Wasn't transference an inextricable element of all romantic love? Wasn't falling in love always partly remembering our first and most powerful loves? Didn't illusion always play a part in attraction? Nevertheless, Freud concluded that love in therapy was based more on fantasy than love in other settings and that for the sake of the therapeutic process, it had to be treated as something to be understood, not something to be acted upon.

Struggling to believe in the transference hypothesis, Lara looks for the connections between Dr. D. and her father, between her significant childhood relationships and what goes on in the room with Dr. D. These connections remain murky. Belief in love comes more readily. Years of cultural training have taught Lara that love, especially romantic love, is too precious and rare to waste, that the love of a powerful man offers the ultimate fulfillment, that love is curative in and of itself, and that the very capacity to sustain love is proof of a woman's mental health. So if she can love Dr. D. and he can love her back, she will not even *need* to be in therapy.

What distinguishes Lara, a woman in love with her therapist, from any other woman in love is that the particular rules of the therapeutic relationship place her in danger of becoming stuck—suspended at the moment of falling in love indefinitely. She is unable to collect the necessary information—by dating Dr. D., learning about his past and present life, seeing him in diverse situations—that would either erode her love or allow it to develop into a more balanced and mutual attachment. Instead, she sees him only during rationed and expensive segments of time during which their connection is emotionally wrought and the very air in the room thick with meaning.

In real life a woman in love with a man who does not reciprocate eventually finds the strength to move on. But a woman in love with her therapist is likely to receive mixed signals. After all, he is concerned and kind and completely focused on her during sessions. He does care. And yet she does not see him in between sessions, and seeing him requires an outlay of cash. The therapist seems to be saying both: I am here completely for you and I am completely unavailable to you in any real life sense. A woman in love with her therapist may feel that she can only resolve the situation by determining how the therapist *really* feels and so can become obsessed with seeking out the signs of true love that lurk beneath the therapist's clinical demeanor.

Despite the intimacy that occurs during sessions, a woman who loves her therapist is always loving from afar. It is like having a crush on a movie star or rock singer. The words her idol sings may be tender and a woman can imagine that they are directed at her alone, but in reality the star is unreachable, his or her offstage life a mystery.

To resolve her impasse, a woman in love with her therapist may attempt to collect enough evidence about the therapist's life outside of the consulting room to determine if she would still be in love if she knew her therapist better. She hopes that a larger dose of reality might break the transference spell. Lara laughs, "If I knew that Dr. D. listened to Donna Summer records or spent his weekends mowing the lawn in polyester madras shorts, it would be over quickly." A woman in love with her therapist may be cagey in sessions, torn between the therapeutic requirement to be honest and her interest in remaining lovable.

There is one maddening question that a woman in love with her therapist feels that she must resolve and that she cannot resolve: Is the only thing keeping us apart the artifice of the therapeutic relationship, or is it only the artifice of the therapeutic relationship that is making me want my therapist in the first place?

Lara asks herself this question time and time again. She wonders if the very nature of the therapeutic relationship is not a set-up inducing her to fall in love and then ensuring that her love can never be satisfied. In her worst fears, Dr. D. is a sadist who takes pleasure in getting her to love him and then refusing to satisfy her love:

> My feelings range from intense sexual attraction, adoration, awe, affection, to shame, anger, confusion, hurt, dependency. To feel so many strong things for someone who is, by definition, out of reach, who encourages you to feel these feelings but plans from the beginning to frustrate you, is like having your heart professionally broken.

## A Desire-Inducing Machine

Is Lara right that therapy is a way of having your heart professionally broken? The very tension between the seeming intimacy of the therapist–client bond and the restrictions imposed on it can serve as an excruciating trigger of desire. This is the very same tension that drives Edith Wharton's novels, such as *The Age of Innocence*, in which society's oppressive and rarefied rules are always about to explode with the passion seething below the surface. And of course it is the oppressive and rarefied rules that heat the passion up.

It is no accident that much soft-core pornography traditionally has been set in staid institutional surroundings where there is a prohibition against the free expression of desire. One typical plot takes place in a library. The librarian, tired of a lifetime of whispering, flings off her glasses, her inhibitions, and her blouse in one fell swoop. She wraps herself around the shy professor, liberating herself from the boundaries of the institution and of herself in a glorious, heart-pounding sexual act.

The therapist's office is such a library—marked by freedom and bounded by restriction. There is a built-in tug between the act of verbal self-revelation, emotional exposure, and the limitations placed on the relationship. There is an inherent disproportion between the client's vulnerability and the therapist's power, between the longings the client inevitably feels and the therapist's refusal to gratify them.

Desire is fueled by obstacles. As sexologist Jack Morin writes in *The Erotic Mind*, "attraction + obstacles = excitement." The mythos of love also teaches that true love must overcome obstacles. Princes cut their way through forests, kill rivals, buck prohibitions to win love. The beloved's own resistance is often greater than that of any external force—sometimes the lover must be seduced and coaxed, made aware of his or her own repressed feelings—and taught *how* to love.

In their essay on the hidden codes of romance, Linda Barlow and Jane Ann Krentz, authors of numerous successful romance novels, endorse these observations. They found that the plot lines of the most popular romance novels "place a woman at risk with a powerful, enigmatic male. Her future happiness and his depends on her ability to teach him *how* to love." This plot line sounds a lot like the traditional client–therapist relationship: The therapist is powerful, enigmatic, and reticent to express feeling. The very boundaries of therapy, the therapist's very restraint in the room, may make it seem as if he or she simply needs to be taught how to love. A woman in therapy can become confused between the "plot line" of therapy, with its ambiguous notion of "cure," and that of romance, with its conviction that "love cures all."

## Conditions for Love

In the 1970s social psychologist Dorothy Tennov studied romantic love to delineate its inner workings. She found that certain conditions could produce obsessive, tortuous love, which she called "limerance" to differentiate it from more realized and mutual forms of love. Tennov found that obsessive love is most likely to occur when obstacles or prohibitions stand in the way of consummation. These obstacles may be worldly impediments—social class differences (as in Emily Brontë's classic romance *Wuthering Heights* and, more recently, in the film *Titanic*) family feuds (as in Shakespeare's

*Romeo and Juliet*), geographic distance, an existing but loveless marriage, or psychological resistances.

The potential lover himself may offer the most formidable obstacle, as did, for example, Mr. Rochester, the enigmatic and imposing patriarch of Charlotte Brontë's classic Gothic novel *Jane Eyre*. If the love object responds ambiguously with some signs of encouragement and others of disinterest, as the always-brooding Mr. Rochester did, that is also likely to fuel limerance and keep the would-be lover suspended between hope and despair. That was how Jane Eyre found herself, wondering what she had to do to be worthy of Mr. Rochester's love, intimidated (and excited) by his wealth and social standing, frightened (and excited) by his moodiness and unpredictable behavior.

And yet whenever Jane was about to give up, Mr. Rochester would do something to suggest that they were twins and that he had the power to see directly into her soul. A competitor lurking in the wings can also fuel limerance. Jane Eyre had to contend with two, a rival girlfriend and Mr. Rochester's mad wife locked away in the attic.

*The Thornbirds*, a best-selling historical romance of the 1970s, also follows a similar pattern. Father Ralph is powerful (a Cardinal by the end of the book), enigmatic, and resistant. This is not to say he is not drawn to Meggie's love; the problem is that he has a higher calling—God and the Catholic Church. The fact that Meggie's charms are great enough to compel him to turn away from God from time to time is testament to her lovableness and to the greater power of romantic love.

The plot of *The Thornbirds* also resembles the dynamics of romantic love in psychotherapy. The therapist is a father figure with a higher calling. To express romantic love for his client, he must break the vow of abstinence he has made to his profession. To a client, the fact that her therapist would risk his life's work and reputation for love may constitute ultimate proof of her desirability.

According to Tennov, the victim of limerance becomes obsessed with fantasies of the moment of reciprocation, when the loved one declares that yes, despite any evidence to the contrary, he or she loves too. She may hope against hope for this moment, search out subtle signs of hidden love, may even rationalize that the lover's overt rejections signify only that the love object is afraid of love or does not know his or her own mind.

Tennov sees the psychotherapeutic relationship as providing a rich milieu for the development of this sort of obsessive, unrequitable love. She writes, "[T]he very nature of the situation provides both obstacles and a rationalization for his [the therapist's] reluctance to admit any positive feelings he may have for a patient." It also provides a wealth of unseen competitors—the therapist's other clients.

The psychoanalyst, of course, might respond to Tennov by saying that those conditions she's identified as breeding unrequited love do so precisely because they re-create the original oedipal situation. The parent is the most powerful, the most enigmatic, figure in a child's life. The child can never get the exclusive love from the parent that she craves. The beloved parent puts out equivocal signals: "I love you completely but maybe not in the way that you wish to be loved; I also love Mommy, and that love may have particular pleasures with which your love cannot compete."

Whether oedipal dynamics are always behind Tennov's conditions for obsessive love is an unprovable hypothesis. It is certainly not that difficult to see resonances between the oedipal situation and many classic love stories. And the conditions that Tennov sees as capable of obsessive love certainly exist in the psychotherapy relationship.

There are ample reasons why a woman in psychotherapy might give herself over to love rather than to the more problematic connection of psychotherapy. Love seems to promise a surer, quicker, more pleasurable road to health and happiness than the rigors of treatment. When a woman enters therapy partly because of difficulties in loving and being loved, there is a certain logic and efficiency in bypassing the middleman and believing that the solution lies in securing the therapist's love. "If the arbiter of mental health loves me," she may think, "I must be okay; if the one who knows me better than anyone else loves me, I must be supremely lovable."

The therapist can become the repository for all a woman's wishes and hopes about love—the ideal love that would satisfy all her needs, the love she has been deprived of all her life. The therapist can come to represent the Über-Lover, the culmination of her personal love story. The woman imagines that the relationship with her therapist will be different from her previous failed romantic relationships; the therapist's understanding of her psychological issues will provide insurance against those very problems that have plagued her in the past.

Transforming therapist into lover has the added benefit of correcting all that is frustrating and tragic about the therapeutic relationship: its price, its boundaries, and the fact that it must end. In women's fantasies of turning their therapists into lovers, the couple does not necessarily stop performing the process of self-examination that is psychotherapy. Quite the contrary—they may get to engage in the process all the time without the troublesome boundaries and without the woman ever having to pay for it.

There seem to be ample reasons why therapy can serve as a desire-inducing, fulfillment-frustrating machine. This was certainly the case for Lara. Let's leave her for the time being, suspended at the moment of falling madly in love with Dr. D., and consider the case of Hannah, for whom therapy also became a way of having her heart professionally broken.

## Hannah's Story: Return to Sender

At first glance, Hannah's is not the typical therapy love story. She was sixty-five and recently retired from a long career as a successful school principal. She had lost her loving and supportive husband of thirty-five years to cancer a few years previously, and then when Hannah's mother died as well, she fell into despair. Feeling isolated and lonely, she sought a therapist with whom she would have something in common. She looked for someone close to her own age, who was married or had been married, who also had grown children, someone who would understand Hannah's life experience without her having to explain too much.

Hannah had not experienced homoerotic feelings since college, when she'd had a crush on another student. Her story exemplifies just how mysterious the combination of factors may be that conspire to create romantic love in therapy. Take the unique set-up of the therapeutic relationship, Hannah's childhood vulnerabilities, and the grief over losing her mother and combine them with the style and demeanor of Hannah's therapist Eve, and you have a recipe for love. Eve's rejecting response to Hannah's love worsened the situation.

Eve fit Hannah's initial requirements for a therapist. She was within a few years of Hannah's age and when asked, disclosed that she had been married and had grown children. Hannah recalls the first six months of her therapy with Eve as rather uneventful. Hannah sometimes felt that she had to keep Eve amused with anecdotes to hold her attention. Although Hannah is hesitant to describe Eve as cold, there was something detached about her style, some emotional distance that Hannah could never bridge.

About six months into therapy, Eve issued what Hannah perceived as an invitation:

> I remember the day that she said it. She thought I had some deeper problems that she could help me with, and she wanted me to think about her and my feelings about her, and tell her everything that I felt and thought.

It sounds as if Eve was ready to use her relationship with Hannah in the therapy, as if she were encouraging Hannah to focus on her transference. Ever the good student, Hannah began to ruminate about Eve, to carry her image around with her in her head, and to keep a running narrative of the events of her daily life for Eve. "Eve invited me to think about the relationship with her and so I did—obsessively," Hannah recalls. Almost imperceptibly, Hannah moved from preoccupation with her therapy to romantic obsession with her therapist. Hannah soon had to admit that she had "fallen in love" with Eve. "It was like a teenage crush at age sixty-five," Hannah recalls. "It was a terrible, terrible experience, feeling trapped in my obsession with her."

What she longed for most in the face of her love was "a show of tenderness," a mere empathic gesture short of reciprocation. Hannah would fantasize about Eve simply reaching across the room to touch her hand during a session.

Between sessions Hannah took to driving past Eve's house to catch a glimpse of her and to feel a part of her other, "secret" life. Eve was often out tending her garden, oblivious to Hannah's presence. Hannah would admire Eve's garden and then feel like a guilty trespasser; the garden belonged to Eve and Hannah was unwelcome there.

Although Eve had initially invited Hannah to think more about their relationship, she seemed totally unprepared to deal with the onslaught of emotion she had unleashed. When Hannah told Eve about driving to her house and feeling guilty for looking at her garden, Eve became even more remote. The more intense feelings Hannah expressed toward Eve, the more Hannah seemed to want from her, the less Eve seemed capable of empathizing with her. The more Eve withdrew, the more lonely Hannah felt, the more desperately she tried to solicit Eve's tenderness and empathy. Hannah wished that Eve could simply acknowledge that she and Hannah were alike in some essential way, that Eve was no stranger to the emotions Hannah described. One image came to represent validation in Hannah's mind: walking arm-in-arm through a garden with Eve when the magnolias were in bloom and the air was crisp, silently appreciating their moments together. Hannah's love was marked by this hunger for twinning, for an experience in which she was so certain that she and her female companion were feeling the same way that they did not have to speak at all.

While out of town on vacation, Hannah sent Eve a "love letter." She hoped that the letter might touch Eve, and she expected that when she came back for her next session that the letter would serve as a point of departure for a conversation about her own feelings. Hannah had been reading about transference in the professional literature and was willing to explore her feelings in this context.

Instead, when Hannah got back into town, Eve simply handed the letter back to her and said, "I suppose you're sorry you wrote this." "Oh, but I hadn't been," Hannah recalls. She had been glad that after so much loss, she had been able to love so passionately again and that she had been able to express her love so freely. And she was excited by the possibility of exploring that love in therapy with Eve.

Eve never said another word about the love letter. Neither did Hannah. Sad and humiliated, she simply quit therapy a few months later. By giving Hannah back her letter, Eve communicated not only that the love Hannah craved was impossible in therapy but also that Eve could not empathize with it, could not tolerate hearing about it, could not even rejoice in Hannah's restored capacity to love. Love was irreducible and impossible to open up—even in psychotherapy. Worse, it was almost shameful.

By taking an empathic position with Hannah, Eve could have minimized the disproportion in the relationship that intensified Hannah's longing. By responding to Hannah's declaration of love with a show of tenderness and with concern, she could have mitigated Hannah's sense of isolation. If Eve had been able to explore the childhood origins of Hannah's love, they might have come to some understanding of why Hannah longed for validation though a twinning experience.

Hannah and I were left to speculate about her childhood. Together we tried to puzzle out the origins of her obsessive love for Eve. Hannah had always been her father's girl, never identifying with nor feeling understood by her mother. When Hannah was three, her sister Elizabeth was born, and Elizabeth and her mother formed a special alliance from which Hannah was excluded. They shopped together, planned parties together, laughed behind closed doors together.

When Hannah was eight her father, whom she adored, entered a tuberculosis sanitarium where he remained for nine years. In his absence, her mother grew more and more estranged from him, angry that he had not left her well provided for. Hannah missed him, defended him in his absence, and walked five miles alone twice a week to visit him in the sanitarium.

One day, she recalls, she came home from visiting him to find the doors to the house locked and the shades drawn. She went around to the side door, which opened onto her mother's bedroom.

After Hannah pounded on that door, her mother finally emerged, wearing only a bathrobe, and accompanied in an equal state of undress by a friend of her father. Hannah was shocked. She saw that her mother was not as she had seemed—proper and prudish and Victorian in her attitudes toward sex. She had betrayed Hannah's beloved father in a secret, sexual life from which Hannah had also been excluded.

In her love for Eve, Hannah expressed some of the unresolved issues of her childhood relationships: her estrangement and alienation from her mother, her envy and fear of the secrets her mother shared with others. A show of tenderness from Eve represented some form of reconciliation with her mother, a measure of the kinship she had never been able to sustain with her. She envied and feared her therapist's secret life partly because of having been excluded and betrayed by her mother's secrets. If these childhood events do not entirely explain Hannah's love, Eve and Hannah could certainly have begun their exploration by looking at them together.

Instead, Eve withdrew from the intensity of the fray, in some ways re-creating Hannah's mother's rejection and, perhaps, her father's abandonment when he entered the sanitarium. Seeing no place for her feelings within the confines of therapy, Hannah became convinced that she could satisfy them only by transforming the relationship with Eve into some other kind of bond. Her love became an agenda—to get Eve to be her friend, to get Eve to accept her, to get Eve to acknowledge the ways in which they were twins, and to teach Eve how to love. The mission was futile and the therapy was lost.

Hannah found some solace the following winter when she discovered, among her late mother's things, the diary of Hannah's great-aunt. In the daily entries of triumph and despair, Hannah found a compatriot in her family who had also been a tomboy, whose mother had misunderstood her, who'd had to chart an independent course as an intellectual adventurer. Here was the twin she had longed for in Eve. Hannah was able to create the narrative of her life that she had attempted to forge in therapy. "I've been able to construct my own autobiography around the diary," she says, "by comparing my experience with hers."

Hannah never resolved her relationship with Eve, never understood why the manner with which Eve invited her love and then withdrew from its intensity was such a particular trigger of obsession. She is wary of therapy now, regarding it as a set-up for inducing unrequitable love.

Hannah is right, of course. The very nature of the approximate relationship—its power inequity, disproportion of feeling, the inherent tension between the formality of the relationship and its call for intimacy, the very fact that love is forbidden—can evoke love in the susceptible. The therapist is the perfect love object, mysterious, enigmatic, ripe for the projection of fantasy, sender of ambiguous signals, inherently depriving. And the genuine pleasures and rewards of the relationship, the prospects of being understood in all one's vulnerability, can also lead to love.

That said, what is a woman in love with her therapist to do? First, she should subject her feelings to the therapeutic process by revealing them to her therapist and opening them up for discussion. Unfortunately, as in Hannah's case, she may not be able to rely on her therapist to help her understand her feelings and may need to do some therapeutic work on her own.

A woman in love with her therapist needs first and foremost to recognize the distinction between a feeling and an agenda. Love is a feeling; attempting to get the therapist is an agenda. A woman may not be able to control how she feels, but she does not have to allow the romantic agenda of getting the therapist to supplant the goals of her therapy. She should not conclude that her love is irreducible and requiring action until she has attempted to explore its every possible symbolic meaning.

She can ask herself: Are these the sort of feelings I've had before in relation to superiors, coaches, teachers, doctors, clergy, movie stars, those in authority or with power? What was the outcome of those situations? She can remind herself of all that she does not know about her therapist, of how much she is basing her feelings on fantasy. She can take the fantasy to its ultimate conclusion and ask herself what would happen after that key moment when the therapist dropped the professional mantle and made the declaration of love? Taking the fantasy to its likely real life conclusion—Am I the stepmother to his belligerent teenage son? Am I at home waiting for her while she does therapy with everyone else?—may help her to understand that the wish is not about anything possible in real life. Chances are the man or woman she is in love with is no mere mortal.

She can also consider what would happen if the relationship were suddenly divested of romantic yearnings. What would be left? How would she feel? A woman may discover that underneath her striving is tremendous grief or fear or anger that the romantic fantasy is shielding her from feeling.

Sometimes a woman simply must grieve what she cannot have and, in so doing, accept what she may have lost long ago. Dana, a woman now in her forties, was in love with her therapist Bill for several years. She described to me the process of letting go of that love: "I had to accept that I was never going to get Bill—not as lover, not as mother, not as rescuer, or magical transformer. I had to grieve and grieve, and then I had to give up the ghost."

I am convinced that in nearly every case, therapy-love would not survive outside of the room, would not survive the transition to another sort of relationship, and that even if it did, a real life love with her therapist would not satisfy a woman's longing.

A woman I know lost a leg in an accident when she was a child. The leg still hurts. The pain is real, but it cannot be emanating from the severed limb, although that is exactly how it feels. Love in therapy can be something like this phantom pain, a longing for that which was long ago severed, a throbbing of absence that is suddenly present again in the person of the therapist.

# 10

# The Lessons of Love

*It is madness in all women to let a secret love kindle within them, which, if unreturned and unknown, must devour the life that feeds it; and if discovered and responded to, must lead, ignis-fatuus-like, into miry wilds whence there is no extrication.*

Charlotte Brontë, *Jane Eyre*

*Dear Dr. H.,*

*I am writing this note to tell you about loving feelings I have been having for you. Please don't talk about this in our sessions because if you say anything that sounds understanding, I might think that something romantic could happen between us, and if you say anything negative, then I'm going to feel rejected.*

*Chloe*

Based on a woman's note to her therapist

Freud may have described romantic love in therapy as both real and unreal, like and unlike love in the outside world, but he was unequivocal in his advice for managing it. The therapist must neither reciprocate nor reject the client's love. Instead, the therapist should regard a client's love with the same equanimity brought to bear on her other feelings. The therapist should be interested, curious, and engaged, without becoming personally invested. "He must take care not to steer away from the transference-love or to make it distasteful to the patient," Freud wrote, but he must not reciprocate or find personal gratification in it. Love was something to be analyzed, never acted upon if therapy were to proceed.

Chloe, a young woman in therapy today, instinctively concurred with Freud's opinion when she declared her love in a note to her therapist, Dr. H. She warned him that any hint of either reciprocation or rejection would be the wrong response. The trouble was that she could not imagine anything right that Dr. H. could say and yet she had to let him know how she felt. Still she could not imagine any way for the therapeutic relationship to accommodate her love.

Accommodating love, even at its most erotically insistent, is just what must happen if a therapeutic relationship is to survive. When a client declares her love, a therapist must maneuver between the seemingly inevitable poles of reciprocation—"Yes, I love you back" —and rejection—"No, I don't." The client's love must serve not as an irreducible end unto itself but as a point of departure for therapeutic exploration. The therapist must let the woman know that her love is normal, acceptable, understandable, but that it will not subvert the therapeutic mission. The goal of therapy is not to get the therapist but to examine the woman's own desire so as to improve her capacity to give and receive love in the world.

This requires a therapist to be Buddha-like in the ability to look on the woman's desire without personal investment, accepting it but not partaking of it, as Buddha is said to look on all things. If Buddha-hood seems too great a stretch, at the least the therapist should behave the way a good father does when confronted by his daughter's budding sexuality. He acknowledges it and its glorious powers without appropriating it for himself. "Your sexuality is beautiful, but it is not for me," the good father says. In the same way, a skillful therapist does not fear or denounce or deny the woman's capacity for love. Instead, the therapist celebrates it, without taking too much pleasure in being its object.

A therapist who maintains an empathic position is far more interested in understanding exactly *how* it feels for that *particular* woman to love, exactly what her love requires, than in being its recipient. Quite simply, the therapist sacrifices the pleasure of being loved in the interest of the woman's therapy.

Often, however, a therapist confronted by a client's declaration of love either withdraws, as Eve did when Hannah declared her love (as we saw in the last chapter), or becomes too personally invested in being loved. A frightened therapist may become a punitive boundary enforcer, laying down the law as to the limits of the relationship. At the opposite extreme, a flattered therapist's ears may suddenly prick up with an unprecedented level of interest. "Oh, you love moi?" he says. "Tell me more!" In either case, empathy breaks down.

Psychologist Michael Kahn told me that therapists make mistakes whenever their behavior is seductive or punitive. In the case of therapy love, both errors are likely. The seductive therapist may lure the client in, fanning the flames of her love, while the punitive therapist makes the client feel ashamed for having loved at all.

Paula, a forty-seven-year-old lesbian, recalls very distinctly the day she declared her love to her therapist Hillary:

> Since the very frightening experience of confessing aloud to her my attraction during the first year of therapy, I haven't had any sexual or romantic fantasies about her. The experience was an antidote to desire and dreams.

The therapist effectively quashed Paula's romantic intentions by letting her know that therapy was not the proper arena for the pursuit of romance. However, she also made Paula feel that her love was a poison requiring an antidote—hardly a therapeutic lesson.

I asked Margaret Baker, Ph.D., a professor of psychology at the University of Pennsylvania and a proponent of Kohut's self-psychology, what she does when her clients fall in love with her. She confided that a therapist she had consulted as a young woman provided a very useful role model. Dr. Baker herself had fallen in love.

"I was absolutely crazy about him," she recalls. "I wanted to marry him. I wanted his wife to drop dead." She was ruthless, "willing to do anything" to make him her own. And, like many women who fall in love with their therapists, she felt stuck. Her romantic agenda was threatening to supplant the therapeutic one.

Fortunately, her therapist was skillful and empathic. She recalls his response with great fondness: "He was able to open it up, so it went somewhere. I felt that he liked me very much and wasn't disgusted by my feelings, and that having them was certainly okay, but that's not what we were there to do." Baker's therapist let her know that although her loving feelings could not be satisfied, they could be accommodated within the context of the therapeutic relationship.

## The Therapeutic Response

Glen O. Gabbard, M.D., professor at the Menninger Clinic and a major authority on therapists' sexual transgressions, suggests that the proper therapeutic response to a client's declaration of love should go something like this: "I know it is difficult and painful for you to have these feelings without being able to gratify them, but if we can explore them together, we may be able to help you to understand more fully the problems that brought you here."

Delivered with finesse and sensitivity, this sort of statement can open the way to further therapeutic exploration. If read like the Miranda warning, of course, it can be hurtful. It is bound to seem somewhat evasive: The woman has gathered up all her courage to declare her love and find out if her feelings are reciprocated, and her therapist's answer skirts the question altogether.

Some of the expert therapists I interviewed might go further in some instances to own their own humanity and to take responsibility for the feelings in the room. In doing so, they would acknowledge the intimate aspects of the relationship, its potential to spur desire.

For example, if a woman expressed feelings with a decidedly erotic edge, the therapist might say, "There is something sexual going on in this room. We need to look at these dynamics carefully. I can take care of myself and my feelings; you don't have to take care of me. We need to keep looking at your feelings together."

Therapists don't always respond with such clarity and thoughtfulness. They can be most dangerous to their clients when unaware of their own feelings and motivations. Just as some therapists become convinced that they can cure their clients with perfect parenting, others are tempted to believe in the curative power of their love.

Sometimes therapists are unaware of the mixed messages they are sending. Alice Brand-Bartlett of the Menninger Clinic was the adviser to a young and handsome therapist in training. He was dark, brooding, narcissistic—a combination apt to prove irresistible to many young women. In fact, the gossip was that several of the therapist's colleagues harbored romantic fantasies about him. Given the added charge of the therapeutic relationship, how could his clients be immune? In fact, Brand-Bartlett suspected from his account of sessions that at least one of his clients had already fallen in love with him. The therapist in training was oblivious. He wasn't actively flirtatious. He wasn't consciously *doing* anything. Yet Brand-Bartlett felt that he had to take more responsibility for what he was unconsciously communicating as well.

Brand-Bartlett sat him down and told him, "This isn't the first time and it's not going to be the last that a patient falls in love with you." She advised him to consider more closely in his own therapy the unconscious messages he was sending. "If he wasn't being seductive, he was being blind," she explains.

## Lara's Story, Part II: The View Between the Rabbit's Ears

Whether seductive or blind, therapists who respond equivocally to a client's declaration of love can make matters worse. This brings us back to Lara. A beautiful woman of twenty-eight, Lara had fallen in love with her therapist, Dr. D. Her feelings were "more intense" than in any other romantic relationship she had ever had. When she first declared her feelings of love and sexual attraction to Dr. D., he attributed them to transference. But that was not all he was to say and do. Now Lara is torn between her agenda to get Dr. D. and her desire to understand herself through her therapy.

Lara tries to take all the blame for her therapist's behavior. In sessions she has been overtly seductive, wearing low-cut dresses, "showing some cleavage," she explains. During one session, she made the strongest case she could muster for Dr. D.'s giving up the therapeutic relationship in favor of a romantic liaison. Lara recalls pleading her case: "I was in the mood and I made it very plain. I told him there was something real and strong between us. I was very convincing."

Dr. D. maintained nobly that the relationship had to remain professional. However, he seemed unaware of the cross-signals he was sending and utterly blind to their impact on Lara. At the end of one session, this exchange took place:

> As Dr. D. got up to walk across the room, he reached over and patted my knee. I was wearing a silk skirt and these slick Donna Karan hose and his hand slipped up under my skirt and brushed the inside of my thigh.
> "That was really awkward," I said. "Why did you do that?"
> "I wanted to make some kind of contact with you," he said.

Dr. D. kept telling Lara that her feelings were transference but then he touched her provocatively at the end of a session. As a result she was overwhelmed by feelings, not all of them good. Despite Lara's repeated attempts to seduce Dr. D., her desire was by no means unequivocal. When Dr. D. appeared to be reciprocating, Lara's reaction was equal parts shock, fear, and excitement. Even when Lara felt sexually aroused during her sessions, she always felt scared at the same time. "My desire never stands alone," she said. "It is wrapped up with all of my feelings about sex: shame, fear, sex as a threat."

This was not the first time Dr. D. touched Lara. Once, as she was sobbing, he gripped her forearm and held it for several moments, presumably in an effort to console or stabilize her. A few nights later she had nightmares about being grabbed with a grappling hook and clawed in the place on her arm where Dr. D. had held her. When Lara told Dr. D. that she desired him or that she was in love with him, the word "love" actually covered a multitude of intense and conflicted feelings roused by their closeness. Anger, confusion, fear, hurt, and shame were virtually inseparable from love. To assume that Lara's "love" was irreducible or that it could be satisfied simply by "getting" him would be a naive and dangerous position for Dr. D.

to take. As her therapist, it was Dr. D.'s job to help Lara unravel that complex bundle of feelings that went by the name of love. By doing so, perhaps they could free her capacity for love from the guilt, shame, and fear that had always driven—and also impeded—it.

When Lara fantasized about Dr. D.'s love, it seemed far more than the mere love another mortal could provide. It represented the promise of a love liberated from conflict and ambivalence. In the safety of her own home, Lara purified Dr. D.'s touch of her shame and fantasized "very different endings" to the session in which he touched her leg. She imagined Dr. D. "dissolving into tears," as he confessed that he had also fallen in love with her. He had done everything he could to resist her sexual seduction out of his noble dedication to the ethics of his profession. But he now knew that there was a higher form of love possible between them. He had not been taken in only by her beauty and sexual allure; he had seen beyond it to appreciate her deeper attributes.

At this point, Lara's fantasy jumps ahead three years. Dr. D. and she are in a setting of domestic harmony, totally committed to each other. He is financially secure and able to take perfect care of her. "The more details I add to the fantasy, the more oedipal it seems," Lara admits. In other words, for the fantasy to be most fulfilling, Dr. D. must behave as much like a good father as an ideal lover. He must cherish Lara, appreciate her, and take care of her. Although he desires her back, there is something Buddha-like in his capacity to subordinate his sexuality for the sake of a greater love. The perfection of Dr. D.'s caretaking, the absence of any conflict between them or within Lara, harkens back to the golden fantasy.

A look at Lara's childhood can help to decipher the meanings of her therapy-love. When Lara was six, her parents divorced and her father abandoned the family. He remarried and he and his second wife quickly had another daughter. After that, Lara rarely saw him. She imagined that he was totally devoted to his "new" daughter, and she watched enviously from afar as he and his second family moved into the best part of town. Meanwhile, she and her mother struggled to survive. She remembers her mother pleading with her father over the phone to send child support checks to pay for groceries. Lara's mother made her feel that their very survival depended on the good will of a powerful and unpredictable man who did not love them enough.

Lara has few positive early childhood memories of her father. She cannot remember his ever holding her on his lap or sitting side-by-side with her while they read a book, images that still evoke longing. Lara recalls the warmth between them when he would tuck her into bed, but she has mixed feelings about his little "bed-time ritual." He liked to wrestle with her, to mock-smother her in the bed. He would press her pillow over her face playfully until she would laugh hysterically and scream, "Daddy, stop! Daddy, stop!" When he stopped she would giggle all the more uncontrollably. But once she felt as if she really were suffocating and screamed out in genuine terror.

In the smothering game, Lara may have learned to associate physical pleasure, which was on the very cusp of pain, with submission and fear. The powerful provider of this pleasure-pain then abandoned her in favor of another, more lovable daughter. This left Lara with yearnings for a father whom she perceived as unavailable, indifferent, and potentially sadistic.

The divorce left Lara's mother emotionally unhinged. Lara felt as if she had to grow up to take care of her. Then just a few years after Lara's father left, her maternal grandfather sexually molested her. She has learned only recently that he had repeatedly molested her mother as a child as well. From this experience she learned to be ashamed of her own sexual feelings and to distrust men further. They simply could not be relied on to control their own impulses to protect the innocence of children.

In the early 1970s, Lara's mother joined the sexual revolution. Lara remembers lying in bed night after night listening to her mother make love to a procession of lovers and feeling more like a participant than an observer. By age twelve Lara was sexually active herself. Divorced from affection, sex was a way of getting some of her needs met by other people, a way of getting some semblance of love. When Lara fell in love herself, her feelings were intense, her relationships tempestuous and short-lived.

Given Lara's background, it's not hard to understand why she might be torn between sexualizing every significant relationship in an effort to get love and fearing the expression of sexuality. Of her relationship with Dr. D., Lara says,

> I want to be touched and I don't want to be touched. I want it to be sexual and I don't want it to be sexual. There is in me a child wanting to be held but afraid of being molested and a woman wanting to express love and unable to do so without making it sexual.

Lara is trapped between the child for whom love has been contaminated with adult sexuality and the woman who compulsively acts out sexually in an attempt to master the events of her childhood. Although Lara dreads being sexually objectified by Dr. D., she fears his rejection even more. Irresistible sexual allure is the means by which she can ward off the possibility of Dr. D.'s rejection and get him to really, completely, perfectly love her. Once Dr. D. falls in love with her, he will appreciate far more than her sexual gifts. He will provide the profound recognition and acceptance that she never got from her own father and for which she continues to yearn.

Aware of the conflict underlying her romantic agenda, a part of Lara also knows what she needs from Dr. D. as a therapist. She needs for him to respond to her sexual feelings in the same way that he responds to her other expressions of affection and caring: with serious concern and tender compassion. The problem is that his reactions to her expressions of sexual desire are markedly different:

> When I am in a girlish, flirtatious mood, Dr. D. gets all giggly and pink. When we talk about intense feelings that are not sexual, he is very careful and therapist-like. That says to me that he finds the sexual element more gratifying.

By not responding with equanimity to Lara's sexual feelings, Dr. D. has reinforced her belief that she can only get love through the calculated employment of her sexuality. He has convinced her that the psychotherapeutic relationship cannot accommodate her sexual and romantic feelings but can only be corrupted by them.

Whenever Lara flirts or behaves seductively, Dr. D. loses his empathic position as an ally and second self and reacts as the flattered object of her desire. He does not ask the therapeutic questions—"What does it mean to love?" or "What is your fantasy about getting me?"—because he is too caught up in being desired. There is nothing Buddha-like, nothing good father-like in his reactions. Does he see the childlike vulnerability, the wish for love and caring beneath the sexual invitation, the grieving for the lost father beneath the grasping for him? Is he blind to the symbolic meanings of Lara's love?

Once Lara was ranting and raving to Dr. D. about how painful it was to be in love with him when he would never feel the same way. Some therapists might argue that what was called for was a show of therapeutic empathy. Yes, he could understand how she felt; yes he could acknowledge the sadness, the isolation, the impossibility of Lara's sexual quandary. Yes, he could see how the very set-up of the psychotherapy relationship, which denied reciprocation of her love, evoked Lara's longings and how her childhood predisposed her to see the object of her desire as indifferent, rejecting, or sadistic.

Instead, Dr. D. sighed and said, "You're not alone."

"What do you mean?" Lara responded. "*You're* not having to go through any of this."

Lara recalls Dr. D. taking a deep breath, looking off to the side and then saying, "Well, I'm going to take a chance and tell you that I have been struggling with my own intense feelings of affection and attraction for you." Dr. D. added that Lara need not worry, he had sought consultation with another therapist to help him work through his feelings.

Perhaps Dr. D. made this admission so that Lara would feel less alone, less isolated by her feelings. Perhaps he made it out of his commitment to authenticity, his belief that therapists should not deny their deeper feelings, particularly if such feelings have become apparent to the client.

Whatever his intentions, Dr. D.'s confession could not help but prove seductive. We have to wonder if he wasn't also torn between a belief in the mythos of love and a belief in the mythos of transference. As with his touch, Dr. D.'s declaration of "love" excited, frightened, and confused Lara. It fed the fantasy that his love was all that she needed, that loving and being loved by him could heal, clean, restore, and redeem her life. So how could Lara possibly continue the therapy on an even keel? How could she not be tempted to simply cast aside the therapeutic work and put all her energies into the romantic agenda?

None of the expert therapists I interviewed could see how, given the situation, Dr. D.'s confession could serve Lara's best therapeutic interest. After Dr. D.'s declaration, Lara's longing intensified. When she tried to throw herself into a relationship with someone else, she thought about Dr. D. When she had sex with someone else, she imagined she was with Dr. D. With her eyes closed while she masturbated, she saw Dr. D.'s face at the moment of orgasm. The image of his face was not enough to resolve her troubled feelings about her own sexuality, however. Lara confides, "I never have an orgasm without feeling bad afterwards. It's a feeling of overwhelming badness; there are no words to describe it. And I've never been able to tell Dr. D. that."

It is unfortunate that Lara cannot safely talk to Dr. D. about her most fundamental sexual feelings. Some might interpret the fact that Lara now sees Dr. D.'s face at the moment of orgasm simply as an expression of her sexual yearning. I think that to read it only this way would be to miss much of its symbolic meaning. By taking the reassuring image of Dr. D. into the frightening territory of sexuality, Lara uses him as a talisman to take the fear and danger and conflict out of sex. This is not so different from the story of the woman afraid of flying who always imagines that her therapist is sitting in the back of the plane. Even the desire to have sex with Dr. D. may emerge as much out of Lara's wish to magically transform her negative feelings about sexuality as out of sexual desire for Dr. D. In seeing only the sex in a sexual fantasy, we might miss the ways in which a sexual fantasy is like other fantasies women report of their therapists as internalized icons. In each of these fantasies, the therapist has some symbolic power to right the situation, to make it safer, to offer the woman sustenance.

Since Lara cannot bring herself to talk about her deepest feelings about her own sexuality with Dr. D., to imagine having sex with him may be the only way that Lara can take him with her into the realm of feeling where she is the most troubled. In this way she could *show* him how she feels. Sexual conflict seems to require a sexual solution. If she were to have sex with Dr. D. he would get to see how she really feels, and maybe his love would magically "fix" her.

After his declaration of attraction, Dr. D. continued to send Lara mixed signals. Because he treated children, Dr. D. had stuffed animals in his office. During Lara's sessions he would sometimes pick up a little gray rabbit and absentmindedly stroke it between the ears. Lara found this disarming and sexually suggestive. When he ran his finger down the little v-space between rabbit's ears, she could only picture his hand stroking a woman's genitals. She imagined that he was imagining stroking her genitals or, worse, making her imagine his stroking her genitals if only to torture her by increasing her sense of deprivation.

One day Dr. D. brought the rabbit right up to his face, parted the ears, and peered at Lara from the space between them. He was smiling a big toothy grin. Lara asked him to stop. In playing with the bunny's ears that way, Dr. D. seemed to be both extending a sexual invitation and mocking Lara's sexuality. He refused to understand why his playful gesture carried so much weight for her.

"You're being provocative," she said.

"Am I?" he asked innocently. "Why does this bother you?"

Lara could imagine only two explanations for Dr. D.'s behavior: Either he was intentionally testing her reactions to sexually suggestive material in a manipulative, sadistic manner, or he was out of control with his own sexual yearning. Either he was like her sadistic manipulative father or he was like her sexually abusing grandfather. In either case, as far as Lara could tell, Dr. D. had given up being the adult in charge. He was failing, in the words of psychologist Michael Kahn, at one of the principal tasks of the therapist, "to mind the store."

Dr. D. may have thought that he was simply being spontaneous and playful. He may have assumed that his behavior would help "normalize" Lara's relationship with him. He had told her that she needed to examine why she was so troubled by his casual, mildly sexual comments, to look at why his every word and gesture were so charged for her. She needed to become more comfortable with her own sexuality, he suggested, to become more comfortable with the casual flirtations of others, to integrate her sexuality into other aspects of life.

Ultimately, this was probably a worthwhile goal for Lara. Sexuality did carry too much weight, did seem the focus of too many of her social interactions, and was the source of much of her bad feeling about herself. But for Dr. D. to simply behave as he might in a casual relationship outside of therapy was to trivialize the symbolic weight that he carried for Lara. She needed to understand why she attributed the meanings that she did to his actions. To expect her to have a "normal" relationship with him was to abdicate his therapeutic responsibility. By virtue of his therapeutic role, Dr. D. has become more than just another attractive man—he has become a stand-in for the important men of Lara's past and a symbol of what any man would ever be able to provide her. That's why his casual flirting has very serious consequences. Dr. D. and Lara both need to respect and appreciate the symbolic meaning their relationship has for her if she is to ever have a relationship with a man that is less burdened by her past.

Unable to tell if her feelings for Dr. D. were "impeding the therapy" or if they were "at the heart of the therapy," Lara sought consultation with several other therapists. She did not want to leave therapy with Dr. D. because she was so attached to him, and in many respects and many situations he had been loyal and trustworthy and caring.

The therapists Lara consulted all looked in a legalistic way for grievous boundary violations in her relationship with Dr. D.—rather than evaluating his overall expertise in handling Lara's therapy-love. Had he touched her? How had he touched her? Where had he touched her? Had he extended her sessions? None suggested that she and Dr. D. should seek consultation with another therapist together. They all sent her back into the ring with Dr. D. "to resolve the situation," presuming, despite evidence to the contrary, that he had the skill and self-knowledge to help her do so.

## Therapists' Sexual Attraction to Their Clients

How common was Dr. D.'s sexual attraction to Lara? Was his disclosing his attraction to Lara typical? In 1986, three psychologist-researchers sent written surveys to 1000 psychologist-members of the American Psychological Association. Of the 575 members who returned the survey, 87% (95% of the men, 76% of the women) reported having felt sexual attraction to a client on at least one occasion. More than half (63%) reported feeling guilty, anxious, or confused by their own feelings. Only 9% felt that the training they had received enabled them to handle the situation well. Many reported having received no training to prepare them for this eventuality. Fifty-seven percent of the therapists did what Dr. D. did—sought consultation with another therapist to help them cope with their feelings. The research did not determine whether this consultation proved helpful or effective.

The therapists who participated in the survey expressed the belief that disclosing their feelings was potentially harmful to the client. They also seemed to believe that they could hide their feelings beyond their clients' ability to detect them: Seventy-one percent of the therapists who had been attracted to a client were sure that the client remained unaware of their attraction. It would be very informative to survey those clients, of course, to determine what they suspected about their therapists' feelings.

Eighty-three percent of the therapists stated that the attraction they felt was mutual. The survey didn't ask them to explain the basis for this assumption. Had their clients declared their love, or were the therapists simply going on the basis of observation? How did the attraction begin? The survey also did not ask if the attraction continued throughout the course of the therapy, if it was a feeling that only flared up on occasion, or if it was resolved. The research could not assess the ultimate impact that the attraction had on the therapy.

What can be extrapolated from this study is that therapists do not acknowledge that they suffer very often from unreciprocated love or desire for their clients. Their answers suggest that they are attracted only to those patients who are attracted to them. By implication, they don't seem to want to acknowledge that the attraction ever *begins* with them and that the client is merely responding to their nonverbal communication of desire. How could the client be responding, these therapists might argue, when therapists are so adept at hiding their feelings?

The notion that attraction begins with the client, and that the therapist merely responds yea or nea, reflects a very old bias in the psychotherapeutic literature. Most of the professional articles on the subject begin with this interesting and untested premise: The client makes the first overture, feels the first attraction, and communicates it, and the therapist responds. In Freud's classic depictions of the woman in love with her therapist, she is always the instigator. Just exactly how Josef Breuer felt prior to Anna O.'s revelation of her pseudo-pregnancy will always remain a mystery.

In Freud's telling of romantic/erotic transference in therapy, the woman patient's "love" is one more issuance from the irrational underworld that psychoanalysis must tame. The patient's desire, her very female sexuality, threatens to pull the analyst down. By resisting, the analyst protects the patient's honor, his own authority, and the discipline of psychoanalysis. At the same time, he upholds the oedipal taboo, the fundamental standard of civilized society.

This bias about desire as always emanating from the patient and "infecting" the therapist is still apparent in much of the professional literature on romantic and sexual feelings in therapy. It is not based on any legitimate research and can only stand in the way of our understanding the subtleties of the love and longing that develop in therapy.

Admitting to having had sexual feelings for a client in an anonymous survey is far different from talking about such feelings in any detail. Getting therapists to discuss their romantic and sexual feelings for their clients with me was no mean feat.

Michael Sussman, Ph.D., psychologist and author of the book *A Perilous Calling: The Hazards of Psychotherapy Practice*, was courageous enough to talk to me about a case in which he felt himself romantically drawn to a client. The client was also attracted to him, and try as they might, they could not resolve the attraction in therapy. The woman disclosed her feelings first and sensed that they were shared. At some later critical juncture, Sussman felt compelled to declare that he had strong feelings for her. They maintained a therapeutic relationship for two years after their mutual declarations.

Sussman struggled in his own therapeutic work to regard his attraction as a form of countertransference. He had a tendency to want to be a rescuer, he knew, and some aspects of his relationship with this client allowed him to assume this role. When he had been younger, he'd had an exploitive, emotionally intense relationship with his own therapist. Perhaps he was now reenacting that relationship in reverse.

Dr. Sussman's feelings extended beyond sexual attraction, he told me. He felt a bond, a strong connection that in any other context would have been the basis for a romantic relationship. "Of course, there were transference and countertransference dynamics operating," he said, "but aren't there transference dynamics in every romantic relationship?" Ultimately the sexual energy in the room interfered with Sussman's ability to conduct therapy. He wanted to terminate the therapy; the client, perhaps afraid that she would lose him from her life altogether if she lost him as her therapist, fought to continue.

The American Psychological Association's Code of Ethics stipulates a two-year waiting period before a therapist can consider embarking on a personal, romantic relationship with a former client. Such liaisons are to be undertaken only with great caution. The American Psychiatric Association is less lenient; no waiting period is considered sufficient—once a patient, never a lover.

Dr. Sussman finally prevailed and terminated the therapy. "It had me off balance as a therapist," he said. "I wasn't able to get back on track. I was never worried that I would actually violate the boundaries of the relationship but it no longer seemed possible to be sure that I was conducting the therapy in a responsible, well-thought out manner."

## Resolving Therapy-Love

Sometimes it would seem that therapy-love is the monster that refuses to die no matter how many times it is whacked over the head with reasonable interpretations. Nevertheless, a woman in love with her therapist may be able to achieve some kind of resolution short of quitting the therapy or turning her therapist into her lover. That resolution may not always be as clean as the model that Freud described: A woman in love with her therapist comes to understand—intellectually and emotionally—the origin of her feelings in her oedipal strivings for her father. She accepts that she cannot have her therapist just as she could not have her father, grieves the loss, and goes on to choose more appropriate objects for her love.

The women who participated in my research suggest that therapy-love is more difficult to resolve than this model might suggest. A woman may work through her love for one therapist only to discover that she has a readiness to fall in love with the next.

To resolve her romantic feelings, a woman may have to acknowledge other feelings about her therapist that her romantic love has masked, such as hostility, anger, rage, even hatred. If love is blind, love in therapy is sometimes a way of refusing to see. By feeling only love, a woman can protect herself and her therapist from the consequences of her less attractive feelings.

In an earlier chapter of this book, Ariel's striving to turn her therapist into a perfect mother protected her from having to grieve the failings in her relationship with her own mother. The past is not over if there is any hope of being able to reverse it in the present. A woman may also use the romantic agenda unknowingly as a way of denying what has already been lost, what her parents may have failed to provide. Romantic love may also mask other needs that are more difficult to articulate. What a woman wants ultimately may not be sex, but sex can be the easiest thing to ask for.

One woman I interviewed told me that in sharing stories about their therapy, she and her friend had had a revelation: Whenever they started to want something, something in the therapy, something else from the therapist, perhaps even something in their extra-therapeutic lives, they first experienced their desire as a sexual impulse toward their therapists. As they were able to articulate what they really wanted directly in their therapy, the sexual desire faded.

Beneath romantic love may be a longing for maternal succor or for the perfect love that can satisfy a woman's every need. Once a woman and her therapist begin to honestly explore her fantasies about consummation, she may realize that she is longing for a good mother as much as for an ideal lover. As Dana wrote,

> As soon as I gave up the sexual fantasy and realized that I was never going to have a love affair with Dr. B., another sort of longing hit me in the center of my chest. It was a terrible, hopeless, child's longing for a mother. I was no longer angry with Dr. B. because he wouldn't sleep with me; I was furious that he was so inept at taking care of me.

Sometimes romantic feelings in therapy fade as they might in any infatuation, as the woman sees enough of the therapist's "real self" to become disenchanted or as the therapeutic relationship becomes too valuable to risk for the uncertain prospects of romance. A driven romantic love can cool to a more temperate attachment; the woman may still love her therapist without feeling that the only way to "fix" her life is to get him. Michael Kahn describes the process of resolution this way: "Hopefully, the demanding erotic feelings convert to a nondemanding set of attenuated feelings and eventually evolve to some kind of warm and gentle gratitude toward the person who went through this trip with you."

Women ask, "Is being in love with my therapist good for me? Is it necessary or therapeutic?" Not in and of itself, I would have to answer. There is no magic in simply enduring a painful romantic transference. Whether therapy-love proves helpful depends entirely on what a woman and her therapist are able to make of it, sometimes on what a woman is able to make of it *despite* her therapist.

Even when a woman and her therapist are able to work productively with her romantic feelings in therapy, that may not be the only or best way to understand the psychological obstacles that are getting in the way of love in the outside world. Experiencing an intense romantic transference is certainly one way of getting those issues into the therapy, but they come at the front end of a barreling train.

Whether a woman will take any lessons away can rely greatly on the skill and the comfort of her therapist, and research suggests that many therapists are not all that skillful at handling therapy-love. When romantic feelings prove intractable, it is often as much because of the therapist's reactions as the client's proclivities. The therapist may simply enjoy being loved too much.

# 11

# Sexual Transgressions in Therapy

When a woman is in the throes of therapy-love, the prospect of actually having sex with her therapist may hold the promise of transformation. Rose, a married woman in her 60s who fell in love with her therapist, recalls the first time he kissed her:

> It was much more than thrilling. It was as if the most perfect thing in the world had happened to me. A person who knew everything about me loved and accepted me exactly the way I was. It was magic, the completion of something I had been waiting for all my life.

For Rose, physical union with the therapist carried the promise of perfectly attuned caretaking, the golden fantasy of unconditional love. It was both the culmination of her adult life and a reunion with some state of bliss she only half-remembered.

If psychotherapy seems to offer the possibility of transformation, the notion that sex might be the medium for effecting this transformation does not seem to require that great a leap of faith. After all, the sexual act itself *is* transformative. Having sex transforms one's physical state *and* one's state of mind. To have sex with the powerful and symbolically charged therapist, someone who may possess a special capacity for transforming others, becomes a doubly transformative act. And a therapist can certainly feed a woman's transformation fantasy by promoting the curative benefits of his or her love.

Even when not motivated by therapy-love or by the fantasy of perfect fulfillment, women who have sex with their therapists hope that the involvement will prove somehow therapeutic. At the least, they try to convince themselves that the therapist is no mere exploiter but has their best interests at heart.

Apparently, some therapists try to convince themselves as well. In a 1986 survey of 1,423 anonymous psychiatrist-respondents by Nanette Gartrell and others, 6.4% (7.1% of the men and 3.1% of the women) acknowledged having had sexual relations with at least one patient. Of this group, 19% claimed that they were motivated by therapeutic, if not altruistic, interests—by their desire to improve the patient's self-esteem or otherwise help. A larger percentage, 73%, admitted to having been motivated by love or pleasure. About 65% of the practitioners reported that they had been in love with the patient at the time, while 92% were sure that the patient had been in love with them. Only 40% of the therapists regretted their tresspasses.

When asked how their patients perceived the sexual encounters, transgressing therapists downplayed the harm. They reported that their patients experienced the sexual acts as caring in 50 cases, helpful in 29, and therapeutic in 9, as opposed to exploitive in 11 cases, harmful in 8, and inappropriate in 5.

When women who have had sex with their therapists report on the experience, they do not describe it as curative or therapeutic. In contrast, it is almost always profoundly countertherapeutic. Nearly every study that has looked at clients who've had sex with their therapists has found negative and often long-lasting psychological consequences. When Rose's therapist broke off their affair suddenly, withdrawing the promise of golden love, Rose fell into a deep despair. It took her several years to recover from the sense of self-dissolution and shame that followed her blissful immersion in the golden fantasy.

A woman may imagine that by having sex with her therapist she can equalize the power imbalance in the relationship by getting the therapist to need her as much as she needs him. This desire to gain some power in the relationship was one motive mentioned by women who fantasized about seducing their therapists. But when therapists and clients actually have sex, it would seem that therapist-lovers retain the power advantages of their role. Although some researchers have found otherwise, my research suggests that transgressing therapists tend to retain the role of therapist, striving to have it both ways: therapy *and* a love affair, or rather therapy with a sexual involvement messily superimposed upon it. They seldom make a clean break with the therapeutic role and segue into the other. Perhaps this allows them to rationalize that by continuing to conduct some bastardized form of therapy, they have not abandoned their professional obligation altogether.

I suspect that holding on to the role has certain advantages. The therapist maintains control over the therapy relationship and is also relieved of the usual obligations of being in a romantic relationship. A woman who becomes sexually involved with her therapist may want to continue to have some of the soul-searching dialogue of psychotherapy with her therapist-lover, but for the most part, women involved with their therapists do not want to keep it both ways, struggling instead to disentangle the two relationships.

Historically, sexual transgressions have been all too common among therapists, with anywhere from 1% to 12% of therapists acknowledging sexual involvement with a patient (or prior patient) in studies based on anonymous self-report. In general, male therapists have reported significantly higher rates than have women. These numbers have all been based on surveying therapists about their own pasts; no one has ever surveyed a large group of clients to assess the prevalence of client–therapist sexual involvements.

We might like to think that the least trained, least experienced therapists are the most common perpetrators, but the statistics do not bear out any such reassuring conclusions. The most highly trained, most distinguished practitioners, such as the heads of East Coast psychoanalytic training institutes, have brought scandal on their houses through sexual involvement with their patients.

As news of therapists' sexual exploitation of their clients has become common knowledge, the public, and to some extent the professions, have focused their attention on the sexual acts themselves, as if the harm comes at the instant of penetration. In adjudicating sexual misconduct malpractice cases, the courts have been as obsessed as the parents of teenagers with "how far" it went, rather than with the overall character of the relationship. From my perspective, sexual transgressions are not isolated events, but the most grievous and graphic markers of more endemic weaknesses in psychotherapeutic practice. Sexual transgressions occur when therapists fail to respect the significance of therapeutic boundaries in protecting the client and their own ability to perform competent work. They happen when therapists fail to fully appreciate the subtle symbolic dimensions of their role, their potency as transference objects.

## Why Don't Women Just Walk Away?

Those women who've never slept with a boss, or a professor, or a coach, or a mentor, those who've never fallen in love with the person behind the podium only to find that person much diminished at home in bed, might ask why women don't just walk away, why they cannot just say no. Don't they smell the whiff of catastrophe in the air? Don't they know that the odds of turning a patient–therapist liaison into a healthy romantic bond are less than the chances of running into a burning building and not singeing one's feet?

What's been underreported is the fact that many women *do* say no. My own findings suggest that the incidence of client–therapist sex would probably be much higher if many women did not find the strength to say no. Delia, a woman in her thirties, was seeing a therapist, also in his thirties, for five months when she "started to get these cues." It was the way he stood and stretched languorously in the doorway of his office and made a point at the end of a particularly hard session of touching her. One day, five minutes before the end of a session, he asked Delia if she'd like to go out for a cup of coffee and "continue this on a more personal basis." Apparently she looked confused, so he elaborated: "I'm really attracted to you and I'd like for us to go out and . . . I think that I could really help you." There was, even in the invitation, the confusing prospect of a dual relationship, the suggestion that a _personal_ involvement would be _therapeutic_. Delia was not taken in: "Yikes!, I thought. My therapist was making a pass at me! Did I need this? I walked out of the office and never went back."

Although no one has conducted any sort of large-scale survey of therapy clients, I would guess that many women, like Delia, do say no to enamored therapists. In my survey, 7 out of a total of 280 women (2.56%) reported having had sex with a therapist. Four reported having learned, either during the course of therapy or afterward, that a therapist they had seen had been sexually intimate with another client. But a much greater percentage, 16 (4.4%), reported that a therapist had propositioned them or had made a sexually suggestive comment at least once in the course of their therapy. Of course, there's always the chance that some of these women misinterpreted their therapists' remarks. But I would guess that women in therapy say no, in overt and subtle ways, every day. They take a walk, like Delia did, or change the subject. Sometimes they endure the therapist's sexual innuendos on the remote chance that they are motivated by therapeutic intent.

Marcia, a woman in her thirties, told this story about a therapist she saw for several years:

> He managed to always bring up sexually related topics. Once, to give me an example of how we can't just be impulsive in the world, he said, "You and I might want to be fucking on the couch right now, but we're not going to do that because it's an ethical line we cannot cross." Well, I was twenty-five and he was seventy-two; fucking him on the couch was not something I particularly wanted to be doing.

If Marcia had been more receptive, might her therapist have found that ethical line less formidable?

When women are unable to say no, or to leave the therapy, or to let the therapist know that sexual suggestions are unwelcome, it is often because of the therapist's greater power in the relationship, and because of the symbolic meaning carried by the therapist's love.

## An Old Problem

Sexual transgressions in therapy are as old as psychotherapy itself. After all, Freud did much of his writing about transference under the shadow of his colleagues' sexual acting-out with patients. Jung had a particularly well-documented affair with at least one young patient, Sabina Spielrein, who went on to become an analyst herself. Ferenczi's "experimentation" in mutual therapy culminated in a messy romantic triangle with a mother and daughter who were both patients and lovers. After much back-and-forth, he married the mother. Poet and novelist Anais Nin's diary chronicles torrid sexual interludes, some of them interspersed with high-minded analytic sessions, with two of her analysts, Rene Allendy and Otto Rank. Poet Anne Sexton had a protracted affair with a respected Boston psychiatrist who continued to treat her at the same time.

In the sexually free-wheeling 1960s and 1970s, when a number of therapists had sex with their patients behind closed doors, two had the audacity to publish works attesting to the therapeutic efficacy of the act. In "Overt Transference," analyst James L. McCartney conveniently argued that "in order to get well, the patient must emotionally grow up and accept full sexuality." The therapist could facilitate this "maturation process" by serving as "the love object and a sexually mature individual." It would seem that McCartney was attempting to justify client–therapist sex as a particularly literal kind of corrective emotional experience. In a book called *The Love Treatment*, psychiatrist Peter Shepard interviewed eleven patients who had slept with their therapists and concluded that "intimacy with a therapist can indeed be useful." He laid out rules for the therapist and for the patient in these encounters. Among those for the therapist, he offered, "Being available is one thing; being insistent is another," while the client should apply this rule of thumb: "If he is suffering more than he was before the intimacy began, he should break off the relationship."

At no other time in the history of psychotherapy have transgressing therapists been quite this bold, but for many years the profession publicly disapproved but did little to punish therapists who slept with their clients. When practitioners learned of a trespass, the tendency was to look the other way or even to identify with their poor colleague, who had fallen victim to a client's feminine wiles. Clara reported in my survey that her trusted internist had referred her to a therapist. Horrified when, after a few sessions, the therapist asked her to have sex with him, she returned to her internist to complain. "Oh, Dick's fucking his patients again!" the internist replied, unapologetic for having made the referral.

Since the late 1970s, the profession has taken a firmer position on sexual boundary violations, partly in response to the feminist movement's exposure of errant therapists in books like Phyllis Chesler's classic *Women and Madness*. Feminist theorists considered therapist–patient sex simply one more instance of patriarchal subjugation of women. The proliferation of civil lawsuits against therapists has also had an impact, resulting in the professional associations and licensing boards taking stronger disciplinary action. The current ethics codes of the major professional associations for psychiatrists, psychologists, and social workers unanimously condemn sexual activity between therapists and clients. In fifteen states sex between therapist and client is now a criminal offense.

Nevertheless, women who have filed complaints with their state licensing boards report that the process of filing is laborious and that boards act very slowly. My conversations with California state enforcement authorities made it clear that they are inclined to give therapists every benefit of the doubt and that the burden of proof continues to be on the victim. Of the complaints filed, boards drop the majority for inadequate evidence. Of course, how much corroborating evidence can there be when most relationships take place in the sanctity of the therapist's office? I would guess that a therapist usually commits multiple boundary violations and may even have sex with several patients before getting caught.

## The "Courtship"

As in an extra-therapeutic romance, sexual acts in therapy tend to follow a courtship period. In contrast to some women's fantasies, therapists don't usually stop midsentence, bound across the room, and sweep their clients into their arms. I could find no instances in which a therapist conducting competent, productive, boundaried therapy suddenly compromised the process by having sex impulsively with the client.

Relaxation of the other therapeutic boundaries characterizes the courtship period. The therapist may suggest leaving the office to "stretch our legs" or get coffee, extend the length of sessions, reschedule sessions for the end of the day, or encourage contact in between sessions. Fees may go unpaid or be reduced, and conversations in therapy may meander.

The single most predictive boundary crossing is excessive, inappropriate self-disclosure. Gary Schoener, licensed psychologist and director of the Minneapolis Walk-In Counseling Center, which has screened more cases of sexual misconduct in therapy than any other institution in the country, says that excessive self-disclosure occurs in 98% of the relationships prior to sexual acts. "Whether the therapist is a sleazy sociopath using it as a come-on or just a needy neurotic, they all do the same thing," Schoener says.

The self-disclosures that foreshadow sexual involvement may be of a particularly intimate nature. The therapist may reveal a dark secret, prefaced by a conspiratorial "please don't tell, but . . ." or "I know I shouldn't be telling a client this, but . . . or "I wouldn't tell any other client but you this . . ." The confession often pertains to the therapist's own romantic life. The gist of the remark may be, "My wife doesn't understand me" or "My lover just left me and I am feeling so blue," something to suggest the therapist's loneliness and availability. By asking the client to keep a special secret, the therapist effects a subtle reversal of role. Soon the client feels that she must protect the therapist and minister to the therapist's needs.

To a client the therapist's self-disclosure may be very seductive. It may seem to reveal the therapist's "real" self peeking out from behind the screen. The client may perceive in it the therapist's plea to be seen, to receive the recognition and acceptance for which clients come to therapists. "I want you to see who I *really* am," the therapist seems to be saying, "not just who I appear to be in the room." Such a disclosure can be intoxicating. The client feels special, singled out from all the therapist's clients, rewarded with some bonus beyond the limited economy of the approximate relationship.

These intimate disclosures are also apt to make the client uncomfortable, as she intuits that some crucial line has been crossed. She may wonder, "Why exactly is my therapist telling me this?" Underlying the disclosure is an unspoken request to satisfy a not yet clearly articulated need of the therapist's. Without any context in which to evaluate what she has heard, afraid to press for more information because she knows she is not supposed to have heard what she has heard, the client has no way of verifying the veracity of the therapist's confession. In fact, these revelations seem just as likely to be half-truths or self-aggrandizing fantasies as honest self-revelation.

The courtship period may also involve physical contact. A pat on the back or a comforting squeeze of the arm may escalate into something more overtly erotic. What were once routine end-of-session hugs may last longer and longer, sometimes evolving into blatant sexual activity without either party ever saying a word.

Some studies have suggested that the stereotypic perpetrator of this courtship is a middle-aged, predatory man often in the midst of a divorce, depression, or other personal crisis. Psychiatrist Glen O. Gabbard has said that he has never seen a therapist who is content in a personal relationship engage in a sexual relationship with a client. This middle-aged male stereotype only holds true up to a point, however; of 250 cases seen by the Minneapolis Walk-In Counseling Center, 14% of the perpetrators were women. Of these,

12% had become sexually involved with a female patient. In the 1986 Gattrell survey of 1,423 psychiatrists, 88% of the sexual transgressions were between male therapists and female patients, 3.5% were between female therapists and male patients, and 1.4% were between female therapists and female patients.

The conventional wisdom seems to be that sexual transgressions in therapy will diminish with the feminization of the therapy profession, as if sexual predation were a function of masculinity. This is probably true as an overall trend, but at least in isolated cases, women therapists are fully capable of becoming sexually involved with their clients. When they do so, the pattern and dynamics are very much the same as with male therapists: the therapist abuses her power and takes advantage of her role and her symbolic significance to the client.

## Wendy's Story: No One Left to Trust

Wendy's story fits this pattern. In her pretherapy scheme of the world, men had the potential to be power-hungry exploiters and women were loving nurturers. Her experience with Arlene taught her otherwise.

Wendy began therapy while in college to facilitate her process of "coming out" as a lesbian. The university counseling service assigned her to Arlene, a well-respected, distinguished woman in her sixties who had been employed there for twenty years. She had a forthright, cut-to-the-chase manner, penetrating gray-green eyes, and cropped gray hair. A few weeks after Wendy "came out" to her friends and family, Arlene "came out" (and came on) to her, disclosing not only that she was a lesbian but also that she was available. Wendy recalls Arlene's pointed disclosure: "Arlene said, 'My lover just left me. *She . . .*'"

This self-disclosure left Wendy feeling flattered and, at the same time, a little frightened. As Wendy says, "There was something wrong about her suddenly telling me so much about her personal life." The disclosure had seductive undertones—what did Arlene want? Sympathy? A replacement lover? Wendy felt bound to keep two secrets for Arlene: that her lover had left her and that she was confiding about her personal life to her clients.

Secrets already had a painful significance for Wendy. She explains,

> My father was an alcoholic and to protect the family we had to keep that a secret. The other secret was incest. My father said that if I ever told anyone he would hurt my mother. It took twenty years for my sisters and me to talk and realize that he had abused all of us and gotten us to keep his secret the same way.

As the next step in their courtship, Arlene invited Wendy out to dinner after a session. Again, Wendy was flattered but frightened; here was the most popular, most accomplished counselor at the center wanting to spend time with her. But were therapists really supposed to have dinner with their clients? Over dinner, Arlene spewed forth a steady stream of compliments: "You're one of my favorite clients," she said. And "I think you're a very sexy woman." A duality was introduced: Was Wendy a favorite client or a potential lover? Could these two roles be compatible?

Flattery such as Arlene's is also a common element of the therapist's courtship. At first, the client may imagine that the compliments are offered therapeutically—to boost her self-esteem. Because they come from a therapist who has been vested with a certain authority and symbolic weight, these compliments are so charged as to seem irresistible.

When Arlene invited Wendy over to her house, Wendy was too confused, too thrilled, to say no. Wendy had no sooner entered the house than Arlene put her arm around her and started kissing her and touching her breasts. "And," Wendy recalls, "she kept talking about *our* secret, saying that if anyone found out about our involvement, it would be her 'professional suicide.' " Meanwhile, Arlene made no attempt to terminate the therapy.

Growing up in her father's house had taught Wendy how to tolerate a relationship with two faces; her father had functioned as a strict paternal authority by day and a crazed alcoholic sexual tyrant at night. Wendy continued with the therapy, never mentioning the "other side" of their relationship in sessions. As she had struggled to keep the daytime and nighttime fathers separate, she now struggled to please Arlene the lover in bed and to keep her secret so as not to lose Arlene the therapist. Meanwhile, Wendy felt guilty for this turn of events; her father had always told her that her "bedroom eyes" were what had driven him to incest. Wendy now feared that her bedroom eyes had overcome her therapist.

Arlene clearly kept the power advantage she gained by virtue of the therapeutic role in the extra-therapeutic relationship. This was no love affair between equals—Arlene set the rules for what was and wasn't admissible in bed, and elsewhere. After a while, Wendy found the strain of keeping the two relationships impossible. She proposed to Arlene that they give up the therapy for the sake of their romantic relationship, or if Arlene preferred, they could go back to simply being therapist and client. Arlene wanted to keep it both ways.

At the end of the year, Wendy's parents threw her a graduation party and she invited Arlene. One of Wendy's former lovers was suspicious of what Wendy had told her about the relationship and confronted Arlene, "This doesn't seem like therapy," she said. "What are you doing with Wendy?" Arlene denied everything, resorting to psychobabble, which incensed Wendy's friend all the more.

After the party, Wendy left town for a brief vacation. When she returned and called Arlene, Arlene would not return her calls. Wendy panicked, feeling abandoned, frightened, and guilty. Mutual friends of Wendy and Arlene induced Arlene to come over to their house for a confrontation with Wendy. "Yes, I *had* a romantic relationship with Wendy," she confessed to the group, "and now it's over."

Wendy ran out of the house sobbing. Arlene followed her and started talking in her dry, clinical, professional voice. Wendy was desolate—she had lost her confidant, friend, lover, and therapist in one fell swoop. She recalls the feeling, "When even your therapist rejects you, you are absolutely alone."

Apparently Arlene had decided to terminate the romantic relationship and so simply retreated to the therapist's role. At the same time she downplayed any damages to Wendy by representing the relationship as no more than a failed love affair. Of course, the stakes had been much higher for Wendy. Although she did not realize it at the time, she had been caught in a reenactment, an attempt to reverse the damages of her father's crimes against her through the curative power of Arlene's love. Sex with Arlene had all the undercurrents of her incestuous relationship with her father. She explains, "I had a very deep wound from what happened with my father and I thought that Arlene could be a band-aid for that wound. I thought her attention could heal me." Wendy thought that Arlene was the opposite of her father: gentle where he was rough, understanding where he was indifferent. Her father had made her feel worthless; Arlene made her feel important, special, singled out. In her attempts to effect a magical, transformative cure, Wendy had actually been victimized again: "I realize now that Arlene did exactly what my father did. I grew up believing that men were monsters and women were nurturers. After Arlene, there was no one left to trust."

Wendy finally went to another therapist to help her sort out what had happened with Arlene. She helped her to feel less guilty for "seducing" Arlene, less guilty finally for what had happened with her father. Wendy explains, "My therapist said that even if I had walked into a session with all of my clothes off, Arlene's job was to tell me to put my clothes back on and to talk to me about what I was feeling."

## Analogous to Incest?

For psychoanalytic thinkers, a woman does not have to have been a survivor of childhood incest for sex with her therapist to be analogous to incest. The therapist always represents a parent, and so, as Glen Gabbard says, "sexual involvement with one's therapist is always symbolically incestuous." The mixed feelings that accompany it and the distress that follows it may also be inherent in the act. Analyst Charles Wahl of Los Angeles says, "A woman might think she wants to go to bed with daddy but in reality she does not. There is a feeling of horror and disgust and revulsion afterwards."

Even if we choose not to buy completely into psychoanalytic theory regarding the oedipal conflict, the parallel between incest and client–therapist sexual involvement seems clear. The therapist is forbidden as a sexual object, has significantly greater power, and assumes an authoritative, if not parental, role. Like a parent in relation to a child, the therapist is duty-bound to put his or her own needs aside in deference to the client's. A woman who has slept with her therapist tends to blame herself for corrupting the therapist with her desire, just as an incest survivor blames herself for seducing her parent. A woman who has become sexually involved with her therapist may rationalize to herself and lie to others to protect the therapist's reputation, just as a child will do everything to retain even a fragment of an image of the most abusive parent as good.

The dynamics of incest usually include a third party—the other parent—looking on or refusing to see. Therapist–client sexual involvements also seem to have a built-in tendency toward triangulation. This third party may be the focus of guilt or of titillation— the therapist's wife, who is always on the verge of discovering the illicit goings-on in his office, or the client's partner, who is being betrayed. The third party may be what one of the women in my survey called "the silent policeman in the room," the abstract parental authority who disapproves of the therapist's clandestine sexual activities. This authority may be the therapist's training institute, the licensing board, or the profession of psychotherapy itself. For some therapists, the therapeutic boundaries themselves come to represent an authoritarian parent, and sex with the patient the ultimate form of adolescent rebellion.

The psychological impact is also comparable to that of incest. A woman whose sexual relationship with her therapist ends is apt to feel far greater pain than if she had simply been involved in a disappointing love affair. The professional literature suggests that she may feel abandoned, betrayed, and unable to trust. Women who have slept with their therapists may feel, as incest victims feel, that the natural order has been sundered and the rules no longer pertain.

Sexual transgressions hurt not only the women directly involved but potentially all of the therapist's other clients if they find out about the sexual trespass and consequently question their own relationship with the therapist. Even when a therapist performed admirably in a woman's own care, she may find it difficult to reconcile her experience with the knowledge that he slept with one of his other patients. She may even feel jealous—Wasn't I special enough? Why didn't he pick me?—although being singled out for exploitation hardly seems a prize.

Indirectly, transgressing therapists hurt every client who must enter the therapeutic process suspicious of the profession and afraid to fully trust their therapists.

## Are Some Women More Susceptible?

If sexual relations in therapy tend to resemble the dynamics of incest, some researchers have postulated that a history of childhood incest or other sexual abuse predisposes a woman to this form of sexual exploitation. The woman may be more likely to reenact her seuxal abuse in the hopes of mastering or reversing her trauma. Victims of prior abuse may not know how to say no or draw a boundary. Psychiatrist Richard Kluft found that a significant number of women who had become sexually involved with their therapists had a family history of incest. He referred to these women as "sitting ducks" because of their increased vulnerability to sexual misconduct. Others have questioned Kluft's findings, as the reported incidence of incest is inordinately high among *all* female psychotherapy clients—not just those who are exploited.

Some critics are wary of any research that searches for common characteristics among abused clients because this kind of data can be turned around so readily to blame the victim. Gary Schoener insists there is no discernable pattern among victims. "No client characteristic predicts sexual involvement with a therapist," he says. According to Schoener, the issue is power and the abuse of power, and any client is vulnerable to a therapist who doesn't play by the rules.

Other studies have contended that victims of therapist–client sex with a history of incest suffer more profound psychological damages than those without such a history. These findings have not been borne out consistently by other research. For the moment, what seems clear is that women with childhood histories of incest and abuse need therapists with particularly reliable boundaries and an informed respect for transference-countertransference dynamics.

### Tina's Story: You Be the Daddy and I'll Be the Baby . . .

Like Wendy, Tina was a childhood incest survivor. Her stepfather sexually abused her from early adolescence until she fled his house as a teenager. She went into therapy because of an aversion to sex with her husband and panic attacks whenever she went out in public. She and her therapist Andrew used the hermetically sealed environment of therapy to create a world where the fantasy of a return to childhood reigned. Their relationship evolved into a sort of shared madness between lovers, a *folie à deux*. The promises Andrew made were too good to be true, and their play-acting was to have adult consequences.

Tina was raised in the South, and the hint of an accent remains. She was thirty-six when she went into therapy with Andrew, whom she did not find at all attractive on her first visit. In fact, she thought he was one of the strangest looking men she had ever seen:

> Andrew was a rather small man and very, very thin. He was bald, but he took this little bit of hair that was left and let it grow real long and then combed it up over the top of his head to cover the baldness. He looked kind of sickly. He was always smoking his pipe. His trademark was a silk handkerchief in his jacket pocket. God knows how many silk handkerchiefs that man had!

There was one thing about Andrew that Tina liked, though. When he came out to the waiting room to get her, he was wearing a fine, gold bracelet. Desperate to believe that Andrew would be able to help her, Tina fled to the realm of magical symbols and took the bracelet as a sign that Andrew was gentle and sensitive—the opposite of the brutal, domineering men in her family.

As Tina got to know Andrew better, he did seem to be the man the bracelet foretold. He was so gentle, she recalls, that when she would talk about sad circumstances in her life, the tears would roll down his cheeks. The more painful the experience was for her, the more painful it seemed to be for Andrew. After a few sessions, when Tina would begin to cry, Andrew would come and sit next to her on the sofa with a box of tissues on his lap.

A few sessions later, Andrew again intensified the intimacy by gently stroking Tina's hair while she cried. Later he began to vow eternal care. Tina recalls that over and over again when she expressed anxiety, Andrew would say, "I love you and I'll always be here for you. I'll never do anything to hurt you. Everything is going to be okay."

Andrew seemed to be promising perfect, eternal, unconditional love, the kind of care that mothers provide infants, or, more accurately, the golden fantasy of perfect maternal care. Such love is impossible, of course, among mortal human beings. Andrew not only failed to observe the usual therapeutic boundaries by touching Tina and by self-disclosing, but he also breached probably the most essential boundary of all human interactions—that between self and other. When Tina felt pain, Andrew cried harder than she did. He leapt right past therapeutic empathy to a state of willfully induced confusion about who was whom. He seemed as drawn as Tina to the illusion that two people could merge and so escape the pain of their own individuality. Tina wallowed in this illusion. Her anxiety abated. As she says now, "I really thought our hearts were one." However, Tina was not becoming any more capable of independent life, which had been one of her original goals in seeking therapy. Instead, she was growing more and more dependent on Andrew, as he became "my father and mother, my whole family."

In his boundary crossing, promise of eternal love and safety, and seductive fantasy of merger, Andrew denied the approximate nature of the relationship between client and therapist. He never helped Tina come to terms with its inherent limits, nor with any of the other limits implicit in adult life. Instead, he encouraged her to regress more and more into a fantasy of infancy, until during some sessions she imagined herself still "a baby in her mother's womb."

The irony was that Andrew, the all-encompassing, all-protecting daddy-mommy, was also Andrew the baby. He seemed so fragile, so sensitive that Tina soon felt bound to take care of him. Not far into her therapy, Andrew confessed a dark secret: When he was a child, his mother had been so depressed that she was unable to get out of bed, so depressed that she had ignored her sensitive little boy. No matter how hard Andrew had tried, he had been unable to rouse her. Now he was on a crusade to save depressed women in the memory of his mother, whom he had not been able to rescue.

Andrew told this story about himself as testament to his selflessness and his love of women. In fact, it would seem that he was using his work and his clients in an ill-fated attempt to resolve his childhood relationship with his mother. He pretended to *be* a perfect mother in hopes of *getting* a perfect mother. His attempts to save his patients were selfishly based on the fantasy that by doing so he would finally receive the love he still craved and so redeem his own childhood.

The impossible agenda that Andrew brought to psychotherapy prohibited his treating his clients responsibly. And as much as Andrew may have been motivated by the fantasy of rescuing poor, depressed mom, he probably also wanted to punish her for abandoning him. This vengeful side of Andrew's agenda would ultimately express itself in his relationship with Tina.

During some sessions Andrew and Tina just sat with their arms around each other, not saying anything. Sometimes they listened to music on the cassette player Tina brought to the office. On Andrew's birthday Tina baked him a cake. After he blew out the candles she told him how much she loved him and asked, "Why couldn't you have been my father?" "I would have liked that," he said. "What would you have named your daughter?" "Amanda," he said. Tina decided that Amanda was a beautiful name.

Tina and Andrew had created a *folie à deux* of early childhood bliss in which they played together and comforted one another in complete isolation from the concerns of the outside world. This was shattered suddenly the day Andrew announced he was not really a mother-father-baby but an adult with a more grown-up need. While holding Tina in his arms, he pulled away and said, "I can't hold you like this anymore." Tina recalls being devastated:

> "Why . . . Why . . . Tell me why," I asked.
>
> "Something happens to me," Andrew said. "I don't want to frighten you, but whenever I hold you I get an erection."
>
> "Well, that's a slap in the face," I responded. "Don't you have someone else for that?"

Since adolescence when her stepfather had sexually abused her, Tina had not enjoyed sex. She had learned to dissociate during her grandfather's abuse, to take herself away from her body and to become numb. With Andrew's gentle ministrations, she had begun to allow herself to feel again, but she still regarded his wanting to have sex as a form of betrayal. Feeling that she had to "grow up for Andrew or lose him," she relented.

If Tina had had a responsible therapist, she would have been working to understand the psychological impact of childhood incest and the toll that never being able to trust a parent had taken on her life. Instead, her therapist insisted that she reenact the worst event of her childhood—the corruption of father into lover. Her total dependency on Andrew, and on the fantasy world they had created in his office, made it unbearable for her to say no, and sexual intercourse became an element of their sessions.

Then one morning after a three-day weekend Andrew came in for Tina's "appointment" as "white as a sheet." He explained that he had gotten married over the weekend and that, under the circumstances, they were going to have to stop seeing each other. "Therapy is over," he announced. Andrew had promised over and over again that he would never leave Tina. She told him that she couldn't survive without him, that if she lost him she would lose her mind. After several more sessions of pleading with him not to leave her, Tina told Andrew that she would need to see another therapist to get her through the process of separating from him.

Andrew protested vigorously, "No, you can't talk to anyone else about this. Being a therapist is the most important thing in my life and you can't take it away from me. Other people just aren't going to understand what we've been doing in here."

She would no longer keep his secrets, she said. "Go ahead then," he shouted. "No one will believe you anyway. You're the one with the psychiatric diagnosis."

Then Andrew the baby started crying and talking about his poor depressed mother, how he was doing all this for his mother. A few days later, Tina attempted suicide by taking an overdose of sleeping pills. When she woke up in the hospital, the nurse asked her if she knew who she was. "Yes," she said, "my name is Amanda."

At the end of therapist–client sexual involvements, the underlying disjunction between the client's needs and the therapist's needs becomes most apparent. The therapist, as if recovering from a love potion, snaps out of it and returns to the outside world. The client may feel as if there is no natural order to which to return, as if the bottom has fallen out of the world. She needs a therapist for help in understanding and grieving the relationship. The therapist's primary concern is in keeping the trespass a secret. The client suddenly recognizes the truth of the situation: The therapist hasn't been acting in her interest all along. When it finally comes down to the client's mental health versus the therapist's career, transgressing therapists tend to fight for their own survival.

So much for Andrew's vow of infinite love, eternal care. The gallons of tears he had shed on Tina's behalf meant little; he had always know that they were just playing a game, and now it was time for their little *folie à deux* to be over. If he could not save one more depressed woman, at least he could stop her from taking him down.

For Tina, the stakes in the game had always seemed life and death, sanity and madness. If the illusion of merger with Andrew had brought feelings of perfect gratification and wholeness, separation carried the terror of a psychic annihilation worse than physical death.

When Tina sued Andrew in civil court, her attorneys found out that he was carrying on similar relationships with several patients. With one, the roles of mommy and baby were reversed. The client pretended to be the mommy, while Andrew lay his head down on her lap and gurgled. This, at least, was a more straightforward expression of his wish for maternal nurturance.

Even without the sexual behavior, Andrew had conducted a reckless form of boundary-less therapy. He had encouraged Tina to regress into childhood, when she needed the rational adult part of herself to do the therapeutic work. He had vowed eternal love, rather than guiding her to work within the constraints of the approximate relationship. In therapy, the past can be understood, and some of its deficits compensated for, but there is no redeeming re-enactment, no reparenting possible. Tina learned a lesson that every woman in therapy should take to heart: The therapist who promises perfect parenting is often a starving infant in disguise.

## Does Termination Make It Okay?

Of the three major professional associations that represent therapists, the American Psychiatric Association and the National Association of Social Workers now state in their codes of ethics that sex with former patients is unethical. In contrast, the American Psychological Association's code states, "Psychologists do not engage in sexual intimacies with a former patient or client for at least two years after cessation" and do not do so even then "*except in the most unusual circumstances.*"

While the American Psychological Association further qualifies their position by stating that the therapist in this situation may be called on to demonstrate that there has been "no exploitation" of the client, they leave the door open to the possibility that therapist and client may, after a suitable waiting period, become lovers.

Perhaps the American Psychological Association had in mind this sort of situation: A behaviorist treats a woman a few times for a phobia using desensitization strategies. The therapy is successful, and three years later she runs into him at a party. They begin to date. Why should the fact that they met as therapist and patient preclude their right to a romantic relationship?

This hypothetical couple may exist. I would hazard to say that Olivia's experience, described next, may be more typical of post-termination sexual liaisons between clients and patients. Her story illustrates how the knowledge that a romantic relationship may occur in the future can turn the therapy relationship into a mere prelude to the fantasied relationship to come.

## Olivia's Story: The Laboratory of Love

Olivia is an exceptionally pretty, articulate, well-educated woman in her late thirties. She comes from a wealthy South American family, speaks several languages, and had already traveled the world by the time she reached her mid-teens. Olivia's parents divorced when she was six because her mother fell in love with another man. He left as soon as her divorce was final, and she sank into depression and hypochondria, dividing her time between her bed and doctors' offices. A progression of servants cared for Olivia, who behaved like a "little adult," cheerfully accepting her father's absence and her mother's incapacitation.

In her heart, Olivia was not cheerful. She missed her father, a brilliant, charismatic, but self-centered entrepreneur who had "a wonderful playfulness." After the divorce, Olivia remained her father's special confidant, entrusted with his adult secrets. He took her on extravagant weekend adventures but only "by appointment," and never again set foot in the house she shared with her mother.

Olivia started therapy with Mac, who had been in practice for only a few years, to find out why she could not seem to find the right man or have a satisfying romantic relationship. Olivia found Mac attractive, charming, funny, smart, and sensitive. She could not help but fantasize that he might well be the man she had been looking for for so long. She declared her attraction in a session several months into the therapy, and Mac acknowledged that he also felt attracted to her. Unsure how to handle the situation, he sought advice from a renowned senior therapist, and then reported back that Olivia could either terminate the therapy or that they could use the "transference," as he called her feelings, to work on her problems with intimacy.

We'll never know, of course, how accurately Mac represented the consultant's advice. The problem was that Mac made it sound as if terminating the therapy at any time so as to enter into a romantic relationship was an option. This is certainly not the intent of the American Psychological Association's two-year waiting period; terminating therapy *in order to enter into a romantic relationship* is considered unethical by the codes of all the professional associations. Nevertheless, this option was to haunt Olivia's therapy.

Olivia was of two minds: She wanted to get help and she wanted to get Mac. In choosing to continue the therapy, she was not operating entirely in good faith, since she did so without giving up the romantic agenda. She was simply afraid that if she quit therapy too soon, Mac might not be motivated enough to pursue the romantic relationship. So Olivia was working to get Mac to fall in love with her as much as she was working to understand herself.

As the therapy progressed, Mac seemed equally torn between the two original options. He was so cavalier about the therapeutic boundaries that he sometimes seemed intent on bending them. He would take Olivia down to the corner to get coffee to go, remove his shoes and put his stockinged feet close to hers on the footrest they shared, groan as he rubbed and rolled his aching shoulders.

Mac also had a habit of talking about himself. These disclosures appeared to be spontaneous but hardly seem random in retrospect. They had a seductive effect: Mac told Olivia just enough to draw her into his life but never enough to dissuade her from pursuing him. He'd allude to being unhappy in his own romantic relationship—"I'm not even sure I believe relationships between men and women are possible," he'd sigh, as if waiting for Olivia to prove him wrong. But whenever Olivia attempted to question Mac directly about the status of his romantic life, he'd invoke the edict against therapist self-disclosure. This placed Olivia in a double bind—when it suited his purposes, Mac kept to the rules, when it did not, he bent them. Being entrusted with her therapist's intimate secrets thrilled Olivia, re-creating her childhood role as her father's special confidant, and it filled her with an old longing.

Olivia only learned later that the woman Mac was living with at the time was his own former therapist! Although there are no data to prove it, it would seem that, like incest, sexual transgressions in therapy recur from one generation to the next. Therapists who are victimized by their own therapists, their own instructors and training analysts, tend to repeat history by victimizing their clients. The single most important predictor of whether a therapist will keep good boundaries and appreciate the symbolic meanings of the relationship—more important than formal education—may well be the relationship the therapist had with his or her own therapist. No wonder Mac seemed equivocal about therapist–client sexual liaisons: To have taken a stand against them would have required that he condemn his own lover's behavior.

About a year into the treatment, on the night before Mac was to leave for a week's vacation, he walked Olivia to the door at the end of her session and said, "I wish you could come with me." Many therapists would argue that the therapy was over the minute the invitation was out of his mouth. It is not so unusual for a therapist to say something he shouldn't, to occasionally confuse his needs with the client's. But there are some statements in some situations that cannot be taken back. Like the jury asked by the judge to disregard a witness's incriminating remark, Olivia could never forget Mac's invitation. His telephone apology later that night did nothing to mitigate its impact.

Mac's haphazardness, his impulsivity in offering the invitation, points out once again the disproportionate stakes for therapist and client. Olivia had invested the therapeutic relationship with the power to resolve her difficulties in romantic relationships. She was understandably confused as to whether this important help would come through the process of doing therapy with Mac or simply as a byproduct of his love. Because of Mac's symbolic weight, and the resonances between her relationship with him and with her father, she could not afford for him to be so casual and cavalier. How could she possibly put his invitation into any sort of realistic perspective?

Over the months, Mac focused more and more on the "in-the-room relationship," depicting it as the laboratory in which Olivia would learn how to love. She would learn to be close to him, he explained, and then she would take that capacity out of the room and love another man. He pushed her to feel more, trust more, express more, give more. "Give me your longing, your pain, your grief, your rage," he said. "I want it all."

This instruction was seductive—all her feelings were suddenly *about* him, directed *at* him, expressed *for* him. His desire, his wanting something from her, was too palpable. Their sessions were soon electrified with connection; Mac struggled to find the superlatives grand enough to describe their bond—it was "compelling," "unprecedented," "charting new therapeutic ground"; they were "flying by the seat of their pants." She revealed a vulnerability to Mac that she had never before allowed any man to see. He cried with her, became indignant at the injustices of her childhood, grew positively high on their encounters.

Olivia was less ecstatic. Although addicted to the connection she felt in their sessions, she was tortured by the "betwixt and between" nature of the relationship. "Intimacy by appointment" with Mac resembled too closely her relationship with her father and evoked an old resolve to do everything in her power to get him back.

Olivia recalls,

> Several months after my father had left us, I missed him so much that late at night I would lie on my bed, draw the curtains, look out into the night sky, and search for a star bright enough to wish on. I would focus all my attention, all my energy on that star, and I would wish and wish and wish that my daddy would come back.

Olivia told Mac that the relationship felt "very dangerous" to her. Rather than exploring where she perceived the dangers to lie as a competent therapist might, he forged recklessly ahead. "Do you think relationships out in the world are any safer?" he said. Olivia hesitated, then said, "I don't want any more partial relationships." But her therapist had an answer to this objection too. "This isn't partial," he said. "Everything will be possible between us except the sex. The feelings are real; I expect to know you the rest of my life."

Therapists get into trouble when they pretend that a therapy relationship can be equivalent to a full-blooded relationship in the world, when they promise their clients everlasting love when what they can offer are only approximations of love. For Mac to say that sex was the only thing missing from his in-the-room relationship with Olivia was a serious—and seductive—misrepresentation. Missing was the difficult meshing of needs that must take place day after day in a real life romantic commitment. Missing was the subtle interplay of two people's internal lives within the demands and constraints of external reality. Missing was the requirement for Mac to confide equally and to present his needs openly. Most notably missing was the accommodation of negative feelings—hostility, anger, aggression, sorrow—that are inherent in any human relationship. Portraying the relationship as perfect afforded Mac a defense against the full gamut of feelings that people must contend with in relationships. The in-the-room alliance was a "virtual" relationship, carrying no risk and comparatively few consequences for Mac.

Upping the amplitude on the relationship in the room only made Olivia's longing outside the room more intense. Laboratory love was so seductive that in-the-world relationships with their struggle and strain paled in comparison. Olivia could not bear the double binds any more, so she decided to quit therapy. Mac issued what seemed like a threat: "If you don't work out your issues about men in here with me," he said, "you're not going to be able to work them out anywhere." After a few more sessions he reversed himself, accepting her decision and declaring her therapy a success. "You offered all your wonderfulness up to me on a platter," he said, "and because I resisted we were able to get to the root of your problems."

Remember what Michael Kahn said? A therapist's seduction need not be overtly sexual to be damaging to the client; seduction encompasses everything that a therapist does to make a client want him. Consciously or otherwise, Mac had done everything in his power to make Olivia want him, to, in her own words, "create the perfect situation for someone to fall in love with him."

Olivia responded with a ferocity born on those nights she had wished on a star. Getting Mac was a way to right the wrongs of her childhood, to deny her father's abandonment and double messages, to prove to herself that she had the power to get whatever she really wanted, to get whoever she really loved to love her back.

For two years, Olivia pursued Mac while he expressed ambivalence. He cared so much about Olivia but felt "conflicted" about "dating a former client"; he wanted to behave ethically; he didn't think he would be "enough" for her; he was unhappy but still living with his former therapist, Ilsa. When they met for an occasional lunch, Mac did most of the talking. He boasted about how many pounds he could bench press; he talked about his plans to write a psychology textbook; he complained about Ilsa's paying more attention to her prize bulldogs than to him. Mac's grandiosity was starting to seem ridiculous to Olivia. Still, she could not let go of her memory of the intense, connected, loving man she had met in the laboratory of love.

With news that Mac had left Ilsa, afternoon lunches escalated to dinners. Once, when Olivia and Mac were together, he insisted they go to his office to pick up some files. Returning to the site of her therapy made Olivia uncomfortable. She was struggling to separate therapy from their post-therapy romance. Mac said the way to accomplish this was to "defile the very place that was being protected." Seeing Olivia in his office again aroused him and he grabbed her and started kissing and fondling her. She withdrew, instinctively aiming to protect the scene of her therapy, and wondering: Who is this man? Have I been seduced by my own seduction?

That defiling the sanctity of Olivia's therapy aroused Mac suggests that some part of him might also have been invested in defiling her therapy even while it took place. How much respect did the boundary-defying Mac really have for the sanctity of the therapist's role or for the symbolic charge therapists carried? When

Mac announced shortly thereafter that he was going back to Ilsa, Olivia asked him to come over and make love to her, just once, anyway. Mac had maintained his "ethics" by refusing to have sexual intercourse with her. For Olivia, this act had taken on ever more magical properties. She believed that it would substantiate the true bond between Mac and her. He agreed to have sex but was in a hurry, as Olivia recalls:

> We pushed into one another. He seemed hungry, rushing and abrupt. We thrashed. I swooned. Our sex had an over-before-it-began feeling.
>
> "You have a nice touch," he said. "You're easy to make love to."
>
> With his clothes off, Mac seemed old mannish and soft, his body curling over on itself. He was smaller in stature than he seemed in his office. It was as if someone had finally let all the air out of him.

In their sexual consummation, the Mac who had existed in the laboratory of love deflated before Olivia's eyes. The spell was broken. Months later Mac called to explain himself. He had always felt ambivalent about love, he said. He had never felt loved by his parents and thus defended against feeling the loss by never completely committing himself to any woman. Loving Olivia so intensely while in the room—and he assured her that he had loved her—allowed him to maintain his out-of-the-room relationship with Ilsa, about whom he had also been ambivalent. The intensity without obligation of laboratory love had served his own psychological purposes well. Mac asked Olivia to see him again; she declined.

"Mac was a loose cannon," Olivia says now, "unwilling to see his own limitations. Even two years after the fact, he wasn't able to take a close look at what had happened in the therapy with me."

Mac waited nearly two years after terminating the therapy relationship before sleeping with a client. In many respects, however, his sexual encounter with Olivia was no different than if it had occurred during the course of her therapy. She was driven by fantasies that had only grown stronger during the years following termina-

tion. The symbolic stakes of the relationship remained disproportionately higher for Olivia. Mac had encouraged Olivia's longings
by behaving seductively while conducting her therapy, implicitly
promising her true love, love beyond the limits of the approximate
relationship, probably beyond the limits of mortal life.

The sex act itself, rather anticlimactic in this case, was not the
source of the harm. The source of the harm was Mac's confusion
between his needs and his client's; his lack of integrity and consistency as a therapist; his disregard, even contempt, for the therapeutic boundaries; and his failure to respect and honor the symbolic dimensions of his role. Mac was like a young boy with a chemistry
set. He just didn't have the skill or the knowledge to control the ex-
plosive forces of the laboratory love his experiments unleashed.

Olivia's story illustrates some of the reasons why many leaders
in the therapeutic community agree that, when it comes to sexual
involvement, "once a patient, always a patient." The client who gains
a lover always loses a therapist—not only the therapist with whom
she has met, but also the therapist that she has internalized. What
happens to that voice of reason, of concern, of positive mirroring in
her head if she and the in-the-flesh therapist have a love affair that
ends badly?

Olivia emerged from her experience bitter, angry, and wary of
the whole psychotherapeutic process. Whatever gains she may have
made in the therapy were undermined by what happened afterward.

The stories in this chapter should serve as cautionary tales to any
woman contemplating sexual involvement with her therapist. There
may be stories with happier endings—women whose sexual relationships with their therapists matured into ordinary in-the-world
relationships with the usual pleasures and problems. The odds seem
very much against it, though, against a relationship that begins with
such an unequal power dynamic ever becoming an egalitarian partnership. The client's fantasy of transformative love is also apt to die
hard and leave some destruction in its wake.

I know a woman who wakes up in the middle of the night and,
in a trancelike state, sees a man standing over her. He seems so real
that every time it happens she has to touch the figure, and only

when her hands goes through the form is she convinced that he is not real. The woman who actually sleeps with her therapist may find that her lover is just such a phantom.

Does this mean that there was nothing real about the Mac Olivia encountered in therapy, that the intuitive, empathetic, insightful man she connected with in therapy was a mere illusion? Maybe not entirely. In some respects therapists are like actors. In their portrayals they may embody nobility, strength, vulnerability that has the power to make the audience weep, to inspire the audience's love. They may even have the power to made the audience change, to bring out the best in the audience's own behavior. Offstage, the actor may be boorish, petty, insensitive. Does the actor's "real" self invalidate the power of the characters he portrays? It is possible for a therapist to embody something greater than his day-to-day self in the room, something that helps other people mobilize the better parts of themselves. Olivia may well have seen glimpses of Mac's best self at his finest moments in the room. In response, she may have been her finest self as well.

# Coda

Since I began writing this book, the status of psychotherapy in our society has changed. Managed care has refused to pay for long-term treatment, and policymakers have attacked therapies that they characterize as open-ended self-exploration or pseudo-friendship.

In this climate, researchers scurry to perform the outcome studies that would prove that particular forms of psychotherapy actually work. As with all medical research, it is easiest to generate clear-cut results when the method, the patients to be studied, and the desired outcomes are narrowly defined. That is why most of the psychotherapy outcome studies that have been done so far link very narrowly defined interventions with equally narrowly defined results.

Given the formerly unregulated state of affairs in the field, this research is a positive development. For too long, psychotherapists have had to pick from a veritable grab bag of methods and techniques with little objective substantiation for their effectiveness. Partly because of the mystery still surrounding human psychology, psychotherapy has seemed exempt from the more rigorous scientific inquiry required to test every other form of medical treatment. Eventually, sophisticated studies may show us not only what works, but ways to apply what works more systematically to improve its effectiveness.

Nevertheless, when I look at the slew of outcome studies that have been published over the past few years, studies that, for example, find ten or fifteen sessions of a specific cognitive behavioral regimen effective in the treatment of "clinical depression," I'm not sure how widely these findings apply. The subjects studied, with their single diagnoses, scarcely resemble the complex women of my interviews. Would these women, who may be more representative of those who seek psychotherapy in the real world, fare as well? In the long term, do the patients in those outcome studies consider themselves cured or happy, able to go on and have more satisfying lives? Or have they simply, perhaps temporarily, learned to define "successful treatment" in their practitioners' terms? Are ten or twelve or even fifteen sessions, conveniently the number of sessions for which providers are willing to pay, enough to change deeply ingrained psychological patterns that are tied to the soul-suffering that the women in my book reported?

In developing therapies that lend themselves to easily quantified results, we run the risk of adopting an overly simplistic view of human beings. What cannot be measured or computed will be denied. Some of the popular short-term therapies already stress conscious thoughts at the expense of feelings. Some seem blind to the impact of irrationality, sexuality, and conflict as driving forces in human lives. Being in these therapies may only force women's true selves further underground. Ever compliant, wanting to succeed and to help their therapists succeed, they may keep whatever doesn't fit in their therapist's paradigm—their desires, rages, fears—a secret. The women I interviewed had a tendency to not tell their therapists what they didn't think their therapists wanted to hear. When a particular therapeutic worldview does not accommodate certain feelings or mental states, a woman who is experiencing them may simply conclude quietly that she is all the more abnormal for having them.

I suspect that some therapies that appear to work in the short term may create more internal conflict in the long term as clients fight with themselves to give voice to only the most rational, most adult part of themselves. As was the case with Anna O. a hundred years ago, therapy continues to be double-edged, a process that can either grant or deprive women their voices.

At the opposite extreme from these newer, very directive, short-term therapies that focus on changing thoughts and cognitive schemas are the more traditional psychoanalytically oriented therapies that may go on indefinitely. They deserve some of the criticism they've received; women in my survey told me of therapies that wandered for months, even years, without a clear course. The therapist rationalizes this drift with the belief that he or she is waiting patiently for unconscious processes to unfold. The client may be too attached to the therapist, too disappointed by her own lack of progress, to leave. Client and therapist may collude silently to not bring up the most painful material, the most uncomfortable problems: Mere duration of therapy is no guarantee of depth.

I was shocked at how many times during the course of interviews women informed me that they had never been able to tell their therapists the "secrets" they were telling me. I was a total stranger, often a stranger they had met over the phone. I was a journalist, not a mental health practitioner. Why could they tell me what they couldn't tell the professional they were paying to listen? Sometimes I think the answer was simply that I enthusiastically and aggressively asked the questions that their therapists refrained from asking.

The problems that plague psychotherapy are partly attributable to the polarization between various schools of therapeutic thought. The movement for therapy integration, which would incorporate the best strands from all perspectives, is promising. If it prevails, psychoanalytic therapists may learn to be more directive and to ask more questions. Cognitive behaviorists may learn to give emotion and conflictual motives as much weight as more conscious thought and to use the client–therapist relationship as a therapeutic element in itself.

Therapists, of all persuasions, must make it easier for their clients to talk to them about sexuality. In a reaction against the Freudian notion that sex is at the root of everything, many therapists now act as if sexuality is completely irrelevant. Some male therapists told me that their fear of being accused of doing something inappropriate with female clients has inhibited their ability to talk to them about sexuality.

Although sex may not be at the root of everything, it is certainly intertwined with other crucial issues in women's psyches. Many of the women that I interviewed told me that excluding sexuality from the domain of their therapy was one way in which therapy rendered them silent.

When psychotherapy is time-limited and more directed, clients may get trapped less often in some of the excruciating conundrums over the therapeutic relationship that are described in this book. They may be less likely to have to ask: Is therapy helping at all, or have I just become too attached to my therapist to leave? How will I ever find a real life relationship to match the emotional intensity of this one? If I'm in love with my therapist but can't have him or her, should I just stay in my long-term relationship and fantasize about my therapist all the time? and so on. When clients and therapists have an explicit understanding of where therapy is heading and of what therapy can realistically provide, surely clients will experience less confusion and pain.

That said, something will also be lost if in the process of making therapy a more directive process, therapists neglect the ways in which clients need to use them symbolically. Something will be lost if therapists are not trained to reflect on or use the relationship in the room as an element of the therapy. Whatever the therapeutic model, it is naive for client and therapist to pretend that their own relationship can be exempt from the dynamics, the interpersonal struggles that characterize the client's relationships outside of therapy and are often what brought the client to therapy in the first place.

The women I interviewed agreed that there is no insight quite as moving, quite as persuasive, as the insight gained by being able to see, in the relatively protected relationship with your therapist, what you are doing outside of therapy in relationships with other significant people in your life. There is no insight as powerful as seeing the past clearly through the present connection. A therapist need not embrace all aspects of the psychoanalytic concept of transference to appreciate the therapeutic power of this experience.

At a recent meeting of psychotherapists, I attended a lecture and videotape presentation of one of the new forms of short-term, cognitive therapy. The presenter was a handsome, appealing therapist, just out of training, energetically committed to his particular approach.

As always, the format made me uncomfortable. There was no one to speak for the client. I may have been the only nontherapist in the room. The therapist showed a videotape that contained several segments excerpted from the course of a therapy session. He stopped the tape at various intervals to offer explanation and interpret the material on screen.

The client in the video was a pretty young woman who had embarked on a twelve- or fifteen-session course of therapy. The problem it seemed was that she couldn't form satisfying relationships with other people. She did not trust that other people were interested in her or wanted to spend time with her. She wasn't able to assert herself in relationships and always felt as if she were being taken advantage of or hurt by the other person.

The woman arrived at her session distraught. With tears in her eyes, she glared at her therapist. He had given her a homework assignment, to plan a weekend getaway with a new female acquaintance whom she admired and desired to have as a friend. She had planned every detail of the weekend trip with great care, had looked forward to it with great excitement, and then, at the very last moment, the would-be friend had canceled.

The client was close to tears as she choked out the details of what had happened and how it made her feel abandoned. The therapist postulated some ways of interpreting what had happened, reasons why the woman might have had to cancel that had nothing to do with the client's lack of desirability as a friend. What were the mental schemas that drove the woman to interpret such ambiguous events as proof of her own social failings?

The client continued to glare at the therapist, clutching her homework assignment notebook to her chest. Her acquaintance's abandonment at the last moment, she said, reminded her keenly of some early experiences with her mother. Her mother never seemed to want to spend time with her. She kept remembering one particular day in a shopping mall. Her mother had parked her in the central plaza to "play" while she went off to shop "for a few minutes." The mother left her there for what seemed like hours. In the wake of this most recent rejection, all she could think about was how it felt to wait there, longing for her mother and knowing that she was off shopping, impervious to her daughter's needs. As she recounted this episode, her voice grew softer and yet more impassioned; tears welled up and spilled out of her eyes. She seemed to really want to talk about that day in the mall, no, she *needed* to talk about it, she needed the therapist to hear the story.

But the anecdote, the woman's obvious emotional distress, scarcely slowed the therapist down for a moment. He gave no sign that her sadness affected him. What must have seemed clear to him was that they needed to move on.

Here was a woman who often felt invisible to other people; here was a woman used to abdicating her own needs for the sake of other people's agendas. In fact, these were the very problems that had brought her to therapy, and here she was in therapy and the same interpersonal process appeared to be happening again. The therapist did not feel what she was feeling; what she needed to talk about was not important to him.

The client made a feeble attempt to return to the subject, but so tentatively, with such a sense of defeat, that the therapist gave it only an instant's attention and then moved on. Perhaps he was also aware of the presence of the video camera and the fact that in addition to helping his client, he must demonstrate certain salient features of the therapy.

The woman continued to glare, pulled her crossed arms in even tighter to her body, and mouthed the answers to the questions the therapist was asking. But she had begun to pull away from him, to withdraw emotionally. There was something else going on in the room that the therapist had not addressed. If this woman had been so devastated because an acquaintance had disappointed her by canceling a trip at the last moment, what sort of feelings was she harboring toward the therapist who had led her into the situation—who had assigned it, in fact? Didn't the acquaintance's rejection have a significant impact on the client's relationship with her therapist as well? For me, the woman's unspoken questions—"Did you set me up so that I could be rejected again?" "Why didn't you protect me?"—were as present in the room as the force of gravity. What if the woman had felt free to voice those questions, and by standing up for herself with the therapist, had begun to learn how to stand up for herself in the outside world? What if by sorting out with her therapist the jumble of feelings she had for him, she had gained a new understanding of the way she functioned in relationships with others, and so found the courage to venture out again?

I grew even more uncomfortable. The woman was now doubly silenced—silenced in the interaction with her therapist, silenced in this room of therapists looking on. I thought again about Anna O., silenced when it came to proclaiming how she felt about the very relationship that should have helped her find a voice. I imagined the pretty young woman emerging from the screen and addressing the therapists in the room. "This is what you, and my therapist, failed to see," she would begin. I wanted to interview her, to simply ask her what had been going through her mind during the session in question. How had it made her feel when the therapist pushed on past her memories? How did it make her feel to know that he was implicated in her most recent rejection?

If the woman on screen was anything like the women I did talk to, then the issues that were causing her pain in her outside relationships were also operating in her relationship with her therapist. If she were anything like the women in my survey, then what she was longing for in the exchange was that the therapist slow down and simply be entirely, emotionally present with her in the relationship, that he be with her, if only for a few moments, as a little girl in a shopping mall forlornly waiting for her mother. Then they could return to the other tasks of the therapy.

Could the therapeutic work proceed with these unspoken feelings in the air? Would the therapist's methods be enough to show the woman how to change her relationships in the world? Or would what was left unspoken in the relationship between client and therapist undermine the work of the therapy?

I only know what the women I interviewed told me. I know how many secrets they harbored during sessions and I also know how liberated they felt when, like Renee, they finally anted up, finally felt free enough to say what they felt and were accepted for saying it.

In too many arenas of their lives women have had to speak their minds indirectly, through symptoms, through other people, through passive-aggression. When psychotherapy effects change, it is partly by giving voice to those aspects of the self that have remained silent, exerting themselves in indirect and destructive ways.

Therapy holds the promise of full exposure in the presence of another person. Such exposure is both dangerous and exhilarating. Sometimes it is only through such an act of being seen and heard completely that we can begin to know how we really think and feel. We gain a self through the very act of articulation.

The women in my book agreed about the one experience in therapy that was the most profound, that held the greatest prospect for change. That was the experience of being "gotten"—of being understood, truly seen and heard in all one's humanity, all one's complexity, all one's conflict—by another human being. Perhaps Marjorie summed it up best: "There was nowhere in me we couldn't go," she said of her therapist Kay. Marjorie could pay her therapist no greater compliment than to allow her to enter into what had once been closed, interior monologues.

I hope that therapists who have read this book will pause a moment the next time the presenter turns off the videotape to consider what the client might not have been able to say, to allow for what the therapist on screen might have failed to see.

And I urge the client who has read this book to become more proactive in her own therapy, to set goals and revisit them and to question her therapist more about the process. And I would ask her to take a chance by inviting and requiring her therapist to enter more fully into her interior monologues. Only by revealing what she is really feeling about herself, her therapist, and their relationship might a woman in therapy have the profound pleasure of being seen and truly understood.

# *Notes*

*Note to the reader:* Unless a quote is attributed to a particular written source, it comes from interviews conducted with the author between 1993 and 1998.

CHAPTER 1

**page 21** "I, a native German girl": Bertha Pappenheim's report on her illness was written in English and is reprinted in its entirety in Albrecht Hirschmüller, *The Life and Work of Josef Breuer: Physiology and Psychoanalysis* (New York: New York University Press, 1978), pp. 296–297.

**page 21** doctor with the "golden touch": Lucy Freeman, *The Story of Anna O.* (New York: Walker & Company, 1972), p. 5.

**page 22** Like the vampire women in the fiction of the period: I am indebted to literary critic Nina Auerbach for pointing out the similarities between vampire women in Victorian fiction and hysterics in physicians' case studies in her book, *Woman and the Demon: The Life of a Victorian Myth* (Cambridge, MA: Harvard University Press, 1982). This book also influenced this chapter in its conceptualization of the empowering freedom that Victorian women gained with "patient" status, albeit at some price.

**page 22** Angel of Death: I have taken poetic license in presuming that Bertha Pappenheim may have shared an awareness of this folkloric notion.

**page 23** "private theatre": Josef Breuer and Sigmund Freud, *Studies on Hysteria* (New York: Basic Books, Harper Colophon Edition, n.d.; reprint of the *Standard Edition of the Works of Sigmund Freud,* Vol. II, translated and edited by James Strachey, with the collaboration of Anna Freud [London: Hogarth Press, 1955]), p. 22. Originally published in 1894.

**page 23** "penetrating intuition," "great poetic and imaginative gifts," "sympathetic kindness": Breuer and Freud, p. 21.

**page 23** "I have a real self and an evil self": I have taken some liberties in making this a direct quote. Breuer and Freud wrote, "she would complain . . . of having two selves, a real one and an evil one" (p. 24).

**page 24** passionately "fond": Breuer and Freud, p. 22.

**page 24** "pampered her": When a physician, now presumed to be Josef Breuer, admitted Bertha Pappenheim to the Bellevue Sanatorium in a small town in Switzerland in July 1882, he left a written case report. Reprinted in its entirety in Hirschmüller, pp. 276–292, the relevant section reads: "very monotonous life, limited entirely to the family; she seeks compensation in passionate fondness for her father who spoils her." Henri Frederic Ellenberger, the historian who first discovered the Bellevue documents, translated the word as "pampers" rather than "spoils" in "The Story of Anna O.: A Critical Review with New Data," *Journal of the History of the Behavioral Sciences*, 8(3), July 1972, pp. 267–279.

**page 24** "The patient, whose life": Breuer and Freud, pp. 21–22.

**page 24** "The element of sexuality": Breuer and Freud, p. 21. In his admissions case history, Breuer wrote, "the sexual element is astonishingly undeveloped; I have never once found it represented amongst her numerous hallucinations. At all events, she has never been in love to the extent that this has replaced her relationship to her father; it has itself, rather, been replaced by that relationship." (Hirschmüller, pp. 277–278).

**page 24** "calm and cheerful": Breuer and Freud, p. 27.

**page 24** "talking cure," "chimney sweeping": Breuer and Freud, p. 30.

**page 24** "the most severe psychical trauma": Breuer and Freud, p. 26.

**page 24** "cheated out of a glance": Hirschmüller, p. 284.

**page 24** "violent outburst of excitement," "greatly changed state," Breuer and Freud, p. 26.

**page 24** "wax figures": Hirschmüller, p. 284.

**page 24** "stove": Hirschmüller, p. 285.

**page 24** "Only for me was she invariably present": Hirschmüller, p. 284.

**page 27** Years later Freud claimed: Freud reported the epilogue in a letter to his friend, writer Stefan Zweig in June 1932; see Ernst L. Freud, Ed., *Letters of Sigmund Freud*, translated by Tania and James Stern (New York: Dover, 1992), p. 412.

**page 27** "seized by conventional horror": E. L. Freud, p. 413. Ernest Jones, Freud's devoted biographer, also retells the story in *The Life and Works of Sigmund Freud*, edited and abridged by Lionel Trilling and Steven Marcus (New York: Basic Books, 1961), pp. 147–149.

**page 28** "derived from the analytic situation": Sigmund Freud, "Observations on Transference-Love," in *The Freud Reader,* edited by Peter Gay (New York: W. W. Norton, 1989), p. 379. Originally published in 1915. I am also indebted to Peter Gay for explaining in the introduction to this essay that part of Freud's motivation for writing it was his concern over the sexual entanglements of his followers with their patients.

**page 29** he complained in a letter: Breuer's letter to Auguste Forel is cited in P. F. Cranefield, "Josef Breuer's Evaluation of His Contribution to Psychoanalysis," *International Journal of Psycho-Analysis, 39,* 1958, pp. 319–322.

**page 32** She has been rediagnosed: Psychiatrist Richard J. Loewenstein rediagnosed Anna O. as suffering from dissociative identity disorder (formerly called multiple personality disorder) in *Rediscovering Childhood Trauma: Historical Casebook and Clinical Applications,* edited by Jean M. Goodwin (Washington, DC: American Psychiatric Press, 1993), pp. 139–167. See also *Anna O.: Fourteen Contemporary Reinterpretations,* Max Rosenbaum and Melvin Muroff, Eds. (New York: The Free Press, 1984).

**page 33** "Love did not come to me —": Bertha Pappenheim's complete poem appears in Hirschmüller, p. 308. The remaining three stanzas read:

> *Love did not come to me —*
> *So I sound like a violin*
> *With a broken bow.*
>
> *Love did not come to me —*
> *So I bury myself in work*
> *And, chastened, live for duty.*
>
> *Love did not come to me —*
> *So I like to think of death*
> *As a friendly face.*

For a vivid portrayal of the medical treatment of hysteria as well as the social milieu of the time, see Hannah S. Decker, *Freud, Dora, and Vienna 1900* (New York: The Free Press, 1991). For a fictionalized first person account of a hysteria-like illness, written in 1899, see Charlotte Perkins Gilman, *The Yellow Wallpaper* (New York: The Feminist Press, 1973).

**page 33** "double-edged sword": This comment is attributed to Bertha Pappenheim in D. Edinger, *Bertha Pappenheim: Freud's Anna O.* (Highland Park, IL: Congregation Solel, 1968), p. 12. The complete quote reads: "Psychoanalysis in the hands of the physician is what confession is in the hands of the Catholic priest. It depends on its user and its use, whether it becomes a beneficial tool or a two-edged sword."

CHAPTER 2

**page 49** Attachment and Dependency: While some attachment and dependency may be a natural outgrowth of the relationship, therapists can also err by fostering too much dependency. See Paul R. Abramson, Monique Y. Cloud, Natalie Keese, and Robert Keese, "How Much is Too Much? Dependency in a Psychotherapeutic Relationship," *American Journal of Psychotherapy, 48*(2), Spring 1994, pp. 294–301.

**page 49** *transitional objects*: D. W. Winnicott introduced the concept in "Transitional Objects and the Transitional Phenomena: A Study of the First Not-Me Possession," *The International Journal of Psycho-Analysis,* XXXIV(Part 2), 1953, pp. 89–97.

**page 57** The Golden Fantasy: Sydney Smith, "The Golden Fantasy: A Regressive Reaction to Separation Anxiety," *International Journal of Psycho-Analysis, 58*(311), 1977, pp. 124–137.

CHAPTER 3

**page 66** social ascription: I am indebted to Marilyn R. Peterson, *At Personal Risk: Boundary Violations in Professional-Client Relationships* (New York: W. W. Norton, 1992), for her explanation of the sources of the therapist's power and the consequences of the power differential; see especially chapters 1 and 2, pp. 11–49.

**page 66** "unregulated industry": Jack Engler and Daniel Goleman, *The Consumer's Guide to Psychotherapy* (New York: Simon & Schuster/Fireside, 1992), p. 73.

**page 69** Until 1973: The American Psychiatric Association only removed homosexuality from its *Diagnostic and Statistical Manual of Mental Disorders* after a referendum of the organization's membership. For a complete account of this historic controversy, and an appreciation for the politics behind psychiatric nomenclature, see Ronald Bayer, *Homosexuality and American Psychiatry: The Politics of Diagnosis* (New York: Basic Books, 1981).

**page 69** therapists claimed that they could "convert": There has been a resurgence of Christian therapies claiming that they can "convert" or cure homosexuals. For a history of therapies directed at converting homosexuals, see Jack Drescher, "I'm Your Handyman: A History of Reparative Therapies," *Journal of Homosexuality, 36*(1), 1998, pp. 19–42.

**page 70** "The First Contact with the Patient": Chapter 3 in Robert Langs, *The Technique of Psychoanalytic Psychotherapy,* Vol. 1 (Northvale, NJ: Jason Aronson, 1989), pp. 51–52.

**page 74** Bronislaw Malinowski's classic study: Bronislaw Malinowski, *Argonauts of the Western Pacific: An Account of Native Enterprise and Adventure in the Archipelagoes of Melanesian New Guinea* (Prospect Heights, IL: Waveland Press, 1982). Originally published 1922.

**page 81** "Darocles": I have changed the name of the deity to protect the identities of the therapist, his colleagues, and his clients. Clients informed me that the channeling was used as part of the psychotherapy sessions and so was billed along with the therapy.

**page 81** therapists use hypnosis: This topic has recently received a lot of attention because accused family members have successfully sued therapists who helped clients recover presumably inaccurate memories of childhood incest. The larger issue of the appropriate use of hypnosis in psychotherapy and the nature of the material "accessed" has not been subjected to adequate scientific study.

**page 82** In her book *At Personal Risk*: See Peterson, chapters 1 and 2.

## CHAPTER 4

**page 87** APA's newly revised Code of Ethics: *Ethical Principles of Psychologists and Code of Conduct,* Rev. Ed. (Washington, DC: American Psychological Association, 1992).

**page 87** any sexual contact: The Code establishes that, in rare instances, sexual contact with former clients, after a two-year waiting period, may not be unethical.

**page 89** a slightly toned-down version: *Ethics & Behavior*, 4(3), 1994, pp. 255–306. The six dissenting opinions were by Bruce E. Bennett, Patricia M. Bricklin, and Leon VandeCreek of the APA Insurance Trust; Debra S. Borys of UCLA; Laura S. Brown of Seattle, Washington; Glen O. Gabbard of the Menninger Clinic in Topeka, Kansas; Michael C. Gottlieb of Dallas, Texas; and Thomas G. Gutheil of Harvard Medical School. In the same issue, Arnold Lazarus responded to the dissent with a rejoinder.

**page 92** the Rat Man: This famous patient of Freud's was so named because as an army lieutenant he became obsessed with images of a prisoner being tortured by rats boring into his anus. His case study appears in "Notes Upon a Case of Obsessional Neurosis," in Sigmund Freud, *Three Case Histories* (New York: Crowell-Collier, 1963), pp. 15–105. Originally published in 1909.

**page 92** Ferenczi's "experiments": The account of Ferenczi's therapeutic experiments is from Judith Dupont, Ed., *The Clinical Diary of Sándor*

*Ferenczi,* translated by Michael Balint and Nicola Zarday Jackson (Cambridge, MA: Harvard University Press, 1988), pp. 34–37.

**page 92** romantic triangle: Kenneth S. Pope, *Sexual Involvement with Therapists* (Washington, DC: American Psychological Association, 1994) pp. 62–63.

**page 93** "corrective emotional experience": Franz Alexander and his concept of the corrective emotional experience is described succinctly in Michael Kahn, *Between Therapist and Client: The New Relationship,* Rev. Ed. (New York: W. H. Freeman and Company, 1997), p. 99. For the full explication of Alexander's views, see F. Alexander and T. French, *Psychoanalytic Psychotherapy* (New York: Ronald Press, 1946).

**page 94** Psychologist Carl Rogers: A good summary of Rogers's approach and influences appears in Kahn, pp. 37–52. Kahn considers the "best single introduction to Rogers" to be Carl Rogers, *On Becoming a Person* (Boston: Houghton Mifflin, 1961).

**page 95** A few practitioners went so far: There were two therapists in particular who wrote seriously on the subject. James L. McCartney's article, "Overt Transference" was published in the *Journal of Sex Research, 2*(3), November 1966, pp. 227–237. Martin Shepard wrote a book called *The Love Treatment: Sexual Intimacy between Patients and Psychotherapists* (New York: Peter H. Wyden, 1971).

**page 96** The Basic Rules: Some model boundary guidelines were proposed in Edward M. Hundert and Paul S. Appelbaum, "Boundaries in Psychotherapy: Model Guidelines," *Psychiatry, 58*(4), 1995, pp. 345–356.

**page 97** Thinking about Boundaries: Psychiatrists Tom Gutheil and Glen Gabbard provide another way of thinking about the subtleties of boundary issues by making a distinction between boundary crossings which may have positive or negative effects and boundary violations which are always harmful. See Thomas G. Gutheil and Glen O. Gabbard, "The Concept of Boundaries in Clinical Practice: Theoretical and Risk-Management Dimensions," *American Journal of Psychiatry, 150*(2), 1993, pp. 188–196. See also Richard S. Epstein, *Keeping Boundaries: Maintaining Safety and Integrity in the Psychotherapeutic Process* (Washington, DC: American Psychiatric Press, 1994).

**page 99** boundaries set limits: See Marilyn R. Peterson, *At Personal Risk: Boundary Violations in Professional–Client Relationships* (New York: W. W. Norton, 1992), p. 46: "Boundaries protect the space that must exist between the professional and clients by controlling the power differential in the relationship."

**page 100** "acts that breach the core intent": Peterson, p. 75.

**page 106** an exhilarating sense of specialness: See Peterson, p. 78: "When the roles are initially reversed, some clients feel elevated in the eyes of the professional. Like a mood–altering drug, the change in status from what they expected feels wonderful. It creates a natural high. Clients mistakenly believe that feeling special stems from who they are as people. They feel validated and chosen."

**page 106** When the boundary slips: Peterson, p. 77: "In a boundary violation, the professional and the client switch places and the client becomes the caretaker. The professional structures the inside of the relationship according to his or her needs. Having reversed roles, the professional now looks to the client for gratification." See also p. 78: "Even though the client becomes the caretaker in a boundary violation, the professional does not give up the control. The professional still defines the parameters of the relationship, determining whose needs will come first and who will meet them. The decision to give priority to his or her concerns is made unilaterally and without the client's full knowledge or consent."

**page 106** Psychologist Michael Kahn: Kahn, in *Between Therapist and Client* (p. 147), attributes the concept of seduction and punishment to the teachings of the Boston Psychoanalytic Institute: "Another bit of wisdom passed around that same institute, one I have held dear for years, was, 'There are only two ways to do real damage to patients: *seducing them* and *punishing them*. If you do neither of those things, you can't get into serious trouble.' (*Seducing* meant more than literally seducing them; it meant working to arouse their desire for you, their admiration for you, their dependence on you. *Punishing* meant anything, however subtle, calculated to hurt them.)"

**page 116** restrictive, legalistic defensive manner: Recent concern over lax boundaries in therapeutic practice may have led to a literalistic overreaction in some institutional and regulatory settings. See Thomas G. Gutheil and Glen O. Gabbard, "Misuses and Misunderstandings of Boundary Theory in Clinical and Regulatory Settings, *American Journal of Psychiatry, 155*(3), March 1998, pp. 409–414.

**page 116** boundaries do protect therapists' interests: How clients may initiate boundary crossings or reenact boundary violations enacted against them and the deleterious impact on therapists is the focus of Tina Chadda and Rodney Slonim, "Boundary Transgressions in the Psychotherapeutic Framework: Who is the Injured Party?" *American Journal of Psychotherapy, 52*(4), 1998, pp. 489–500.

## CHAPTER 5

**page 119** "For they saw, standing in just the spot": L. Frank Baum, *The Wonderful Wizard of Oz* (New York: Alfred A. Knopf Everyman's Library edition, 1992), pp. 147–148. Originally published in 1900.

**page 121** "The most remarkable thing is this": Sigmund Freud, *An Outline of Psycho-Analysis*, translated and edited by James Strachey (New York: W. W. Norton, 1969), p. 31. Originally published 1940.

**page 121** "menacing illusion," Freud, *Outline*, p. 34.

**page 121** "waking dream," "Just as happens in dreams": Sigmund Freud, "The Dynamics of Transference," reprinted in *Essential Papers on Transference,* edited by Aaron H. Esman (New York: New York University Press, 1990), p. 34. Originally published in 1912.

**page 123** Carl Rogers: Carl Rogers, *On Becoming a Person* (Boston: Houghton Mifflin, 1961); and "The Necessary and Sufficient Conditions of Therapeutic Personality Change," *Journal of Consulting Psychology*, *21*(2), 1957, pp. 95–103.

**page 130** "a social-cognitive phenomenon": Jefferson A. Singer and Jerome L. Singer, "Social-Cognitive and Narrative Perspectives on Transference," in *Empirical Perspectives on Object Relations Theory*, edited by Joseph M. Masling and Robert F. Bornstein (Washington, DC: American Psychological Association, 1994), p. 158.

**page 131** What information-processing theory may not yet be able to explain: Several papers by Drew Westen describe the challenges of employing the cognitive perspective to explain the internal conflicts and contradictory behaviors that have been of central significance in psychoanalytic theory. See the note for page 142 for a list of references by Westen.

**pages 131–134** Andersen and her team of associates: The discussion of Susan Andersen's work is based on telephone interviews with her as well as on her published work. See Susan M. Andersen and A. B. Baum, "Transference in Interpersonal Relations: Inferences and Affect Based on Significant-Other Representations," *Journal of Personality, 62*(4), 1994, pp. 460–497; Katrina Hinkley and Susan M. Andersen, "The Working Self-Concept in Transference: Significant-Other Activation and Self Change," *Journal of Personality and Social Psychology, 71*(6), 1996, pp. 1279–1295; Susan M. Andersen, Noah S. Glassman, Serena Chen, and Steve W. Cole, "Transference in Social Perception: The Role of Chronic Accessibility in Significant-Other Representations," *Journal of Personality and Social Psychology, 69*(1), 1995, pp. 41–57; Susan M. Andersen, Inga Reznik, and

Lenora M. Manzella, "Eliciting Facial Affect, Motivation, and Expectancies in Transference: Significant-Other Representations in Social Relations," *Journal of Personality and Social Psychology,* 71(6), 1996, pp. 1108–1129; Susan M. Andersen and Michele S. Berk, "Transference in Everyday Experience: Implications of Experimental Research for Relevant Clinical Phenomena," *Review of General Psychology,* 2(1), March 1998, pp. 81–120; Susan M. Andersen, Inga Reznik, and Serena Chen, "The Self in Relation to Others: Cognitive and Motivational Underpinnings," in *The Self Across Psychology: Self-Recognition, Self-Awareness, and the Self Concept,* edited by J. G. Snodgrass and R. L. Thompson (New York: New York Academy of Science, 1997), pp. 233–275.

**page 134** script theory: Tomkins's example of a script comes from Amy P. Demorest and Irving E. Alexander, "Affective Scripts as Organizers of Personal Experience," *Journal of Personality,* 60(3), September 1992, p. 647. See also S. S. Tomkins, *Affect, Imagery, Consciousness,* 2 vols. (New York: Springer, 1962–1963); and S. S. Tomkins, "Script Theory: Differential Magnification of Affects," in *Nebraska Symposium on Motivation,* Vol. 26, edited by C. B. Keasey (Lincoln: University of Nebraska Press, 1979), pp. 201–236.

**page 134** In 1992: Demorest and Alexander, pp. 645–663.

**page 136** Psychologists Lester Luborsky and: Lester Luborsky and Paul Crits-Christoph, *Understanding Transference: The CCRT Method* (New York: Basic Books, 1990); Paul Crits-Christoph, Amy Demorest, Larry R. Muenz, and Kathryn Baranackie, "Consistency of Interpersonal Themes for Patients in Psychotherapy," *Journal of Personality,* 62(4), December 1994, pp. 499–526; and Deborah Fried, Paul Crits-Christoph, and Lester Luborsky, "The First Empirical Demonstration of Transference in Psychotherapy," *Journal of Nervous and Mental Disease,* 180(5), 1992, pp. 326–331.

**page 142** Drew Westen: See the following by Westen: "Transference and Information Processing," *Clincal Psychology Review,* 8, 1988, pp. 161–179; "Implications of Cognitive Science for Psychotherapy: Promises and Limitations," *Journal of Psychotherapy Integration,* 4(special issue), December 1994, pp. 387–399; "Psychodynamic Theory and Technique in Relation to Research on Cognition and Emotion: Mutual Implications," in *Handbook of Cognition and Emotion,* edited by T. Dalgleish and M. Power (New York: Wiley, in press); "The Scientific Status of Unconscious Processes: Is Freud Really Dead?" (in press); "Integrating Psychodynamic and Cognitive–Behavioral Theory and Technique," in *Handbook of Psychological Change: Psychotherapeutic Processes and Practices for the 21st Century,* edited by C. R.

Snyder and R. Ingram (New York: Wiley, in press); "The Scientific Legacy of Sigmund Freud: Toward a Psychodynamically Informed Psychological Science," *Psychological Bulletin, 124,* 1998, pp. 333–371.

**CHAPTER 6**

**page 143** the 1944 film *Gaslight:* The screenplay for *Gaslight* was written by Patrick Hamilton, John Van Druten, Walter Reisch, and John L. Balderson. The script was based on Hamilton's play *Angel Street: A Victorian Thriller in Three Acts.*

**page 146** As psychiatry critic Thomas Szasz: Thomas Szasz, "The Concept of Transference," *The International Journal of Psycho-Analysis, 44*(Part 4), 1963, pp. 437–438.

**page 150** Analyst Merton Gill: A concise summary of Gill's work appears in "A Re-Experiencing Therapy: Merton Gill," chapter 4 in Michael Kahn, *Between Therapist and Client: The New Relationship,* Rev. Ed. (New York: W. H. Freeman and Company, 1997), pp. 53–85. See also Merton Gill, *The Analysis of the Transference,* Vol. I (New York: International Universities Press, 1982).

**page 151** As psychiatrist Arnold Cooper: Arnold M. Cooper, "Changes in Psychoanalytic Ideas: Transference Interpretation," in *Essential Papers on Transference,* edited by Aaron H. Esman (New York: New York University Press, 1990), p. 522.

**page 166** seducing them and punishing them: Kahn attributes this rubric to the Boston Psychoanalytic Institute. See note for page 106.

**CHAPTER 7**

**page 173** Stone Center: For more information on the Stone Center's theoretical and clinical work, see Jean Baker Miller, *Toward a New Psychology of Women* (Boston: Beacon, 1976); Jean Baker Miller and Irene P. Stiver, *A Relational Reframing of Therapy* (Wellesley, MA: Stone Center, 1991); Judith V. Jordan, *Relational Resilience* (Wellesley, MA: Stone Center, 1992); Jean Baker Miller, Judith V. Jordan, et al., *Work in Progress: Some Misconceptions and Reconceptions of a Relational Approach, No. 49* (Wellesley, MA: the Stone Center, 1991); Judith V. Jordan, Alexandria G. Kaplan, et al., *Women's Growth in Connection: Writings from the Stone Center* (New York: Guilford, 1991); Jean Baker Miller and Irene P. Stiver, *The Healing Connection: How Women Form Relationships in Therapy and in Life* (Boston, MA: Beacon, 1997).

**page 174** Jacqui Schiff: Jacqui Schiff (with Beth Day), *All My Children* (New York: Harper & Row, 1975); and Jacqui Schiff, *Cathexis Reader: Transactional Analysis Treatment of Psychoses* (New York: M. Evans, 1970).

**page 179** Heinz Kohut: For a concise review of Kohut's work, see "The Meeting of Psychoanalysis and Humanism: Heinz Kohut," chapter 5 in Michael Kahn, *Between Therapist and Client: The New Relationship*, Rev. Ed. (New York: W. H. Freeman and Company, 1997), pp. 87–123. See also Heinz Kohut, *How Does Analysis Cure?* (Chicago: University of Chicago Press, 1984); and *The Analysis of the Self* (New York: International Universities Press, 1971).

**page 183** the golden fantasy: Sydney Smith, "The Golden Fantasy: A Regressive Reaction to Separation Anxiety," *International Journal of Psycho-Analysis*, *58*(311), 1977, pp. 124–137.

**page 183** "Such a blissful state was actual": Smith, p. 124.

**page 184** "Stepford" moms: The *Stepford Wives* was a 1975 film based on an Ira Levin novel that was part science-fiction thriller, part social satire. In it, the husbands of a suburban community conspire to turn their wives into robots so that they have no selves or desires of their own beyond serving their husbands' needs perfectly.

CHAPTER 8

**page 190** the visual bridge experiment: See *Social Referencing and the Social Construction of Reality in Infancy*, edited by Saul Feinman (New York: Plenum Press, 1992).

**page 191** Melanie Klein: For a concise explanation of Kleinian and other object relations theories, see Glen O. Gabbard, *Psychodynamic Psychiatry in Clinical Practice* (Washington, DC: American Psychiatric Press, 1994), pp. 37–51. See also Klein, *Developments in Psychoanalysis*, edited by J. Riviere (London: Hogarth Press, 1952); *Psychoanalysis of Children* (New York: Grove, 1932, 1960); and *The Selected Melanie Klein,* edited by Juliet Mitchell (New York: The Free Press 1987).

**page 192** Margaret Mahler: For a brief summary of Mahler's work, see Gabbard, pp. 49–51. See also Margaret Mahler, "Symbiosis and Individuation: The Psychological Birth of the Human Infant," *Psychoanalytic Study of the Child, 29,* 1974, pp. 89–106; "On the First Three Subphases of the Separation-Individuation Process," *Journal of the American Psychoanalytic Association, 15*(4), 1972, pp. 740–763; "On Human Symbiosis and the Vicissitudes of Individuation," *Journal of the American Psychoanalytic Association*, *15*(4), 1967, pp. 740–763.

**page 194** Daniel Stern: Daniel Stern, *The Interpersonal World of the Infant* (New York: Basic Books, 1985), pp. 18–34. See also Daniel Stern, *The Motherhood Constellation: A Unified View of Parent-Infant Psychotherapy* (New York: Basic Books, 1995).

**page 195** D. W. Winnicott: D. W. Winnicott, *The Maturational Processes and the Facilitating Environment* (New York: International Universities Press, 1965), pp. 44–50.

**page 196** Winnicott suggests that the therapist: Winnicott, p. 240.

**page 202** A child's mirroring needs: Heinz Kohut, *How Does Analysis Cure?* (Chicago: University of Chicago Press, 1984), pp. 192–193. See also Michael Kahn, *Between Therapist and Client: The New Relationship*, Rev. Ed. (New York: W. H. Freeman and Company, 1997), pp. 91–93, 115–120.

**page 206** "unthinkable anxieties": Daniel Stern offers a complete catalogue and interesting discussion of these anxieties in Daniel Stern, *The Interpersonal World of the Infant* (New York: Basic Books, 1995), pp. 199–200. See also D. W. Winnicott, *The Maturational Processes and the Facilitating Environment* (New York: International Universities Press, 1965), pp. 57–58.

**page 207** twinning experiences: Kohut, pp. 192–193; see also Kahn, pp. 95, 115–120, 192–193.

## CHAPTER 9

**page 213** H. D.: Hilda Doolittle, *Tribute to Freud* (New York: New Directions, 1984), pp. 15–16. Originally published in 1974.

**page 222** Even Freud struggled: Freud, "Observations on Transference-Love," *Essential Papers on Transference*, Aaron H. Esman, Ed. (New York: New York University Press, 1990), p. 45. Originally published in 1915.

**page 225** "attraction + obstacles = excitement": Jack Morin, *The Erotic Mind* (New York: Harper Perennial, 1996), p. 50.

**page 225** "place a woman at risk": Linda Barlow and Jayne Ann Krentz, "The Hidden Codes of Romance," in *Dangerous Men and Adventurous Women*, edited by Jayne Ann Krentz (Philadelphia: University of Pennsylvania Press, 1992), p. 17.

**page 225** Dorothy Tennov: Dorothy Tennov, *Love and Limerence: The Experience of Being in Love* (Briarcliff Manor, NJ: Scarborough Books edition, 1981), p. 26.

**page 226** *Jane Eyre*: Charlotte Brontë, *Jane Eyre* (Rutland, VT: Charles E. Tuttle, 1991). Originally published in 1847. Mr. Rochester alternates between shows of empathy for Jane and utter neglect. On page 177, not unlike a good therapist, he perceives the depression she attempts to hide:

> "I am tired, sir." [Jane says]
> He looked at me for a minute.
> "And a little depressed" he said. "What about? Tell me."
> "Nothing—nothing, sir. I am not depressed."
> "But I affirm that you are: so much depressed that a few more words would bring tears to your eyes—indeed they are there now, shining and swimming; . . . If I had time, and was not in mortal dread of some prating prig of a servant passing, I would know what all this means."

Four pages later, after Jane has fallen even more in love with the perceptive, yet enigmatic, Mr. Rochester, she laments, "[H]e had ceased to notice me—because I might pass hours in his presence, and he would never once turn his eyes in my direction."

**page 226** *The Thornbirds*: Colleen McCullough, *The Thornbirds* (New York: Avon, 1978).

**page 226** the moment of reciprocation: Tennov, pp. 119–120.

**page 227** "[T]he very nature of the situation": Tennov, pp. 194–195.

## CHAPTER 10

**page 235** "It is madness in all women": Charlotte Brontë, *Jane Eyre* (Rutland, VT: Charles E. Tuttle, 1991), p. 156.

**pages 235–236** "He must take care": Sigmund Freud, "Observations on Transference-Love" in *Essential Papers on Transference,* edited by Aaron H. Esman (New York: New York University Press, 1990), p. 43. Originally published in 1915.

**page 248** three psychologist-researchers: Kenneth S. Pope, Patricia Keith-Spiegel, and Barbara G. Tabachnick, "Sexual Attraction to Clients: The Human Therapist and the (Sometimes) Inhuman Training System," in *Sexual Feelings in Psychotherapy: Explorations for Therapists and Therapists-in-Training*, edited by Kenneth S. Pope, Janet L. Sonne, and Jean Holroyd (Washington, DC: American Psychological Association, 1993), pp. 205–236. This book is one of the few sources that attempts to discuss the topic of sexual feelings in therapy without a strong theoretical bias, and it is valuable reading for clients as well as practitioners. Originally published in *American Psychologist, 41,* 1986, pp. 147–158. The same survey was repeated in 1994 with 453 social workers, with very similar findings. See Ann Bernsen, Barbara G. Tabachnick, and Kenneth S. Pope, "National Survey of Social Workers' Sexual Attraction to Their Clients: Results, Implications, and Comparison to Psychologists," in *Ethics & Behavior, 4*(4), pp. 369–388. Also see Nancy A. Bridges, "Meaning and Management of Attraction: Neglected Areas of Psychotherapy Training and Practice," *Psychotherapy, 31*(3), Fall 1994, pp. 424–433.

**page 250** Michael Sussman: See Michael Sussman, *A Perilous Calling: The Hazards of Psychotherapy Practice* (New York: Wiley, 1995), a fascinating anthology on the personal psychological challenges of practicing psychotherapy.

**page 250** Code of Ethics: *Ethical Principles of Psychologists and Code of Conduct,* (Washington, DC: American Psychological Association, 1992), pp. 9–10. The code goes on to read,

> Because sexual intimacies with a former therapy patient or client are so frequently harmful to the patient or client, and because such intimacies undermine public confidence in the psychology profession and thereby deter the public's use of needed services, psychologists do not engage in sexual intimacies with former therapy patients and clients even after a two-year interval except in the most unusual circumstances.

**page 250** The American Psychiatric Association: On the subject, this code reads,

> [T]he necessary intensity of the treatment relationship may tend to activate sexual and other needs and fantasies on the part of both patient and psychiatrist, while weakening the objectivity necessary for control. Additionally, the inherent inequality in the doctor–patient relationship may lead to exploitation of the patient. Sexual activity with a current or former patient is unethical.

*The Principles of Medical Ethics with Annotations Especially Applicable to Psychiatry* (Washington, DC: American Psychiatric Association, 1998), p. 4.

Similarly, *The Ethics Code of the National Association of Social Workers* (Washington, DC: NASW, 1997), p. 11, reads,

Social workers should not engage in sexual activities or sexual contact with former clients because of the potential for harm to the client. If social workers engage in conduct contrary to this prohibition or claim that an exception to this prohibition is warranted because of extraordinary circumstances, it is social workers—not their clients—who assume the full burden of demonstrating that the former client has not been exploited, coerced, or manipulated, intentionally or unintentionally.

## CHAPTER 11

**page 256** In a 1986 survey: Nanette Gartrell, Judith Herman, Silvia Olarte, Michael Feldstein, and Russell Localio, "Psychiatrist-Patient Sexual Contact: Results of a National Survey, I: Prevalence," *American Journal of Psychiatry 143*(9), 1986, pp. 1126–1131.

**page 256** Nearly every study: See Jacqueline Bouhoutsos, Jean Holroyd, Hannah Lerman, et al., "Sexual Intimacy Between Psychotherapists and Patients," *Professional Psychology: Research and Practice, 14*(2), 1983, pp. 185–196. This study, which asked licensed psychologists to report on clients with past histories of sexual involvement with a therapist, reported ill effects for 90% of the 559 patients who'd had a prior sexual involvement. Some critics have argued that studies that base their understanding of consequences on patients who seek further therapy or those who file complaints are flawed because those women who are *not* damaged may not seek further help or take further action. See also Roberta J. Apfel and Bennett Simon, "Patient–Therapist Sexual Contact, I. Psychodynamic Perspectives on the Causes and Results," *Psychotherapy and Psychosomatics 43*, 1985, pp. 57–62. For an overview of the research on consequences, see Kenneth S. Pope, *Sexual Involvement with Therapists: Patient Assessment, Subsequent Therapy, Forensics* (Washington, DC: American Psychological Association, 1994), pp. 117–156.

**page 257** 1% to 12%: Pope, p. vii. Figures on the incidence and prevalence of sexual transgressions have varied widely from survey to survey partly because the survey questions have defined sexual relations differently, and have not always encompassed sex with *former* as well as current clients. A table summarizing the major national studies appears in Ann Bernsen, Barbara G. Tabachnick, and Kenneth S. Pope, "National Survey of Social Workers' Sexual Attraction to Their Clients: Results, Implications, and Comparison to Psychologists," *Ethics & Behavior, 4*(4), p. 377.

**page 260** Sabina Spielrein: For the complete story, see Aldo Carotenuto, *A Secret Symmetry: Sabina Spielrein Between Jung and Freud* (New York: Pantheon, 1984); for a summary, see Pope, pp. 60–61.

**page 260** Ferenczi's "experimentation": See my notes for p. 92. For a summary, see Pope, pp. 62–63.

**page 260** Anais Nin's diary: See Anais Nin, *Henry and June: From the Unexpurgated Diary of Anais Nin,* with an introduction by Rupert Pole and biographical notes by Gunther Stuhlmann (New York: Harcourt Brace Jovanovich, 1986); and Anais Nin, *Fire: From A Journal of Love,* with a preface by Rupert Pole and biographical notes by Gunther Stuhlmann (New York: Harcourt Brace, 1995).

**page 260** Poet Anne Sexton: See Rachel T. Hare-Mustin, "Cries and Whispers: The Psychotherapy of Anne Sexton," *Psychotherapy: Theory, Research and Practice 29*, 1992, pp. 406–409; and Diane Wood Middlebrook, *Anne Sexton: A Biography* (Boston: Houghton Mifflin and Company, 1991).

**page 260** "Overt Transference": James L. McCartney, "Overt Transference," *The Journal of Sex Research,* 2(3), 1966, pp. 227–237. It seems fair to point out that McCartney was published in a journal devoted to sex research, not in a peer-reviewed journal dedicated to psychiatry or psychotherapy.

**page 261** *Women and Madness:* This 1972 classic by Phyllis Chesler was reissued in 1989 (New York: Harvest/Harcourt Brace Jovanovich) with a new foreword by the author.

**page 261** criminal offense: The 15 states in which client–therapist sex is now considered a crime are Arizona, California, Colorado, Connecticut, Florida, Georgia, Iowa, Maine, Minnesota, New Hampshire, New Mexico, North Dakota, South Dakota, Texas, and Wisconsin.

**page 262** a courtship period: This pattern of progressive boundary breakdown, sometimes referred to as the "slippery slope" has been reported by Glen O. Gabbard, Gary Schoener, and others. See L. H. Strasburger, L. Jorgenson, and P. Sutherland, "The Prevention of Psychotherapist Sexual Misconduct: Avoiding the Slippery Slope," *American Journal of Psychotherapy 46*(4), 1992, pp. 544–555. The fact that sexual boundary violations may begin with relaxation of other boundaries does not mean that every instance of lax boundaries necessarily leads to sex.

**page 267** Analogous to Incest?: The parallel between incest and therapist–client sexual involvement is ubiquitous in the literature. A good summation of the analogy as well as a comprehensive bibliography on sexual transgressions can be found in Pope, pp. 20–23. See *Sexual Exploitation in Professional Relationships*, edited by Glen O. Gabbard, (Washington, DC: American Psychiatric Press, 1989) and Ellen T. Luepker, "Sexual Exploitation of Clients by Therapists: Parallels with Parent-Child Incest," chapter 5 in *Psychotherapists' Sexual Involvement with Clients: Intervention and Prevention* (Minneapolis: Walk-In Counseling Center, 1989), pp. 73–79. The latter book, while dense and somewhat redundant, is a rich source of information on the subject of patient–therapist sex.

**page 269** Richard Kluft: Richard Kluft, "Treating the Patient Who Has Been Sexually Exploited by a Previous Therapist," *The Psychiatric Clinics of North America, 12,* 1989, pp. 483–500.

**page 275** Does Termination Make It Okay?: See notes for page 250. The subject of post-termination sex is discussed in the following articles: Glen O. Gabbard, "Reconsidering the American Psychological Association's Policy on Sex with Former Patients: Is It Justifiable?," *Professional Psychology, Research and Practice, 25*(4), 1994, pp. 329–335; Laura S. Brown, "Harmful Effects of Posttermination Sexual and Romantic Relationships between Therapists and Their Former Clients," *Psychotherapy, 25,* 1988, pp. 249–255; Paul S. Appelbaum and Linda Jorgenson, "Psychotherapist–Patient Sexual Contact after Termination of Treatment: An Analysis and a Proposal, *American Journal of Psychiatry, 148,* pp. 1466–1473; Melba J. T. Vasquez, "Sexual Intimacies with Clients after Termination: Should a Prohibition be Explicit?," *Ethics & Behavior I*(1), 1991, pp. 45–61.

# Acknowledgments

Thanks first must go to the women who trusted me enough to complete the survey questionnaire and to allow themselves to be interviewed, often at great length on very intimate matters, for this book. I am grateful for their bravery, frankness, curiosity, humor, and intelligence in articulating the dilemmas and exhilirations of psychotherapy. Their stories moved me, gave me nightmares, enraged me, and often made me rethink everything I thought I had come to know up to that point about the subject. As I found myself unintentionally thrown into the role of a therapist, I came to appreciate even more the artistry, skill, subtlety, and compassion required to perform the role well.

I am very grateful to my content adviser, Marie M. Cohen, who was a great teacher, a wise counselor, and a steadfast friend. Her acute mind and kind heart significantly shaped this project.

To the therapists and researchers who answered the hard questions I posed to them with much grace: Keith Ablow, Deborah Andersen, Judith Armstrong, Margaret Baker, Mindy Benowitz, Teresa Bernardez, Debra S. Borys, Alice Brand-Bartlett, Nancy Bridges, Andrea Celenza, Stanley J. Coen, Paul Crits-Christoph, Estelle Dische, Rena Folman, Richard P. Fox, Donna Frick, Deborah Fried, Glen O. Gabbard, Judith H. Gold, Thomas G. Gutheil, Janet Hadda, Constance Hammen, Lylette Hofkin, Jean C. Holroyd, Michael Kahn, Arnold Lazarus, Richard J. Loewenstein, Charles McGaw, Wayne Myers, Marilyn R. Peterson, Lisa Post, Nancy Ronne, Norman Schaffer, Gary Schoener, Janet L. Sonne, Alan Spivak, Irene Stiver, George Striker, Michael Sussman, Lenore Terr, Shari Thurer, Meredith Titus, Charles Wahl, and Drew Westen. To Jan Wohlberg for sharing her knowledge of sexual transgressions in therapy and for affording me access to women willing to talk about their experiences.

To my long-time research assistant and friend, Robert Ruckman, who worked diligently on every stage of this project; to Rachel Ross, who enthusiastically and energetically helped to gather and assess the survey respondents and interviews; to my UCLA intern, Jill McCall, whose curiosity and energy were enlivening; and to Patti Brooks, who provided data-base programming and analysis.

Thanks too must go to my good friend Gretchen Henkel, who developed some of the concepts and ideas behind this book with me and then allowed me to write it on my own; to the members of my writers' group for keeping me honest and halfway sane: Hope Edelman, Toni Frank, Karen Kasaba, Danny Miller, Spencer Nadler, Marilyn Reynolds, and Lynn Shook; to Bernard Cooper, for the inspiration provided by his own work and for reading early drafts of this material and offering astute critical judgment; to Marcia Seligson for acting as a mentor and for reading early drafts and offering very helpful comments; and to others who read early drafts and offered support and suggestions: Sara Arsone, Jared Diamond, Michael Kahn, Henry and Katherine Kimmel, and Jerome Shapiro.

I am grateful to my family for love and support and to friends and writer-colleagues who stuck with me even when my obsession with this project left little room for friendship: Margaret Hatfield, Katherine Phillips, Scott Wimer, Chris Miller, and Lucy Bradley.

My appreciation goes to the research librarians at the Menninger Clinic and the UCLA Biomedical Library, and to the press officers of the American Psychological Association, the American Psychiatric Association, the American Academy of Psychoanalysis, and the American Psychoanalytic Association for helping me find information and secure interviews with experts. I owe a particular debt to those teachers who allowed me to attend continuing education seminars directed to practitioners. I also must thank my editors at *Psychiatric Times,* Christine Potvin, and at *Psychology Today,* Anastasia Toufexis, for providing me with a forum to write about the subject I love.

I owe a debt to editor Betsy Lerner for recognizing the potential of this project and to Gail Winston, who offered nurturance and guidance along the way. To my agent Jeanne Hanson, for cheer under adversity and an unshakeable belief in my work.

To my editor at W. H. Freeman and Company, Erika Goldman, for seeing very clearly what this book was really about and who it was for and for enabling me to bring it to fruition with her tenacity, hard-headedness, and warmth. Thanks also to my project editor, Georgia Lee Hadler, for getting me through the production process smoothly with good grace and great efficiency. To Sloane Lederer and her superb marketing team, and to my copy editor, Michele Kornegay, for proving over and over again that God is in the details.

And to my husband Gary, simply the best and smartest man on earth.

# Index